Your First 100 Days in Church Revitalization and Renewal

RENOVATE
Publishing Group

Tom Cheyney

Tom Cheyney

Dedication
To Cheryl, my beloved!

My best friend, life companion, and one who challenges me every day to be the best I can be for my Lord. You mean the world to me. There are so many things I truly admire about you as a person, as my best friend and as my wife. Your smile lights up my soul. As a church revitalizer's wife, you have been courageous to go even when the path seemed unclear and yet the hand of God was certain. You have given much and sacrificed more so others might see Jesus.

To the students of the Church Revitalization Doctorial Classes at Midwestern Baptist Theological Seminary and Anderson University: two great schools emphasizing the need to train ministers in the field of revitalization and renewal. Their encouragement to write this manuscript, discussion of the issues, and willingness to serve the Lord in the hard places encourages me every day.

To all of those Church Revitalizers serving in local churches asking God to do great things again and revive their church once more: The course is not easy, but the need is great and our Master longs to see the church restored for future generations.

"For God has not given us a spirit of fearfulness, but one of power, love, and sound judgment"
2 Timothy 1:7 CSB
To God be the glory forever and ever.

Your First 120 Days in Church Revitalization and Renewal
TABLE OF CONTENTS

Acknowledgements

I am blessed to serve each day the Greater Orlando Baptist Association (GOBA). This is a network of churches that is changing the way we have done associational work across Southern Baptist churches. No longer bound by geography, GOBA has raised the bar by working with churches, networks, and partners to plant healthy churches, to revitalize those churches in need of renewal, and to develop leaders equipped for the ministry through the GOAL Leadership Development Training. The Renovate National Church Revitalization Conference is one of these new things that have impacted Christianity cross-denominationally. Spearheaded by the wonderful pastors and laity who have partnered with us for the work of the Lord may I say thank you.

To my many committed Church Revitalization Practitioners who join with me annually to make the Renovate National Church Revitalization Conference the largest conference focused on helping declining churches, I thank you. Your gifts and your passion for hurting churches make my heart leap for such godly compassion. To those just beginning the journey, seek God's best, and become your best for God so you can be a vessel fully developed for the work of a Church Revitalizer.

To Dr. Randy Bennett my editor. Many thanks for taking my manuscript and pouring over it to make it the best possible. I appreciate you so very much.

What Others Are Saying About *Your first 120 Days in Church Revitalization and Renewal*

Tom Cheyney knows churches. As a church leader himself and as an advisor to countless pastors, Tom has developed insights about church life and health that are valuable resources for all of us. In particular, Tom has a heart for church revitalization, which is one of the most pressing issues of our day. I am thankful for the investment Tom Cheyney has made in helping pastors and other leaders breathe new life into dying and declining congregations.

Michael Duduit that's true, Executive Editor of Preaching Magazine and founding Dean of the Clamp Divinity School at Anderson University in Anderson, SC.

During the years I spent as an Organizational Change Consultant, I observed first-hand the kind of impact that leaders can have when they embrace the role of change agent. In ***Your First 120 Days in Church Revitalization and Renewal***, Tom Cheyney gives church leaders tools to take on that critical role. This book will help to increase your confidence to become the kind of catalyst leader needed to lead your church into the future.

Lee Kricher, Author
For a New Generation: A Practical Guide for Revitalizing Your Church

I am convinced that nobody and I mean nobody in America understands Church Revitalization like my friend, Dr. Tom Cheyney, founder of the Renovate National Church Revitalization Conference. He not only understands the intricacies of the revitalization process itself, but the dynamics required of the leaders who attempt this important work. Tom Cheyney is the seminal leader in the Church Revitalization Movement in America today. His vast experience as a church planter and revitalizer, coupled with his ability to communicate within both academia and to the church, uniquely qualifies him to write the official playbooks of revitalization strategies. In ***Your First 120 Days in Church Revitalization and Renewal***, Cheyney has comprehensively identified and described the contemporary strategies for addressing church revitalization in the dying church. Church leaders, looking for guidance as they lead their churches into a revitalization process, will find this work to be an essential and invaluable tool to guide them in the strategy that best fits their settings.

Terry Rials
Church Revitalizer & Pastor of Crestview Baptist Church
Co-Author of *The Nuts and Bolts of Church Revitalization*

I don't know anyone who is more well-versed or written on church revitalization than Tom Cheyney. His advice is solid, practical, and helpful. This is one for your tool chest, pastors.

Ron Edmondson, Blogger
CEO Leadership Network
ron.edmondson@gmail.com

Tom Cheyney does it again! He addresses a critical need in Church Revitalization in a way that is both insightful and practical. In *Your First 120 Days in Church Revitalization and Renewal*, Dr. Cheyney, who is quickly becoming known as the father of the church revitalization movement, writes about this crucial role for Church Revitalizers. Let us never forget the obvious - that church revitalization requires significant change. Readers will discover that much more is being done in the area of church revitalization than previously realized. This book is for and about those whose job it is to lead churches to do what they are reluctant to do. Inspiring and hopeful, this is a must read for anyone who is concerned about the state of rural churches in North America.

Mark Weible, Director of Church Planting Greater Orlando Baptist Association

Tom Cheyney understands Church Revitalization like few others. He realizes the local pastor of the church in search of revitalization is the key. If my declining or plateaued church was struggling and in need of revitalization than I would want to first read *Your First 120 Days in Church Revitalization and Renewal*. Tom leads a growing multi-denominational church revitalization movement that impacts thousands of churches and pastors. He is the leader in the field and the voice that so many turn to when it comes to church revitalization and renewal. This book by Tom Cheyney will be a valuable asset to any pastor desiring to lead his church through the process of Revitalization. This is a book you want to read and want to read it now.

Larry Wynn, Co-author
Preaching Towards Church Revitalization and Renewal
Buy this book; the cost is small in dollars but large in impact. *Your First 120 Days in Church Revitalization and Renewal* is about new paradigms for the declining church. Tom trains revitalization pastors who take action

and bring about healthy change. Cheyney is like few in this world on Church Revitalization. Tom helps me consistently become a more effective leader personally and with churches. He will do the same with you here. It is important to understand that there, are specific "skill sets" that are either learned or acquired by pastors as they walk down the paths of their ministries. Everybody brings something to the table when they arrive to pastor a rural church. However, if they arrive at the table with an inability to analyze, create and adapt, they are going to be in for a rough "Pastor-Life," experience. I have known Dr. Tom Cheyney for over forty years. *Your First 120 Days in Church Revitalization and Renewal* is packed with valuable insights that he has gleaned through the "School of Hard Ministry Knocks." Tired of watching others succeed in changing their situations where you are too scared to lead? Read this book! Don't know how to move your rural church past an entrenched establishment that hasn't changed in years? Read this book! Starting out in ministry and looking to not have to "learn the hard way?" Read this book!

Greg Kappas
President, Grace Global Network
Vice President, The Timothy Initiative
Author *Five Stages for Multiplying Healthy Churches*

No one has worked harder, written more, or studied more in the arena of church revitalization than Tom Cheyney. I consider him THE expert on this vital topic for 21st Century church leaders. Tom tackles the task of restarting dead churches in his latest book, *Your First 120 Days in Church Revitalization and Renewal.* I believe it is a "must read" for anyone who finds himself in the position of leading, helping, or attending a "dead" church.

Steve Holt
Church Revitalization Leader
Tennessee Baptist Mission Board

No one has researched and trained more church leaders in the area of church revitalization than Dr. Tom Cheyney. As you peruse the pages of this book, you will discover how God is calling you to help bring necessary change to your church. Both pastors and lay leaders will benefit greatly from the challenges here offered by Cheyney. May the Lord use this tool in your church's life as it moves toward life!

Joel Breidenbaugh
Author, *Preaching for Body Building*
Senior Pastor and Church Planter

Leading change is one of the most difficult disciplines in rural church revitalization, yet one that cannot be overlooked. In Tom Cheyney's most recent book, *Your First 120 Days in Church Revitalization and Renewal*, he is going to help you understand those necessary principles that will help you be an effective pastor in your church setting. If you find yourself in a place where change is so desperately needed, this is a must have book for you. Through Cheyney's expertise and experience, you will develop an appreciation for the many ways that God can bring about health and vitality in the church. The stakes are high and the challenge is big, but with the perils of wisdom you find within this book, as a revitalization leader you will gain confidence and understanding for how you can see revitalization in your church, for the glory of God.

Dr. Michael Atherton, Pastor
First Baptist Church O'Fallon
Author of *The Revitalized Church*

A critical book for a critical time! *Your First 120 Days in Church Revitalization and Renewal* carries with it a sense of urgency. This book addresses the necessity to act immediately in a dying situation. Church Revitalization takes a lengthy period to bring new life to a declining church. But there are many churches that do not have the years needed to bring revitalization to fruition. Dr. Cheyney's latest book, *Your First 120 Days in Church Revitalization and Renewal*, addresses the immediate call for radical spiritual intervention. While many churches do not want to die, Tom Cheyney outlines how a resurrection can come from a terminal condition. **Except a grain of wheat fall to the ground and die, it remains by itself, but if it dies, it brings forth much fruit** -John 12:24.

Dr. Jim Grant
Executive Director
Galveston Baptist Association

Experience matters. If you are desperately searching for someone to help you renew your church, then Tom is the one. His experience in revitalizing churches will arm you to face this challenging task, not with untested theories, but with a phase-by-phase plan steeped in practical knowledge. In this book you will learn from a man who passionately wants you to be used of God to rebuild a witnessing church in your community.

Dr. Steve Smith, Church Equippers Ministries

Tom Cheyney has done it again! With *Your First 120 Days in Church Revitalization and Renewal*, Cheyney has applied his wisdom and experience to the challenge of replanting a church in a meaningful way. The focus of the author on what it takes and the steps needed to make a renewal effort successful is particularly helpful for any minister who finds himself in this setting. Replanting is not for the faint of heart! Cheyney recognizes this, and with this book added to your revitalization toolbox it will help you to be more effective in partnering with God on this Kingdom adventure.

Dr. J. David Jackson,
Author of *ReNEW: Traveling the Forgotten Path*

Introduction
Time Tested Ways to Keep Your Renewing Church from Advancing

You are initiating the beginning of your church's effort towards church revitalization. You are to be commended for the willingness to save a church from the pain of loss. There are all types of loses for declining churches. There is the loss of long-time church members who have either moved away or passed on. There is the loss of impact in one's community in which the church was planted to serve. Another loss is the mixture of all ages within your fellowship to what now leans further towards the elderly than the young. But perhaps the biggest loss is when your church has not done anything to bring about renewal and eventually it is given away to a church planter which is stranger because the membership and leadership within the church waited too long to act. As you look in the mirror ask the Lord how you are going to be the catalyst for revitalization in the dear church you serve. Beginning the process of revitalization and renewal is a critical time for the church revitalizer. Whether you realize it or not the clock is ticking and the key decisions you make in your initial one hundred and twenty days is imperative. While you have some time on your side might I encourage you to begin day one displaying to your lay church leaders that you are there to lead them out of their demise and towards a better future. You are there to make a difference and if you do not see yourself up to the task then you should begin developing your exit plan.

We should all face it that becoming the leader of a church revitalization effort for the local church is a big challenge. It is a chance for you as the church revitalizer and for the church in need of revitalization to make a fresh start and develop a new vision for a better future. But for you as the one called to lead the church out of decline, it is also a time for intense vulnerability. Making unwise slipups and blunders are missteps you cannot afford at the beginning of your journey. What you do during the opening one hundred and twenty days of your revitalization efforts can either position you for success of jeopardize your leadership which will ultimately lead to failure. This new book written by my dear friend Steve Holt (guest writer of two chapters) and I seek to identify for you the potential landmines and potholes you will encounter and show you how to avoid them. It goes without saying but probably needs to be stated nevertheless that you as the church revitalizer need some early wins in order for the majority of the church to follow your leadership. You have been given a great opportunity by the Lord to seize the opportunity to bring renewal to your church. What you do during the first 120 days sets the stage for the impossible dream to become the possible dream of revitalization and renewal.

Ways to Keep Renewal from Happening in Your Church

But before you rush out to conquer the world of church decline, my desire is to acquaint you with the most practiced ways within the local church of keeping your church from being renewed. There are all types of seminars informing us how to grow a church. The so-called church growth gurus of the 1980s offered up and are still offering up ideas that have never been the catalyst for growth. Think of the large number of church growth consultants out there within every denomination. The actual number exceeds seven hundred organizations and over twenty-five hundred consultants. With such a large number one would think that the need for revitalization in declining churches would never be an issue. Yet, little has been changed by these organizations. All of us attended the majority of these experiences hoping that something that was shared would help the church in need. It is high time the other side of the issue is considered. While I don't guarantee these easy-to-apply steps will always keep your renewing church from advancing and keep growing, they will with proper application, certainly increase the chances. These principles have been utilized by so many churches, which actually wanted to do nothing, or to decline rather than getting back to the work of growing into a healthy renewed and vibrant church once more. Let's take a look:

Reaching Out to People Only in Safe Situations and Members in Other Church's

Many a church revitalizer wants what another church pastor already has. The idea of a stabilized declining church can lead one to take measures that are unbiblical. Trying to revitalize a church in decline by sheep stealing actually is one of the most dangerous things you and your church can do. The reason is because most members coming from other churches are not looking to buy into your renewal vision but are looking for relief from the former place they belonged. These individuals and often groups of individuals actually have a vision of their own and seek to make you fit into their former ideal of a perfect church.

Accentuating Excellence Over the Capacity of Your Worship Center

Renewing Churches that are just beginning to emerge from plateau or decline need to have such a desire to reach new people for the cause of Christ that excellence is developed as you go and the degree of excellence during the relaunch period will not be the final degree of excellence once your church gets growing again and more volunteers can contribute to the effort. For the church revitalizer the gathering of prospects, the reclaiming the formerly active members, and the setting of a new direction are the most important during the initial one hundred and twenty days of revitalization and renewal. Listen to the seasoned church planter when he tells you "gather, gather, and more gathering" is the best expenditure of one's time during the beginning days of a revitalization effort. If you are not able to develop a team of gatherers alongside of you, it will be hard to make the impact that is needed initially. Gathering is essential in church renewal. If you as the church revitalizer spend all of your time trying to develop materials that are the equivalent of a larger church nearby, you are wasting valuable time that could be used for developing relationships with those who need Christ. Great resources and nice curriculum come later!

Insist on Using Only Evangelistic Methods that were used in the Past

While I would be the first to declare that as the church revitalizer you must have the ability to lead someone to Christ and have the gift of evangelism as part of your wiring, there are many new ways to reach significant groups of people in your community with the Gospel.[1] If you do what you have always done, you will get what you have always gotten is the old axiom. Today we have certainly the tried-and-true methodologies of the past that have worked for decades. Yet we are still in great need for new methodologies for reaching the various emerging generations and people groups within our land. Wise church revitalizers know that it is essential to continue to reach a lost world for Christ. New methodologies are coming on the scene every day and it is vital that church revitalizers keep current when it comes to giving an evangelistic witness for Jesus Christ.

---

1 A great book on ways to reach new prospects for Christ has been written by Mark Weible and is entitled: ***Fishing on The Other Side: A Guide to Being the Church in the Digital Age.*** You can order it from Amazon.com or RenovateConference.org/bookstore.

Trying Not to be Welcoming to Visitors and Your Returning Guests

If you want to remain in a perilous situation of rapid decline continue making your guests feel like they are intruding on your close-knit family. Many dying churches are frequented by guests looking for a place to worship only to discover that the church is not open to new people. I am always amazed when I see a church revitalizer that is blind to their inability to build a crowd. If you as a church body need a tiny closed cluster you might not be able to keep your church growing and expanding. Revitalizers who need a small group of people gathered around them often are not able to stretch their tiny group to include new people coming on a weekly basis.

Never Invite New People to Join the Your Church

All of us at one time or another has failed to invite an individual to church. I have worked with many a church needing revitalization that were unable to invite prospects in and become part of the family of God. When a church Revitalizer does this on a regular basis it is a quick road map towards failure. Inviting and tell people about your new story of renewal and the exciting things that are happening in your church is vital to regrowing the church. In one church my wife and I visited in the Atlanta area, we were looking for a church home since we just moved into the area. For three weeks the adult class we were sent to never socialized with us or gave us the time of day. Imagine their surprise three weeks later when the pastor introduced me as their guest speaker. I preached a sermon titled: *What Keeps you Up at Night?* It was dealing with the question can we sleep while men are dying without Jesus Christ?

Develop the Concept that Growth is Entirely Dependent on the Holy Spirit

Far too many church revitalizers have created the idea that we as a church boy need not participate in the work of evangelism. Many declare that the Holy Spirit will reach whomever he desires to reach, and we are off the hook in doing the work of evangelism. Nothing could be further from the truth. I believe the Holy Spirit goes ahead of you as a witness and as a church revitalizer to prepare the harvest field. Yet it is amazing to me today that there is growing number of church revitalizers who do not believe that being an active witness brings results anymore. They just sit back and forget that they need to do their part for the growing of a church. Church revitalizers who can renew a church understand that they have a part in this effort of growth and that they should actively be seeking how to reach their communities for Jesus' sake.

Never Set Goals for Growth

If you do not set a goal as a church revitalizer you most certainly will reach it. Dying churches often stop setting numerical goals for growth. They will say things like "there is no such thing as a small church." As the leader of a church towards renewal you must get yourself first and your people second out reaching other with the Gospel. One way to remain the same in a declining church is to not set a goal of growth for tomorrow today. I would certainly agree that most of us who have grown a church are not totally sure how it happened short of God's incredible anointing, yet a clear vision for a preferred future is vital. I used to say this little ditty all the time as a church planter and church revitalizer: "Always more than the year before!" Some pastors of declining churches do not like that phrase, but it is good to remind us of the need to set goals for growth. Declare it. Pronounce it often. Declare it early. Proclaim it regularly from the pulpit. Declare these goals for growth repeatedly! Set a personal goal and set a goal for you and your church leadership. Then get moving.

Do Not Pray for Growth

It is sad that most pastors and church revitalizers do not pray for real Holy Spirit blessed growth. I always did. As I journeyed along it was critical that I prayed individually for growth. It is critical that others on your staff or deacon body as a revitalizer pray for growth. Furthermore, you ought to keep this before your people to pray for growth. In a training event with church revitalizers a while ago one pastor who was attending shared that he was scared to tell his declining church that he was praying for a certain number of new believers to be baptized and join the church. He understood that a quick way to bring new life to a dead body is the influx of new believers who are willing to go to work. He voiced fear of what the older church members would think. I told my story of how when we were serious about reaching people God would show up and more often than not, do even greater things than we had set as a goal. The Lord began to display His power. Much of that I still feel would not have happened if it were not for us first praying for growth and then publicly declaring it. Keep it regularly before you and your people.

Change the Pastor Every Few Years

You will not have to worry about where you are going to put new people if you keep switching out the pastor in a declining church every two or three years. People will not stay around such a church long enough for you to change out the parts. You usually only get one chance as a revitalizer to revitalize a work so take it seriously, stay in place and wait on the Lord to pour out His blessing in His time. My personal testimony is that if I had run when I wanted to, I would have missed

God's miraculous blessings in my life and ministry. Your victory is just around the corner so enjoy the ride.

Keep Your New Constituents from Serving on the Leadership and Ministry Teams

New people want to belong and feel they are contributing towards something they believe in. If you keep them out of your ministry team or leadership team, you will watch them participate for about six weeks and then quietly disappear in search of something more significant in a church and in a group of people that are more inclusive. Put your new people to work Church Revitalizer. Even a brand-new believer can give out a worship guide the following Sunday of his conversion.

Split Up Your Affinity Groups Regularly

There was a time when splitting up affinity groups helped a church continue to advance. Those days are past as most church participants are looking for worship and service that is multicultural. People today are searching for significant relationships amidst their hectic schedules. There is a failed understanding that by a church keeping natural affinity groups together today they are more successful.

Do Not Send Your Church Revitalizer to Church Revitalization Conferences

Always try to display generosity towards your church revitalizer as a renewing church leadership group. If you have the resources to send them to a conference or seminar it will not only help your church but it will encourage him as well. Try to budget at least one training event of his choice each year and pay for his wife to go along as well. Remember to give him a little spending money for purchasing resources so your church will also profit from his experience.

Do Not Encourage Him to Read Church Revitalization Materials

Give your church revitalizer a book allowance. His reading will aid the work by stretching him personally and advancing your church publicly. The more you can afford the better opportunity you will have to watch him lead your renewal work further and with greater effectivity.2

Trying to Win Every Person in Your Community

When you try to win everyone you usually win no one. Renewing churches that view the whole population of an area as theirs is not realistic. Church Revitalizers who assimilate well, gather in pockets and fishing pools desiring to catch those who already an affinity with each other. As the Lord continues to advance the renewal effort, opportunities will open up and then you can enlarge your scope. The reason so many churches fail in this area is because they want to utilize the reach everyone strategy and the effort fails in reaching anyone.

Do Not Advertise Your Church on Social Media

Most renewing churches are not known so anything they do to advertise is a plus. Just be careful not to waste funds on formats that bring you no return on investment.

---

2 There are many church revitalization resources available at: RenovateConference.org/Resources. The majority of them are free. This is a wonderful place for the beginning learning of the one who is called to lead the church through revitalization and renewal.

Do Not Staff for Renewal and Do Not Make Financial Provisions for Revitalization

Failure to plan for renewal is dangerous. While there is a time to add staff and a time to wait, you need to begin planning for additional staff right away. Caution should be given towards not bringing on staff in areas where volunteers can still function. Far too many church revitalizers are looking for a pal when they need a key contributor. While laity are serving in areas where one day a staff member will serve, begin saving towards that first two years of expenses. You will be glad you did and the church will not feel a crunch in services due to being broke.

Act Like the Lord Does Not Want Your Church to Grow

God desires your church to grow and be revitalized. He blesses those churches with a heart for reaching the lost in this world. Revitalizing churches do the work of evangelism while there is still time to touch individuals with the saving Gospel of Jesus Christ.

These seventeen are the best way to keep your declining church from being renewed. Granted I was being quite cynical in a jesting way but these are prevalent throughout the declining church community.

Wrapping It Up!

As you can see this book on your first 120 days in church revitalization and renewal is deigned to challenge you to release old and outdated theories and methodologies. We will continue to declare that the early days where you transition into this new role of church revitalizer is critical and challenging. But if you begin well you have established a solid foundation of you as the leader, the team you will employ to help you with renewal, and the success you will have going forward. I suggest you begin carrying a small journal that you can write in each day the things the Lord tells you about the revitalization of your church. From these pages will come the strategy necessary for renewal. You will find the importance of setting direction in the renewal effort. Ideas for reaching the culture in your community can be written in this journal. I always use a journal because I believe it is God's way of giving me a head start in the revitalization of the church. I can develop a message for the effort that rings loud and clear with the members of faith as well as those who will come to join us in the days ahead. Ideas on how to align all that needs to be done will be written in this journal. Thoughts about the new message we will declare to our community can be placed there.

Many of you have experienced our, Your First 120 Days in Revitalization and Renewal Retreats. This book is the larger edition in which we often spoke about needing to be included but for the sake of the schedule during the weekend we were not able. It excites me to have a dear friend and one who has journeyed with me in these retreats write this book right beside me. You will be blessed I am sure by his commitment to this book and these retreats.

Until Jesus Comes,
Tom Cheyney, Founder & Directional Leader
The Renovate Group Renovate National Church
Revitalization Conferences
Col. 4:6; 2 Timothy 1:7

Chapter One
Planning Your First 120 Days in Church Renewal

Beginning well in one's initial efforts toward church renewal takes bold leadership and effective planning. The first 120 days as the revitalization leader in a declining church is important. It is amazing what can be accomplished in the initial four months of any Revitalization ministry. Franklin D. Roosevelt, the 32nd president of the United States accomplished much during his first 120 days as the leader of our country. He sent fifteen messages to the Congress of the United States. He delivered ten speeches, guided fifteen laws into enactment, held press conferences and met with his cabinet each week. Further he talked with other heads of states.

Similarly, how you begin your journey into church revitalization and renewal is equally as important. Because if you are going to lead your church in and through total revitalization you will need to invest a minimum of one thousand days in the effort. The way you utilize the first one hundred and twenty days will set the stage towards weather you will be successful or not. You bring to the revitalization effort a leader who will take charge, stand boldly, kneel in prayer daily, build a team carefully, set a new direction towards health, and work towards tiny wins immediately. Whether you realize it or not, the clock is ticking on you as the leader and your ability to initially make a positive impact in the church towards its revitalization sets you in the right position to make a lasting difference. Most church revitalizers who make little or no impact at the beginning find it hard to rally the congregation towards the effort of revitalization and renewal. For most church revitalizers those initial first months are like a tornado. Tumultuous even on the good days. Cyclonic on the bad ones. It takes about one hundred and twenty days to adjust to your new environment and focus on the big picture sensing what needs to be a top priority in the church. Many pastors speak of a honeymoon period. Can I give you a wake-up call? Here it is! There are no honeymoon periods in revitalization if you desire to be successful. If you waste your first four months doing little or nothing the groundwork that should have been laid and the ground that should have been taken will be much harder. No one will tell you this, but those who do nothing often do not make it past the eighteen-month tenure because so little has been accomplished and the members begin to ask themselves if you are the right leader for the effort.

The church revitalizer should begin thinking immediately about what their first one hundred and twenty days would look like. It is important to make a list of who you are going to see, what you are going to do, why you are doing those things to begin with, and when will you begin to gather team members for the initial revitalization effort. You must re-evaluate the churches present strategy for growth and decide what needs to be kept and what need to be dismissed. You will need to evaluate the health of the membership and determine if they are willing and ready to begin the process of revitalization. You and your leadership must re-evaluate where the resources are presently going and decide if these same expenditures are necessary as you move towards revitalization. Things that worked fifty years ago might not work today or even tomorrow and a serious look into every ministry is warranted. Lastly, as the Church Revitalizer, you will need to focus on the innovative and creative side of ministry as you seek a new direction. If you and your leadership are honest with yourselves and your church members, many of the things you are currently doing have not made an impact in the growth and health of your church. Some of those actually need to be let go of so that you will be able to have the manpower and the resources necessary to try new things to reach your ministry area. You must work towards beginning to learn your community's culture while examining you own church's culture to see if they are harmonious or if they need to be redesigned. You must start off well by developing new relationships and learning your church's culture. It is through the development of these relationships that you as the pastor leader will be able to develop a new message and begin to direct the church towards lasting change. Look for those in the church which can help you develop these new ideas so that you are not out there all by yourself. This is where you can begin on Sundays developing your churches new narrative towards growth. You also can begin developing those hooks that your vision and values will hang upon by giving your members worthy talking points for future expansion. Begin praying about whom you would like to ask to serve on the revitalization team. Set your sails towards a new direction and paint the picture of where the church is heading. Begin to deliver the little wins and allow the Lord time to build them into larger wins. Remember they are looking and watching you as they form their individual opinions weather you can lead them towards revitalization and church health.

Think about what you will deliver in your initial thrust towards revitalization in the first four months. There certainly will be the strategizing, organizing, and conducting of a process. The practical moves you make at first can set you up for a better chance for renewal. Begin to own your vision and get your people to begin thinking about what a sustainable vision for revitalization would look like. Look for your early adopters to come along side of you and enlist their ideas and dreams. You must do something each and every day towards revitalization so begin early and work continuously. Nudge the church forward a little bit every day until you see a plan coming together. Here are a set of typical questions most church revitalizers must ask and answer during their first one hundred and twenty days.

In becoming the church's new leader what should be my top concerns going into the work of revitalization?

It is always wise to learn who the players are in any church and get to know those long-time members early in the process. Keeping a journal is a good way to begin working in and on revitalization for the church you have been called to lead. Assessing the opportunities and difficulties in the church would be helpful. I would set up a series of meetings with key leadership groups in the church as a way to hear what they believe are the issues and opportunities. Spend time with your deacons or lay elders. Listen to their ideas, recommendations and worries. This will give you the beginnings of a plan to work with in developing the initial one-hundred-and-twenty-day plan.3

Is there a worksheet of some type that as the pastor I can craft to allow fellow church leaders to input and participation?

Worksheets are a good way for you as the church revitalizer to receive input from key lay leaders without appearing to be giving out orders and delegating to the rank and file. Worksheets are ever changing and considered by most as working drafts always able to be updated and revised at any time. It could have a few low hanging fruit action steps to achieve initially. Most of the items will more than often focus on meeting with present members and the formerly church members. Eventually there will come a time towards the end of the four months where you gather together your entire church leadership teams and any members at large who are willing to spend a day together dreaming and strategizing

---

3 At the back of the book, there is a great worksheet that I developed as an action plan for you to draft out what your first 120 days might look like. This action plan outlines the key priorities to address during that time frame and focuses your efforts on the most important items at hand.

towards a new future. This strategic day of focus allows you to solicit from the congregation ideas that can help form your long-term strategy towards revitalization. It becomes a renewal map that guides you towards the eventual revitalization of your church. While most men are afraid of asking for directions (sorry ladies), the wise church revitalizer will ask for advice early and often.

What should I be doing with my initial days in my office as pastor revitalizer?

Regardless of where your office is officially, I highly recommend you have a plan for office time. Your members will be watching so if you wander around looking lost, they will perceive you as an incompetent leader. If you come in with a plan and are decisive in your actions, they will sense that you know what you are doing and will give you a chance. If you have an assistant that has a long tenure, I will seek to sit down with her and listen to her thoughts and ideas. It can also be a time to let all staff members know what you expect in the future. When I arrived at my present Executive Directors position, I discovered that the entire staff was more interested in their own well-being and not in the best interest of those we serve. I heard from those we serve that the staff was more interested in saying "No," rather than saying, "Yes." They even called former employees Ministers of No. There had become an entitlement complex with most of the staff and something had to be done about it. I met as a staff in staff meeting and in individual meetings to hear what they were doing in their ministry and allow them to ask me any questions. I also shared with them where we were going and why it was more important in finding ways to say yes over declaring that it was too large of an inconvenience so no was in order. I understood that everyone was watching me so I modeled the preferred behavior for the future. Likewise, my eyes were on them to see if they had what it takes to lead themselves out of such a mire of self-focus. If we are more concerned about what is in it for us as the leaders, our followers will question what our real motives are.

How many active members and participants are there currently and what is my plan to contact them as soon as possible?

Get your sermons done quickly each week initially because you have more important things to do with your time initially then sit in your office crafting out deep sermons. Sermon preparation is important but in the first one hundred- and twenty-days meeting people is more important. Formulating of relationships is critical. In my last church that I worked on revitalizing, there were some well-meaning individuals who believed that two men in the church were hard to work with. They advised me to stay away from them. I prayed and the Lord said, "Get to know them." The short story is that these men became two of my best friends and were willing to do the hard stuff. They just wanted a leader who could intentionally lead and not "wing" everything as an unprepared pastor. Then I was visible with these men in front of the entire congregation as they watched us pray, laugh, and make decisions together. I went out of my way to be approachable and loved on the entire congregation and not just a select few. I had coffee with many of the congregation. Lunches were done in a way that I never ate alone and listened to those I was having lunch with. On Sundays I attended a Bible Study Class for its opening activities so I could get to know as many people as possible. We planned ice cream fellowships so we could laugh together and gain weight together. Laughing was brought back to the work of ministry in that church.

Who are the former members that have left in the last few years and do we have their contact information?

I desired to reclaim as many as were willing to come back to the church and give me a chance. Not everyone came back but there were many who did and what they discovered was a renewing church that they desired to make it a home once more. I wanted to know what went wrong and then move on from it.4

How will you launch your ministry with your church's governance board?

Within my denomination the majority of our churches have a body of deacons which function as a servant leadership team and a staff that serve as the leaders of the church. The staff usually interacts with the various leadership committees in the fulfillment of the various management functions of the church. Many a declining church has allowed the deacons to fall into the only decision makers of the church and have placed upon them an unbiblical role that the scripture never intended. Determining early in your tenure how you will relate to these various groups and teams will be important. One of the most important elements of a church revitalizer's success is developing and sustaining a healthy relationship with those who are coleaders in the church. Some of these church members weld great power and can be your greatest influencers for the good of revitalization or the bad. It all depends how you develop these relationships. You need to build the trust together in order to advance the church. Most power brokers hate surprises so keep them informed.

---

4 The Renovate Group has a workshop that is offered entitled: *Reclaiming Inactive Church Members Utilizing the RECLAIM Strategy*. The kit includes a manual, a DVD with thirty-two resources on it, and promotional materials you can use to gather church members who are willing to be participants in this new ministry of renewal.

What feedback and from whom do I need to receive feedback?

Receiving proper feedback to the vast number of questions you have as you begin a new ministry of revitalization is a must. Many early mistakes can be avoided if we are open to feedback and ask questions of one's membership. Church members appreciate you taking the time to ask question and receive feedback. They like to see that their pastor is a learner. Much goodwill is developed when you seek feedback. Your credibility will also rise as members know you will listen to their ideas. Try not to over promise during the first one hundred and twenty days. I formerly worked for an organization that was known for over promising and under delivering. Their unrealistic goals created pressure on the staff and damaged relationship in the field. Much harm can come from that form of action. Think sustainability and progress in a way that everyone can keep up.

Foundations for a Wise Church Revitalizer's Thinking

Every successful revitalization leader has what I call an entrepreneurial spirit. They dream big and they work even bigger. They take risks for the good of the church. Here are a few foundations for wise thinking as the church revitalizer leading a church towards renewal:

Always be looking for the opportunity over the obstacle.

The majority of successful church revitalizers spend their active down time pondering ways to take advantage of the renewing churches distinct abilities and focuses on the things it does best. Have you ever noticed that when God is blessing your ministry the most, there are troubles which follow? Your church is beginning to grow again, but you desperately need a refurbished building. New people are coming to Christ, but you now need volunteers to disciple them. You are tackling some of the greatest evil giants within your community, and now they are starting to tackle back. Maybe you are feeling a lot like Joshua. As God was leading Israel into one of the greatest eras of its history, the conquest of the Promised Land, Joshua was chosen to lead the charge. Yet in the midst of this great time of success came one of the greatest challenges of his life. There were seven larger and stronger nations already there. If he was going to fulfill God's call on his life, he'd have a big obstacle to overcome first. Taking the time when you are at leisure to think more about the opportunities and how to utilize the things your church does well will help you overcome the obstacles which are keeping your church from breaking through. Recognize obstacles as merely a detour to your final goal. Never allow minor obstacles to sidetrack you. It is easy to give up sometimes when you are worn out but it is much harder to stick to the plan. Focus in your thinking on what you can do. Choose an outlook as the church revitalizer that you and your church can prevail. Develop an unwavering belief in yourself, your abilities, and your membership's ability to bring the church back to life. Instead of fighting your obstacles, find a means of making them defeat themselves. That takes thinking.

Develop a down the road mentality that allows you to see what others miss.

It is always wise as the revitalization leader to view adversity as the opportunity for growth. Remember you are about to change the long-term status quo in a church and that will require a forward-thinking mentality. Look down the road as far as the Lord will allow you to see. Remember that He can see further than you and will only give you the direction for today and tomorrow so move ahead with what you can see. Developing a down the road mentality provides you an opening that you can utilize to chive better results.

Learn that you will fail sometimes and other times you will have great successes.

All of us have fallen. All of us have failed in a ministry project. Allow such failure to sharpen us and mold us into the church revitalizer that God can use. The wise church revitalizer looks on their failures as trainings to be celebrated and not mistakes to be bemoaned. If you will take on the outlook of never giving up and never allowing yourself to make the same mistakes tice you are well on your way as successful revitalizer. When you think of the word failure, many in the church see a huge dark cloud behind it. They see this is because, throughout their entire life they have been told that "failure is not an option," but it is. How can you know where you need to improve if you have never failed at something? Things don't just work instantaneously. There is a lot of trial and error in revitalization. When you try something and it doesn't work the first time it provides you with answers on how to implement the situation the next time. However, if you don't even attempt to try the first time how will you know your methods work, you don't. Do not allow yourself as the church revitalizer and your church as the one being renewed to live with a pile of regrets because you were too afraid to try. You want to live out your ministry knowing that you gave it your best shot and when that wasn't good enough you gave it another shot. The best part about failure is you get another shot and another one if you want one. It is up to you to decide how many times you're willing to fail in order to achieve your goal of church revitalization. I say if you really want it you will never give up. Understand that there will be times that you might be thinking, "this isn't working," but it is. It is working because you are constantly learning what you did wrong the last time so the next time you make a mistake it won't be the same one. If there's ever a time where you have the opportunity to give it another go, you have to take it especially when it comes to the goal of revitalizing a local church.

Get over your mistakes, acknowledge them and get back in the game.

The wisest church revitalizers endure the pain of their errors only once. You will have times where your judgement in untested and your decision is not wise. Learn from this but stop suffering from it. None of us working in church revitalization have the time to waste worrying about our yesterdays. Get back in the game and move on. Stop internalizing your mistakes because they have nothing to do with your individual worth to the Lord. Your worth to the Lord is secured through Christ Jesus. Your performance just like the rest of us can get better. Promise yourself to work better, understand the situation more fully, and rise above the circumstances continually. Revitalization is all about learning, doing, growing and stepping out of pre-confined boxes of predictability. If you never have failed at anything in ministry, you will never have learned how to step out of your comfort zones. That is why many a church is declining or dying. They have never learned how to rise above their mistakes. In order to get the outcomes, you are looking for in revitalization you and your church need to extend yourself, so you both can grow.

Try not to close your mind off from ideas that are contrary to yours.

Stop blocking your creativity because of the fear of the unknown. Closing one's mind off from new ideas for the work of ministry is dangerous as the church revitalizer. There have been many times in my revitalization work when the Lord gave me a great idea that moved my church forward in a positive way towards health and growth. New ventures and avenues spring from ideas that are often contrary to yours so listen to others as well. Being open with our eyes, ears, and mind enables us to see what most people of habit continually miss. Many a pastor has cut off a good idea that could become great only because they thought it would require more work from them. Allow people with other ideas to press on and see if it will work for your church.

Dream more of the future church you desire.

Andy Love in his song says, "When your dreams come alive, you're unstoppable. Take a shot; chase the sun find the beautiful. We will glow in the dark. Turning dust to gold and we'll dream it possible, possible."5 Church Revitalizers who dream are usually people of action not inaction. Many declining church members have difficulty seeing the potential of their dreams for a revitalized church. They give up on these dreams because they do not see how the idea of a healthy church again will ever come true. Church revitalizers know that in revitalization there is a large degree of dreaming of what could be possible if they will take the time to embrace possible and watch the Lord do the impossible. While you cannot force

---

5 https://www.youtube.com/watch?v=WcsGV6fP0D4

dreams to transpire, you can take steps toward realizing them. Your dreams as the church revitalizer and your team that is working with you have value. Keep moving toward them, even if you face obstacles and challenges. If you will hold tight to your goals of revitalization, you will discover it is easier to stay on the right track.

Let others know of those dreams.

Once you declare your dreams let others know about your dream for a revitalized church. Get others on board and buying in to a revitalized church. Sharing the adventure in revitalization with as many people as possible allows for a larger group to work towards revitalization. Your early adopters will be a source of strength in the launching of renewal. Sharing the excitement that comes with watching the Lord renew His church is a great thrill for everyone. It is something that gets those who have prayed long and hard for revival in their church in which to rejoice. Bringing others into your dreams of revitalization makes you a wise leader. When your membership can see the serendipitous blessings, hear the delightful sounds of testimonies about how the Lord is working in your church, smell the smells of church fellowship dinners, feel the touch of the Lords hand upon the church, and taste the Holy Spirit's goodness to your church that is a dream worth sharing.

Be a leader who seeks joy and hopefulness.

I have learned as a church revitalizer how important it is that I stay optimistic and positive towards what the Lord is doing in the church. You must believe in yourself, believe in the one who brings about renewal, and believe in the people He is going to use to revitalizer your church. Never lose your joy as the leader towards renewal. It takes a holy anointed confidence that the Lord wants to use you in the revitalization of a church. Live in it and walk worthy of it. I have never seen a pastor who was a worrier be successful in renewal. I have never seen a pastor who was a naysayer be successful in renewal. I have never seen a pastor who is an eternal pessimist be successful in church revitalization and renewal. It requires a positive church revitalizer to lead the effort toward revitalization. Positive church revitalization leaders have the ability to unite the team. They love the entire church and not just the ones that think he is awesome. They have the ability to call out the greatness that is within the congregation. Church revitalizers must lead with enthusiasm. Through adversity, obstacles and challenges joyous and hopeful church revitalizers consistently rally their revitalization team with a shared vision and a greater purpose.

Grow every day through at least one new discovery.

Revitalization requires that the church revitalizer grows each and every day by learning something new that can help in revitalization. I receive so many kind notes weekly from pastors in the work of revitalization thanking me for the tremendous number of just-in-time resources available on our Renovate Conference website. The reason they are there is because we believe that you do not have the funds available to go out and throw down large sums of money to utilize tools for revitalization. Let me tell you a story. When I was planting churches early in my ministry there were all types of groups out there who wanted to sell me their stuff. My church struggled initially for its initial two years and there was little money to be spent on things besides keeping the church building heated, and the lights on. There was a group though that knew me and gave me a few tools. I used them for a long time because they worked and because they were given to a church planter that did not have large dollars provided by a denomination. I prayed way back then that if I was ever in the situation where I could do the same for other pastors, I would do so. The Lord answered my prayer and the Renovate Conference website (RenovateConference.org) lives out this prayer each and every day for those needing just-in time resourcing. Learning something every day is made easier through the resources available to you as a revitalizer. Also, it is important that you spend time with those who have done it so get yourself a coach that has done revitalization. There are a lot of groups out there who are still trying to provide failed methodologies of the 1980's church growth movement as a solution. Be cautious.

Work on your creativity.

 The creative church revitalizer learns how to be playful with ideas and knows that they must gel for a while. Experimentation is revitalization takes place often. Learning that there is always a different and better way to revitalize a church is crucial. You will not be able to develop your creative talents if you do not make time for them. Schedule some time each week to concentrate on some type of creative project that will benefit at least one aspect of your revitalization project. Brainstorming is a common method in both many professions. It could be your most powerful tool for stretching your creativity and imagination. Work on developing the skills you need to advance your creativity. Daily seek inspiration from various resources designed to help you revitalize your church. I try to develop one new thought or idea every day. Keep a journal of your ideas. It takes many ideas to come up with one really creative and useful idea. One thing to ponder each day is a serious question that might bring light to the solution that would renew your church. If you are a morning person those hours will be your most creative time of the day. If you are a night person, the twilight hours will be your most productive time of the day. Always think on your ideas first before you consider others' ideas. I love hanging out with other creative people. They fuel my passion for creativity. Imagination and creativity are the traits that fuel the future. These can help you discover the way the Lord would want you to renew your church.

Never stop thinking connection.

Personal relationships as a church revitalizer will run the process of revitalization. Connections allow you to build rapport with almost anyone. The only connections that work in the local church will be with those you are really involved. If you make halfhearted connections as the church revitalizer, you will in pretty short order, be discovered by the members you are trying to impact as shallow and uncaring.

A new leadership opportunity for the church revitalizer can be stimulating. It can also be overwhelming. Within your initial one hundred and twenty days you have to prove yourself as an asset to the declining church. During that time, you will be examined directly and indirectly by those who make up the congregation. The key leaders of the declining church such as deacons and trustees will be analyzing your efforts and actions. Even those that are volunteer and paid staff members will be assessing your first four months effort.

Not only will the actions you take determine your success as the revitalization leader, but they will also inspire, stimulate, and motivate how others will perceive you within your role as the church revitalizer.

Creating Your First Draft of Your 120 Day Plan in Church Renewal

Not everyone will want to actually take the time required to declare in writing your draft idea of a 120-day plan. Yet, there is strength when you struggle with the issues and concepts that could be part of your renewal efforts. Let me give you four key words that could help you gain focus during the first one hundred and twenty days in a declining church. They are: Learn, Clarify, Alignment, and Build. Additionally, may I give you four concepts for these one hundred and twenty days? They are: Focus on your church members, Rebuild the church's brand, develop strategies for sustainable growth, and Build your revitalization team.

Your First 30 Days as the Church Revitalizer (Days 1-30) – Focus on Your Church Members
Key Word for the Month: Learn

The new church revitalizer has a lot to do their first month as the pastor of a church needing to be revitalized. There are people in which you need to begin developing relationships. There are organizations within the church in which you need to begin to have conversations. It is important that you hit the ground running and try to meet as many church members, both active and inactive, as possible so you can begin sharing your passion of revitalizing the church. During these initial thirty days you should make every effort to relate and connect with as many people in your church as you can. You want to find out who your church members are, what strengths and skill sets they bring to the effort of revitalization, and how united they are with the churches culture. Beginning the process of bonding to present members and former members is important in a church revitalization effort. Come to understand who the players are and what strengths they bring to an effort of revitalization. Learn everything you can from them and ask questions that demonstrate your genuine desire to hear everything they have to say. Strategic learning lessens the timeframe of your vulnerability as the new church revitalizer. It is a vital time for you to get traction. This goes a long way in demonstrating that you desire to learn their values, hear about the previous mission, discover any unmet goals, and learn about former strategic plans. It is also an important time that you are seen and demonstrating that you are available to your membership. This helps to elevate the trepidations and intimidation of you as the new pastor. Showing up among your people is always better than showing off.

One church I worked with always wanted to have a Youth Center and it was something that was never accomplished. The church revitalizer came in and saw the vast numbers of children in the community and realized it was something that should be accomplished as quickly as possible. The good will that he earned by including this as part of his eventual strategic plan coming out of his first one hundred and twenty days was incredible. It became a momentum maker for the church. Your effort at the beginning quarter of your first one hundred and twenty days is towards re-establishing as many church members and former church members belief in the church and the new direction it is headed. First, they need to connect to you as the new leader and even much more importantly, they need to connect to the renewed vision for revitalization of the church. That is a large job and worth committing all of your effort during the first thirty days as the revitalizer in a new church. Just keep asking yourself what am I learning about this dear church and how can I utilize this knowledge for God's glory of revitalizing the church? Spending time with those who are leading and working in the church's organizations is wise. They have been in the trenches for so long and you ought to hear their hearts. They will also tell you what needs to be fixed. Feedback such as this is valuable to you as the church revitalizer. It also allows them to discover your leadership abilities as you seek their feedback. Learning and listening is important during your early beginnings. One word of caution I would add is that you need to leave the naysayers on the sidelines. Nothing distorts your learning more than Mr. or Mrs. Negativity accompanying you on your journey to learn. They will be a liability to your new effort so walk alone and out front to start. You are better prepared to reach your individual conclusions that way. The church revitalizer cannot afford to have individuals that were part of the cause for church decline to accompany them on these visits.

Another thing that I always did in every one of my churches was to initiate and develop the habit of recognizing new church members or returning church members. I had a large bulletin board made that allowed me to take a picture of these new participants and put them on the board so others could see their names below their pictures and begin to learn their names. Developing the habit like this in a church that was declining and now is beginning to come back is a strong way for your people to see that the Lord is still working and moving in the church. Habits and outlooks created during your first one hundred and twenty days are ways to bring a gentle but subtle nudge to the congregation about the things your hold dear. Creating the habit of recognition of new members is a way to model a preferred future of renewal and growth. It takes about sixty days to form a habit so start this early in your effort.

Your Second 30 Days as the Church Revitalizer (Days 31-60) – Rebuild the Church's Brand
Key Word for the Month: Clarify

The new church revitalizer has as their goal for the second thirty days the task of rebuilding the church's brand and refining how such church identity will be shared. This is also where you can begin to display your expectations and beginning of the revitalization plan. As you lay the foundation for revitalization in your church among the church membership, you will begin to see how the church functions as you look for ways to move it off of stuck or being polarized. Rebuilding the church's brand and mission are important things to be done early in your effort while you have the priority time to give it thought and attention. Church Revitalizers must build the new mission and brand from the inside out by engaging the membership in the process. This is where you begin to examine how potential members can join your church and get involved. Most dying churches have such an elaborate form of joining a church that it makes them hard to belong. Teach your members how to say, "yes" to things over "no" to the new things. This is also a good time to look at your assimilation systems in the church and see if one of the early equipping events might be a refreshing of these procedures. Are there things that the church does that are too complicated? If so, work toward ways to simplify such systems. As the church revitalizer you must describe the "why" first and then move on towards the "what" goals as you implement the "how" we are going to do it process.

It is always wise for the church revitalizer to begin acquiring early victories no matter how large or small. Early victories have a way of demonstrating to the membership and leadership of the church that good things are happening and the church is on the right path. Nothing helps the church revitalizer more than when positive things are happening which moves the church closer towards renewal. Trust begins to be given and your credibility quotient goes up. Stay focused on the building of the church's brand. If you take this as an unimportant, your defeat in the process will often be tied to this stage of renewal where you pushed by these items and found yourself at a loss on the other end. Assess the church well, develop a working draft of your revitalization strategy, help the church to adapt to the community, make strategic changes only as they are needed, and gather as many that are willing to join in the process of renewal. I always sought to present another shift in a change for the church right after we had won a significant victory. Change is much easier to embrace when your church members are riding the high of a miraculous victory. Implementing the shift was always easier if we allowed it to follow some sort of success and achievement. A word about change in general relating to revitalization is that you do not layer up a pile of changes and then thrust them upon your people. Too many changes made in revitalization too rapidly will burn out those that are on board with you and cause a stall in the process of revitalization. Tackle the most important ones initially and allow the Lord time to bring the others to fruition. Momentum is the goal so do not load up a long list which will destroy any chance of keeping the big "MO" going. Revitalizing a local declining church means you must become the instigator of change.

Your Third 30 Days as the Church Revitalizer (Days 61-90) – Develop Strategies for Sustainable Growth
Key Word for the Month: Alignment

The new church revitalizer must begin to formulate short-term goals and long-term goals. The key goal during this stage in that gaining of alignment of the membership and developing the strategy for advancement. As you develop your strategy to match your church's unique condition you will be better prepared to present to the church at the end of your first one hundred and twenty days your vision for the revitalization of the church. Think of alignment like a team of seven people out in a large rowboat. There is one who guides the way it should go, and that person is the helmsman. Then there are three individuals rowing on each side of the boat. If all six respond to the helmsmen and row together the rowboat moves in a course which has been set by the helmsmen guiding the tiller. But if three on one side and one on the other side of the boat are rowing together but the other two are either not rowing at all or are rowing the wrong way the boat is going to struggle. That is the way alignment works even in the local church. Gaining alignment is a big deal and should not be taken lightly or expected to be something given just because you arrived to lead the church through revitalization. The goal is to get everyone rowing in the same direction.

Some church revitalizers are *rapid deployment specialists* that tend to threaten the passive declining church. This is often because they are really church planters with the wrong core values. They can plant but will destroy the church unless they kill it first and then begin anew. Some church revitalizers are *sluggish deployment specialists* that tend to threaten the aggressive members in the church because the leader is taking too long to do anything and everything. Many will question if these individuals are more of a maintenance pastor and not a revitalizer. Most leaders of revitalization fall somewhere in the middle of these the rapid and sluggish deployment specialists. But let me be clear. There are times that you must move on an opportunity and take advantage of the open doors the Lord has given. The sluggish deployment specialist hurts the revitalization efforts if they do not react quickly enough. New opportunities seldom present themselves over and over again so be ready for the Lord to open doors. Then there are the cultivators that have the time and can plan with direction, but they are not forced into a quick decision. You will need to function in both planes at times in renewal.

Cultivators have time to plan, plant, and produce without creating a feeling of rushing off the starter's line. Regardless of the posture you take it is vital to remember that you as the church revitalizer are on the offensive side of the football field and not on the defensive side. Defenses are built to stop advancement while offenses are built to score.

Additionally, the church revitalizer should work towards bringing alignment to the church's existing activities. One of the great lessons John Maxwell taught me from his Leadership Conferences was the importance of bringing alignment to the church body. He declared that it was unwise for a church leader to allow the various organizations to do their own thing. He said there needed to be one voice and one sound. Stop allowing the Children's Director and the Youth Minister to have their own websites outside of the main website of the church. My take on both of these examples is that they only create youth or children's hideouts which disconnect them from the rest of the church.

Your Final 30 Days as the Church Revitalizer (Days 91 - 120) – Build Your Revitalization Team
Key Word for the Month: Build

The church revitalizers remaining thirty days of their initial one hundred and twenty days should be spent on discovering, developing, and deploying of your church's revitalization team. It is paramount that you select well. Do not merely ask for volunteers to join you because you will not get that which you really need. Accepting the wrong people on the team will only frustrate the process and could cause you to lose the very people on the team that you really need. The wise church revitalizer looks over the congregation and selects individuals which are tactical and deliberate in their efforts. There is astonishing influence that comes to your revitalization efforts if you pick the right type of individuals to serve on your revitalization team.6 Every successful Church Revitalizer knows the importance of building a great team around them. Poorly selected teams only lessen the chances of renewal coming to your church. If you have a team already and all you seem to do is put out fires, then you have selected poorly and are reaping the benefits of poor selections. You can't do everything yourself so make sure you get the right people on your revitalization team. I was working with a church recently that lost their pastor and they were lamenting that they had no deacons or elders because the pastor wanted to do everything and now, they were left with no leaders in the church. I asked where he went only to discover that he went to a large denominational agency to lead out in an effort. You must have a team and you cannot do it all by yourself pastor. These last thirty days are also a good time to begin rolling out any new slogans and promotion materials designed to share the new things that are going on in your church. You have had ninety previous days to work on your strategy. Your Revitalization Team has been built. Now the work of pastoring, leading, and renewing the church can begin with intentionality.

Wrapping it Up!

Well, you probably need to take some time to reflect on what you have learned here in this chapter. Before you do though, may I say a word of congratulations to you? You have been at the role of the church revitalizer at your new church for one hundred and twenty days and you have made a significant step towards the renewing of your church. Well done. I think that some of the things you learned during these four stages are real eye openers. You may have felt over your head at times and consumed at other times. The learning curve has

---

6 For more on *Determining the Composition of Your Church Revitalization Team* go to: RenovateConference.org/resources and download the resource with the same title.

been set high and yet you have survived with a new direction which will allow you to prosper in the arena of revitalization. Most Church Revitalizers tell me that they also were stretched during those one hundred and twenty days. They were forced in many ways to develop a new set of skills that may not have been needed in their previous church. Now that you have reached the first portion of your thousand-day journey towards revitalization allow me to remind you that you have eight hundred and eighty days remaining where you can edit and redesign this plan as the Lord provides new avenues and venues for you to explore. Let me ask you a few more questions before we close this lesson on utilizing your first days in revitalization wisely. Write down these questions and write down your answers in a tiny journal you can keep with you every day.

1. What are the things that frighten you about revitalizing a church?
2. What is it that you desire to get out of this opportunity to revitalize a church?
3. How will this effort towards revitalization help you in becoming a better pastor for the Lord?
4. Do you see areas in your ministry that need to be strengthened as the result of these last 120 days?
5. Are there gaps in your church revitalization team that need to be filled in the future?
6. Can your Church Revitalization Team learn its way towards revitalization and if so, how are you going to provide such opportunities for learning?
7. Will you invest your time and friendship in these members and their families being all in for the task?
8. Are there some key reasons the church has declined and what are you going to do about it?
9. Would a group like Renovate help you by serving as your coach and mentor?
10. What are the critical issues that keep the church from growing?

11. Would a Discovery Retreat with my leaders help move us forward and unify us together?
12. Are there any men in the church I ought to do the meeting before the meeting with?
13. Who are the individuals I could hand off a task or ministry program and know that it will be accomplished?
14. If you could do something immediately, what are the three most important changes you would make?
15. Will I enjoy the ride of revitalizing a declining church?

Picture with me: The engine fired loud and continuous into my hands as I clutched the tiny roadster for the very first time. Power was at my fingertips that spoke of the unnatural performance that was lying just a few feet away under the cherry red-scooped hood. Was this going to be short-lived excitement of passing days of youthful exuberance? I hoped not. Moments earlier I had just finished paying for the tiny car and now while darkness surrounded me, I had the enjoyment of driving it home, where a garage was waiting for its new resident. There was a small crowd gathered as I fumbled around trying to figure out what each button and switch accomplished. Gone are the days, except in vintage cars, where you must flip switches, pull levers, and push buttons to get an automobile to move. Those around me were asking if I was fearful of driving the "thing" as they called it, home without having had the chance to give it a complete checkout. Within me was a sense of contentment in anticipation of the ride. My mind flashed at the other machines I had considered: Spyder, Cobra 427, Snake, and Invader all with their ominous monikers spoke of prowess and power. Strangely within me was a peace, a sense of guidance, or perhaps contentment that reminded me of days gone by when I had driven a similar machine.

I encouraged those around after fumbling to find reverse; and backed it out of the space where it had been displayed.

Once it was moving forward and I was applying that which I had learned some twenty-five years earlier, thoughts of uncertainty ceased. Humorous print ads and commercial slogans bounced back across my mind. One ad was true, which spoke of "Your Mother Wouldn't Like It!" and I could see my wife as I pulled off a little bit fearful that her usually levelheaded husband, had just taken off in a car that would fit inside her family car. Sounds bristled as I shook the machine down. "Silky smooth and smokin!" By the time I reached the fourth speed it was hauling and I was holding on. It was hard not to smile, since the wind pushed through the cockpit. My clothes were flapping me to death as laughter reminded me just how fun it was and still is to enjoy such a ride. Steal string guitars and acoustical instruments played in my head since I could not figure out in the dark how to turn on the radio. Lyrics rocked my cranial cavity like, "Do You Want to Drive My Car?" "409", "Fun Fun Fun", and "Surfin Safari" all flashed around my mind and caused me to laugh. By the time I reached home my face honestly hurt from the smile of experiencing such a spirited drive. My bald head was whipped and wind burned. Like sailors drawn mysteriously to the sea, enthusiastically I drove her (all sports cars have female names, go figure) into her new berth, having sampled the sweet flavor of a ride that was so complete.

The enjoying the ride principle is simply the principle of joyful contentment right in the midst of all that you are doing. Enjoying the ministry for me is like that drive. It is contentedly enjoying the ride of ministry right where God has placed me. For the Called of God, it is the God given strength to be satisfied with the loving supply of God in any and every situation. Though the road of ministry is often difficult because of its rocks and boulders, the strains and struggles, or even the twists and turns, if you keep on keeping on, you can make it. Yes, there are times when potholes are all around us. There are surprises, accidents, and detours that wait for us along the road. We might sweat a little and sway a little but remember; every road has an end. If we hold on in the midst of the strain, God will bring us to the end. To really grasp the principle, we must be aware of the warning signs. Failure to listen will cause us to fall or perhaps even fail!

One last bit of information about my ride. Listening to the engine is crucial. Just a few miles from my house I stalled the British roadster out and had a rough spot in my enjoying the ride practice. The engine had started to run a little rough and I had a wonderful man stop by and give me a roadside lift in the form of resetting my carburetor. Undaunted and appreciative, I thanked the man for his help and the good advice he gave me about the machine and off I went again with joy, only one last leg until home! Paul declares in Philippians 4:4 *"Rejoice in the Lord always: and again, I say, rejoice."* One of the reappearing themes of the book of Philippians is that of Joy! It is mentioned in various forms over nineteen times in four brief chapters. To put it simply, Paul admonishes us that a Christ-like mind can bring us Christian joy and contentment. Even in the midst of prison Paul was still joyful. In perhaps the most uncomfortable of circumstances, he was still found full of joy.

There are times granted in our lives when we enjoy the ride more than other times. If we are not careful, we will allow things to come into our lives that cause us to lose our joy. Worry has been for many one of those things that rob us of the joy. This is probably why the original Old English word for worry was to *strangle*. Again, contentment and joy will keep us humble in lives lot and will free us from strangulation. When you enjoy the work of the ministry there is that mark of joy for all to see. It has that quality of inner gladness and deep-seated pleasure with what one is doing. Ministry and service should be exactly that. Fun, full of pleasure, and gladness all rolled up into you. It is that deeper sense of assurance and confidence that ignites a cheerful and rejoicing heart. That heart that cheers then leads to continual rejoicing behavior. I have said it this way for years: "I choose joy!" In ministry, we can either enjoy the ride or we can gripe and complain at every junction. That might be all right for some, but for me I choose God's joy! A friend of mine often tells me that even when I am down no one knows.

Have you ever stopped to notice that the world's joy is plagued by incompleteness? There is always something that is lacking, unfulfilled, or missing. The world's joy brings no sense of complete assurance, confidence, or satisfaction. But it is God's joy that is complete. Take a quick look at qualities of joy found in the Enjoy the Ride Principle for Pastor's, Preachers, and Church Revitalizers:

1. God divinely gives Joy and Contentment alone.

    It is the joy that our roots are based in the Lord. We should learn to rejoice always!

2. God gives us His very own joy and that joy overrides all else.

    Circumstances can destroy earthly joy, but when God implants joy into a believer's heart it dwells deep. He says, "Rejoice always" that is, continually; and then we are to rejoice again, that is repeatedly. Joy is the joy in the Lord (Nehemiah 8:10).

3. Joy and Contentment spring forth from faith.

    One who is enjoying the ride and has contentment is *Balanced* (Phil. 2:25). We must be balanced as pastors. I had a man in California the other day say after talking with me for a while how nice it was to see a fellow brother in the Lord who had a fun balanced life. Additionally, when enjoying the ride there must be a *Burden* for others (Phil. 2:26-27).

Lastly, like Epaphroditus a life that is contented is *Blessed* (Phil. 2:28-30). What a great brother he must have been! Epaphroditus proves for us today that the joyful life is the life of sacrifice as we submit ourselves to the Lord and to one another in the spirit of Christ.

Along life's journey towards revitalization, there are some things that will help us become more secure in enjoying the ride: *Right Praying* (Phil. 4:6-7) will help you as a revitalizer. We must see the greatness and majesty of God! We bow before Him as He searches our hearts and minds. *Right Thinking* (Phil 4:8) will help you lead others toward a renewed church. Joy and contentment involve the mind learning to think rightly. Wrong thinking leads to wrong feelings while right thinking leads to right feelings. *Right Living* (Phil 4:9) is where others will see your walk and your talk mess perfectly together. Right living is a yielded heart and mind to the Spirit of God. Such will always bring peace. The great thing about rejoicing is that it places and keeps a person in the presence of Jesus Christ! No matter what may confront us and no matter how terrible the trial, we know that Christ Jesus our Lord is looking us after. So, we know that whatever we face it will never conquer or overcome us. Jesus Christ will give us the supernatural power and strength to overcome it. Walk rejoicing in the Lord no matter what confronts us and remember to enjoy the ride (Romans 8:35-39). Some pastors, preachers, and church revitalizers might be saying, "Someday I will enjoy the ride, but for now I just can't. I am too busy with the work of the Lord to have the time." Ministry is enjoyment! Our Calling is Joyful! If you have always told yourself you were going to enjoy the ride, make sure you do not wait too long. You will be better for it and so will the people God has called you to serve!

Chapter Two
Are You Ready to Lead Your Church to Revitalize?
(Guest Writer Steve Holt)

On a regular basis I find myself sitting across the table from a pastor who has asked for a meeting to talk about revitalization. Most often those conversations stem from the pastor's sense that His church is in trouble and consequently he feels he has the responsibility to find a solution. Typically, the pastor is frustrated because he has been somewhat successful in his former churches, but now he is at a loss to understand why the principles and tactics that led to a measure of tangible growth and fruitfulness in his other congregations are not producing the same results. Sometimes the pastor is so defeated by his current circumstances that he is ready to resign or is actively seeking another church to pastor. Caught in the classic "fight or flight" scenario, sometimes the pastor just wants to run away.

However, most pastors with whom I meet are looking for solutions. They are looking for ways to move their churches off the plateau or to stop the bleeding of decline and start the journey toward greater health. These men love the Lord and they love the people of their churches as well. They are frustrated by their inability to move the church in a positive direction and often they are struggling to figure out what to do next.

One might think the question; "Are you ready to lead your church to revitalize?" would be a simple one for any pastor whose church is in decline. Yet this question is very legitimate and encompasses more than simply a desire to see one's church change for the better. Behind the question is the reality that leading an effective church revitalization process takes more than desire or good intentions. Church revitalization takes passion, commitment, skill, intentionality, and most of all a sense of calling. Just wanting something positive to happen in your church does not necessarily make it a reality.

The Importance of a Call

Several years ago, while attending a conference, I struck up a conversation with a pastor from a different denominational family from mine. As we got to know each other over the course of our time together, we began to talk about our faith journey and how we came to be pastors. As we talked, my new friend asked me the following question, "I have heard other Baptist pastors talk about being 'called' into ministry, what does that mean?" I soon found out that in my friend's faith family the idea of a call from God to ministry was not emphasized to the same degree as it was in my own Southern Baptist tradition. His own experience was one of growing up in a Christian home, being nurtured in his faith by both his biological and faith families, and then choosing to make pastoral ministry his profession. The idea of a distinct or dramatic "call" experience was not the norm among ministers in his tradition.

Among the pastors I know in my Southern Baptist family, most all of them share a true sense of a divine invitation to ministry that led them to pursue pastoral ministry as a vocation. I can remember hearing my childhood pastors relate their stories of having felt or "heard" God speak to them in an unmistakable way that led them to believe He was calling them to serve Him in ministry. Some of those stories were dramatic, "Damascus Road-type" stories that included hardships due to the pastor's failure to immediately surrender to God's call. Other stories were more of a progressive obedience to God's invitation to follow His leadership and say "yes" to the opportunities the Lord put in his path. I don't remember ever hearing a pastor relating how he came to pursue the vocation of pastor simply because HE thought it would be a good idea.

I share that story to reveal my personal bias toward what I believe is an essential element for any pastor who is leading a revitalization effort in a local church—a call from God. As I read the pages of God's word, I see time after time where God revealed Himself to men and women to call them into a relationship with Him, reveal His will and plan to them, and then commission them to serve Him by leading His people. Whether it was Moses, Joshua, Jeremiah, Peter, Paul, or one of dozens of others; each of these people were drawn by God into a relationship which created the context that gave them the capacity to lead God's people. Moses even tried to help his people without a definite call from God and wound up spending 40 years tending his father-in-law's flock on the backside of the desert as a result. It was only after his "burning bush" experience that he learned the true nature of what God intended for his life. You may not have experienced a "burning bush" or "Damascus Road" kind of call to ministry, but I hope you have a definite sense of divine direction in your life and ministry that has led you to pursue pastoral ministry in general and serve as pastor of your current church in particular.

In the next three sections, I want to explore three different callings a successful revitalization pastor should have experienced. First, we will examine our call to faith in Christ. While it may sound strange to start at such an elemental level, I am convinced that many churches are struggling today because of a faulty understanding of what it means to be a Christian and walk with the Lord. The Apostle Peter encouraged his readers to "confirm your calling and election" (2 Peter 1:10) and the Apostle Paul challenged the Church at Philippi to "work out your own salvation with fear and trembling" (Philippians 2:12). These great leaders of the New Testament church understood the nature of saving faith and how essential it is to possess it and to understand its impact on our lives. Second, we will examine what it means to be called to pastoral ministry. I believe one needs to be selected by God to be the pastor of a local church. Then finally, I want to make a case for the importance of being chosen by God to serve as pastor of a specific body. As you will read, I am convinced that a successful revitalization effort will be led by a pastor who has been "hand-picked" by the Father to lead the people of that church.

The Call to Salvation

"I just want to know; have you ever been saved?" That was a question I received during a town hall meeting on the Sunday I preached in view of a call at the second church I served as pastor. The questioner was a thirteen-year-old youth and it was the most important question I answered that Sunday evening. It gave me the opportunity to share how I came to know Christ as Lord of my life. The decision I made to surrender my life to Jesus' Lordship is by far the most important event in my life. Every other major event in my pilgrimage from that point to the present has been colored by that moment. That decision set me on a journey of transformation, challenge, and joy.

As a pastor looking to revitalize your church, I hope you have experienced a call to salvation. Depending on your background that call may look a little different than mine, but hopefully you have given your life to Christ and you are following Him as Lord. The heart of evangelical faith is the belief that humanity has been separated from God by sin and the only solution to that separation is the atoning sacrifice of Jesus on the Cross. Romans 5:8 states, *"But God proves his own love for us in that while we were still sinners, Christ died for us"* (CSB). The most quoted verse in the Bible is most likely John 3:16 which is the "gospel in miniature." *"For God so loved the world, that he gave his only begotten Son, that whosoever believeth in him should not perish, but have everlasting life"* (KJV). By faith in God's revelation of Jesus, we receive the forgiveness of our sin as well as new life in Christ Jesus our Lord. What a deal!

To trust Jesus as your Savior is to make Him Lord of your life. Lordship means He is in charge of your life and you live in submission to His will and follow His commandments as revealed in His Word. Believers need to be a part of a "faith family"/church in which they can be discipled by more mature Christians in how to live the life of faith. Christianity is a "team sport," not a "solo" effort. It is within the context of community that we learn and grow as followers of Christ, find support, encouragement, and purpose. No wonder you and I are so passionate about seeing Christ's body, the church, and experience revitalization!

Your faith journey may have been like mine. I grew up going to church with my family, came to faith at a young age, and then began serving the Lord as a teenager. I have never known life without the influence of a faith community. However, you might have come to faith as an adult or older adolescent, which means your context could be very different than mine. Regardless of when and how you came to faith, your spiritual growth has led you to the place of having a true passion for the church and how to make it more effective. The fact that you are reading these words is indicative of that passion.

As we grow spiritually, we become aware of particular gifts and abilities God gives us as believers. It is His intention that we use those gifts for His glory in service to Him and those around us. Paul exhorted the Roman Christians to put their gifts to use when he said, *"According to the grace given us to us, we have different gifts: If prophecy, use it according to the proportion of one's faith; if service, use it in service; if teaching, in teaching; if exhorting, in exhortation; giving, with generosity; leading, with diligence; showing mercy, with cheerfulness"* (Romans 12:6-8, CSB). Our gifts

35

serve as a platform for us to engage in fulfilling the Great Commission by making disciples. We are all called to live out our beliefs, share our faith, serve others, and disciple less mature believers. All these tasks are a part of the call to salvation. All of them lead to a healthy, vital church as well. Every born-again Christian has a role to play in the life of his/her church. None of us are called to simply be "spectators" in the story of God's Great Plan of Redemption.

The Call to Pastoral Ministry

If there was ever such a thing as an "accidental pastor," I may have been one. I felt a call to ministry on my life when I was sixteen. I grew up in a very rural area in Northeast Tennessee and attended a very small, one room church. All the pastors I had growing up were bivocational—even though none of them had ever heard that term—so I went to college with the idea of becoming a schoolteacher who preached on the weekends. In my naivete, I didn't even consider the idea of full-time pastoral ministry. After college I found a job teaching at a local elementary school and began looking for opportunities to serve the Lord, but few opportunities presented themselves. Eventually, I was asked to preach in a revival at the church pastored by a family friend—he may have felt sorry for me. During that revival I met a couple from a neighboring church who came at the invitation of a family member. After the service, the couple asked if I would be interested in preaching at their church since they did not have a pastor at that time. I said I would love to preach for the church and they asked me to come on a Sunday later that month. After the first Sunday I was asked to come back again. Then after a few weeks of filling the pulpit, I was asked to serve as interim pastor of the church. I prayed about that possibility and believed the Lord was leading me to say "yes." I continued to teach at the elementary school as I served as interim pastor, but I began to sense a definite call to that group of people. God confirmed that call on my life when the search committee approached me and asked if I would serve as their full-time pastor. After a season of seeking God's confirmation, I agreed to allow the church to vote on me as pastor. I received a very positive vote and served the church for a total of seven and a half years. I never sought the position of pastor, it found me.

Reflecting back on my calling to pastoral ministry, even the calling at age sixteen was not something I sought or even wanted. I loved Jesus and wanted to serve Him, but I wanted to find my life's work in a secular profession and serve the Lord as a devoted church member—not as a pastor. However, God had other ideas. I believe He called me into ministry. While not as dramatic or consequential as the calling experiences of Abraham, Moses, or the Apostle Paul, I had an experience with God which caused me to believe He had given me a special assignment to serve Him as a minister. In my limited understanding of calling at that time, I believed it was to be a "preacher of the gospel." I shared my calling with my church family on the following Sunday and began to receive opportunities to preach. My obedience in accepting His call and sharing with my faith family about what God was doing in my life were vital elements of my development as a "preacher" and later as a pastor.

Your "calling story" may be different than mine. Maybe people in your life recognized a special gifting in your life and encouraged you to follow it. Perhaps you ran from God's call for years before surrendering to it. Whatever your story, if you are a pastor you have a calling on your life. That calling comes from God. He is the one who then directs your life through circumstances and times of challenge and change to fulfill His purpose for your life. I believe the calling to be a pastor is a holy calling and the most humbling thing that any Christian can receive from the Lord. While my calling has been a tremendous blessing in my life, it has also been the source of my greatest difficulties and heartaches. But through it all, God has been faithful.

So just what does it mean to be called as a pastor? While much has been written over the centuries about pastoral ministry, perhaps the clearest, most concise word on what it means to be a pastor came from the Apostle Peter in 1 Peter 5:1-4: *"I exhort the elders among you as a fellow elder and witness to the sufferings of Christ, as well as one who shares in the glory about to be revealed: Shepherd God's flock among you, not overseeing out of compulsion but willingly, as God would have you; not out of greed for money but eagerly; not lording it over those entrusted to you, but being examples to the flock. And when the chief Shepherd appears, you will receive the unfading crown of glory"* (CSB). Peter uses three words in this passage that clearly illustrate three distinct roles an effective pastor performs in a local church.

The first is that of "elder." The word elder carries the sense of maturity and experience. It doesn't necessarily mean old or "elderly." Pastors need to be spiritually mature believers who demonstrate wisdom and godly character. Paul said a pastor "must not be a new convert . . ." (1 Timothy 3:6, CSB) When I look back on my first years as a twenty-something pastor, I realize that while my congregation exercised great patience with my youth and inexperience, God did grant me the gift of wisdom and a maturity beyond my years. Our daily surrender to the Lordship of Christ and our effort to live holy lives opens the opportunity for God's Spirit to pour into us the kind of wisdom and character traits that create godly leaders. People respect pastors that demonstrate those characteristics—and they follow them.

Second, Peter uses the word "shepherd" from which we get the word pastor. One of the most used images for pastoral ministry is that of a shepherd. It is a term Jesus used to describe His ministry as well. Pastors are called to take care of God's people as "under-shepherds" of the Chief

Shepherd, Jesus Christ. How does one fulfill such a role? Let me suggest three primary functions of effective shepherds. First, they feed the sheep. Pastors feed the sheep on the Word of God. Nothing we do as pastors is as important as the faithful proclamation of God's Word. We also feed them by discipling them, walking with them through life, and teaching them how to disciple others. Second, pastors tend the sheep by taking care of them, encouraging them, correcting them when they need correction, and keeping them connected with the rest of the flock. Third, they guide the sheep. Without a shepherd, sheep will wander away from the flock and jeopardize their safety and survival. Sheep need a shepherd to help them navigate through life. Congregations need leaders to keep them together, moving in the right direction, and focused on fulfilling the Great Commission.

The third word Peter uses to describe the office of pastor is the word "overseer" from which we get the word "bishop." Some denominations use this word to describe a person who gives oversight to multiple congregations and pastors, but for our purposes in this discussion let's focus on the element of oversight that is inherent in every pastor's ministry. The care of souls is a great responsibility and requires great humility and a true servant heart. The writer of Hebrews indicates that pastoral leaders will be held to a higher standard than other believers when he says, *"Obey your leaders and submit to them, **since they keep watch over your souls as those who will give an account**, so that they can do this with joy and not with grief, for that would be unprofitable for you"* (Hebrews 13:17, CSB emphasis mine). Pastoral authority does not mean autocratic control, but responsible, compassionate oversight. I like to think of this kind of oversight as being similar to a lifeguard at a swimming pool. The lifeguard is there to make sure everyone is safe and no one acts in a way that endangers themselves or others. A good pastor provides servant leadership under the authority of Christ. Paul encourages the Corinthians to *"Imitate me, as I also imitate Christ"* (1

Corinthians 11:1, CSB). I believe pastoral authority flows best from a Christ-like life.

Receiving a call from God to follow him as a pastor is a great blessing. I don't believe there is a higher calling a Christian can receive. Serving as Christ's under-shepherd in the lives of the men, women, boys, and girls that make up His church is a great responsibility, but it brings tremendous blessings as well. Being the instrument God uses to help His people grow in their faith, discover His purpose for their lives, and celebrate the significant moments in their faith journey is such a joy. If you are a pastor, take a moment and thank God for calling you into that sacred ministry.

The Call to Pastor a Church

As I reached year six in my seven-and-a-half-year journey at my first church, I started to experience a sense of restlessness. The church was stable, and I had no significant issues or problems, but I began to crave a new challenge. I shared my resume with a handful of churches, none of which even bothered to contact me. The restlessness grew more intense, as did my frustration at the lack of opportunity for a new assignment. Eventually, the director of missions of my local Baptist association called to tell me he had the perfect church for me. My excitement was brief as he proceeded to let me know it was a small church in a community just ten miles from the church I pastored. I knew a lot about the church and felt that it would be a "lateral" move at best. My ego began to get the best of me. I wondered why I had bothered to pursue further education and develop myself to simply pastor the "same church in a different location." I am so thankful that God was patient with my whining and self-centered complaining—He could have just zapped me on the spot!

I received another call; this one from the chairman of the search team at the church my director of missions had felt was perfect for me. He asked me to send him my resume and then asked me to meet with the search team the following week. I believe it was God's grace, not my obedient spirit that led me to mail the chairman my resume. I wasn't excited about the possibility of being pastor of that church. However, something happened as I moved forward in the process with the team. Every contact drew me closer to them and to the church. I began to sense God birthing a vision in my heart for how He could use me there. My wife was also reluctant at first about the possibility of moving there, but she experienced the same kind of drawing I had toward the church and the opportunity to serve there. Every step was further confirmation of God's plan for the church and my family to come together. I accepted the call and served there for ten years. I have no doubt that God meant for me to be their pastor.

How about you, Pastor? What's your story? How did God orchestrate your circumstances to get you to the church you currently serve? Do you have a strong sense about why you are there? As I stated earlier and as I have illustrated above, I have a strong bias toward divine direction and calling when it comes to pastoring a church. I believe God calls men to specific churches for specific reasons and He uses circumstances—and even search teams—to put pastors and churches together. From a practical standpoint, it's hard to imagine how a search team can discover "God's man" from the hundreds of resumes the average church receives, but it happens. I have worked with many search teams in the seventeen years I have served on the staff of a state convention and I can tell you it is amazing to watch how God works to bring the right man to the right church at the right time.

So, what's next, Pastor? Because the vast majority of evangelical churches in North America are either plateaued, declining, or even dying; there is a great chance you are currently serving in a church that needs to experience a season of renewal. If it were easy to lead a church to make such a turnaround then every pastor would be a revitalization pastor. Unfortunately, it is not easy to lead a church through revitalization. This is because the heart of revitalization is CHANGE, and change is not easy. No one wants change except a baby. We are all subject to falling into routines of behavior that become imprinted on our brains and feel very secure and comfortable to us. The idea of disrupting or even destroying those patterns is very threatening and requires steady leadership, a sense of mutual accountability, and God's sovereign direction. Revitalization is not for the faint of heart. The good news is God wants His church to be healthy and productive, so He will be with you as you go through the renewal process.

One of my favorite revitalization verses is Luke 12:32: *"Fear not, little flock; for it is your Father's good pleasure to give you the kingdom"* (KJV). Don't you love that? Jesus is telling His disciples that God wants to give them the kingdom (God's rule over human hearts). The context of the verse is trusting in God's provision and not worrying about how we are going to live. The truth is that God wants His church to thrive, so why is it not thriving? I believe it is because it is being "artificially hindered." A church is a living thing and just like all living things it needs the proper conditions to grow. Light, nourishment, water, etc. are essential for growth. When those things are not present or are in short supply, the organism in question suffers. A bonsai tree is a perfect example. The bonsai expert has learned how to manipulate the conditions surrounding the tree in such a way that keeps it small. Ironically, it takes a lot of time and effort to maintain a bonsai tree in that state.

In a similar way, churches are kept small and unproductive by manipulating the conditions in which they exist. We get into patterns of thinking that are very inwardly focused and self-centered. We subconsciously function as though the purpose of the church is to meet our needs and we fail to reach out into our communities with the gospel. Our churches take on the feel of "country clubs" that primarily exist to meet the needs of their members. Consequently, the mission of the church to make disciples is relegated to lip-service and the church's health is artificially hindered. Ironically, just like the bonsai tree, it takes a lot of time and resources to maintain a church in that condition.

A church stuck in a "maintenance" mode needs a leader that can lovingly lead the body to understand its current reality and take steps toward reclaiming its God-given mission to impact the world with the gospel. Such a leader needs to be equipped to face questioning, resistance, and even hostility. However, the Lord has told us He will be with us and it is His will that the church be healthy, winsome, and fruitful. Having examined the importance of calling in church revitalization, let's look at four things every revitalization pastor must have to be successful in leading a turnaround process in his church.

A Surrendered Heart

During the American Civil War, Ulysses S. Grant rose to prominence as a great military leader in the Union Army. He first captured the attention of the nation during the battles of Fort Henry and Fort Donelson in the early months of 1862. After surrounding the Confederate forces under the command of General Simon Bolivar Buckner at Fort Donelson on February 16, 1862, the Confederate forces asked General Grant for terms or conditions under which he would accept their surrender. Grant's response to General Buckner's request became popular throughout the Union,

"No terms except an unconditional and immediate surrender can be accepted." This response led to the general becoming known from then on as "Unconditional Surrender" Grant.7

As followers of Jesus Christ, we are commanded to "unconditionally surrender" to His Lordship over our lives. That kind of surrender is based on our absolute dependence upon Christ for our life and salvation as well as our complete trust in His ability to guide and direct our life. Our surrender to Him is not a one-time act, but literally a moment-by-moment decision to submit ourselves to His authority and control. The Apostle Paul described Lordship to the Church at Galatia this way, *"I have been crucified with Christ, and I no longer live, but Christ lives in me. The life I now live in the body, I live by faith in the Son of God, who loved me and gave himself for me"* (Galatians 2:20, CSB).

The Bible uses the word "heart" to describe the seat of human emotions and will. The writer of Proverbs states, "For as he thinks in his heart, so is he" (Proverbs 23:7, NKJV) and Jesus said, *"A good person produces good out of the good stored up in his heart. An evil person produces evil out of the evil stored up in his heart, for* **his mouth speaks from the overflow of the heart"** (Luke 6:45, CSB emphasis mine). In many evangelical traditions we talk about "giving our heart" to Jesus. So, Pastor, have you surrendered your heart to the Lord? Are you following His will for your life and ministry? Has He captured your heart?

God captured Nehemiah's heart one day as he heard his brother Hanani's "report from home" about the condition of God's people and the city of Jerusalem. As he sat in the Persian citadel in Susa, he wept uncontrollably and mourned for days. God used his brother's report to arrest Nehemiah's

---

7 Jean Edward Smith, *Grant* (New York: Simon & Schuster, 2001), pp. 143-162.

attention and capture his heart to serve as His instrument of deliverance for the people of Judah. As the king's cupbearer, Nehemiah was strategically placed to have a great impact on the future safety and security of his homeland as well as lead them to experience a season of spiritual renewal and awakening.

Church revitalization begins with a burden for the spiritual condition of a local church and the great spiritual famine in the surrounding community. A strong sense of concern will lead to a high degree of commitment to do something about it. A pastor's sense of calling plus this kind of divine motivation leads him to be willing to follow God's leadership wherever it leads him. Just like Nehemiah, you can be confident that the Lord will direct your steps and open any doors necessary to get you and your church headed in the right direction. But it all starts with your unconditional surrender to His Lordship.

A Disciplined Mind

Have you ever been around a truly disciplined person? You know, the kind of person who can maintain his/her focus regardless of what is going on around them, spend whatever amount of time it takes to get the job done, and sacrifice his/her personal comfort or preferences for the sake of the cause. I have worked with a few people like that over the course of my life and they are amazing. Focus, passion, and persistence are all characteristics these people have in abundance. They know what needs to be done, what it requires, and they stay on task until it is completed.

A disciplined mind is a huge asset to a pastor in the midst of church revitalization. Pastors have a multitude of demands made upon their time during any given week. Whether it is sermon preparation, hospital visitation, counseling, outreach, committee meetings, family crises, staffing issues, weddings, or funerals, there is always something on the pastor's mind to keep him from being able to focus on the church's future. It's what Stephen Covey has referred to as the "Tyranny of the Urgent."8 It takes a tremendous amount of discipline to keep one's own mind focused on transformative issues amid the "day to day-ness" of pastoral ministry. This is where daily surrender to the Lordship of Christ is essential. Surrender helps create an internal environment where a pastor can be disciplined and focused.

After Nehemiah asked the king for permission to go to Jerusalem and rebuild the wall around the city, he ran into many obstacles and challenges along the way. However, he never lost focus on his calling and purpose. He knew that God had uniquely positioned him in the king's palace in order to be able to secure not only permission to rebuild the wall, but to get the king to donate the needed materials as well. While that was no small feat in itself, he then had to rally the people of Judah to work together to rebuild the wall, manage the project, govern the people, and deal with hostile neighbors who were not happy to see the city of Jerusalem be re-fortified. This sounds a lot like pastoring a church to me! Time after time in the book of Nehemiah we see him first call on the Lord and then address whatever crisis or decision he faced. Nehemiah gives us a great illustration of how surrender and internal discipline work together in the life of a leader.

An effective revitalization pastor is able to discipline himself in such a way as to not lose sight of his calling from God to lead his church to fulfill the Great Commission. That does not mean he never visits church members in the hospital or attends committee meetings. However, it does mean he is able to remain focused on God's vision for the church's

---

8 Stephen R. Covey, *Seven Habits of Highly Effective People* (Free Press: New York, 1989).

future as he fulfills the routine tasks of pastoral ministry. Not only is he able to maintain his focus, he can also lead the people of his church to stay committed and engaged with God's vision as well. How does he do it? He follows Nehemiah's pattern of maintaining a close relationship with his Heavenly Father which allows him to have the internal focus necessary to remain clear about his calling and purpose. In short, a surrendered heart leads to a disciplined mind.

Willing Hands

Jesus called them over and said to them, "You know that those who are regarded as rulers of the Gentiles lord it over them, and those in high positions act as tyrants over them. But it is not so among you. On the contrary, whoever wants to become great among you will be your servant, and whoever wants to be first among you will be a slave to all. For even the Son of Man did not come to be served, but to serve, and to give his life as a ransom for many." (Mark 10: 42-45, CSB)

Jesus left His disciples with a wonderful example of servant leadership. He wanted them to know how to lead by meeting needs and empowering others. That kind of leadership was very different from what most First Century Palestinians would have experienced from both their secular and religious leaders. Their Roman overlords exacted oppressive taxes from them with little given back in return. The Herodian kings were corrupt, greedy tyrants. In addition, Jewish worshippers were even gouged by moneychangers when they offered sacrifices at the Temple. In contrast Jesus wanted His disciples to be known as leaders who serve, who go the second mile, and who lift people up—not push them down. He modeled servant leadership by healing the sick, feeding the hungry, identifying with the oppressed, washing feet, and finally by giving His life "as a ransom for many." He led by demonstration, not decree.

Nehemiah is another great example of what a servant leader looks like. In chapter four of Nehemiah, the work is threatened by the enemies who lived adjacent to the city of Jerusalem. Verse 8 says, *"They all plotted together to come and fight against Jerusalem and throw it into confusion"* (CSB). Nehemiah prayed to God and rallied the people to work together to both protect the city and continue the work on the wall. He also remained personally vigilant by being present with the builders each day and standing guard over the city through the night. He kept the trumpeter close to himself at all times and told the people, *"Wherever you hear the trumpet sound, rally to us there. Our God will fight for us!"* (Nehemiah 4:20, CSB). That meant Nehemiah planned on being in the thick of the battle if Jerusalem was attacked. A servant leader is willing to put his/her hands to the work and sacrifice his/her comfort to make sure the job is completed.

In chapter five, Nehemiah addressed a situation that arose in which some of the wealthier people of Judah were taking advantage of the poor. These individuals had loaned money to the poorer people to enable them to feed their families while working on the wall. This placed tremendous hardships on families, to the point where children were sold into slavery to pay back creditors (Nehemiah 5:5). Nehemiah was appalled at this injustice and called those guilty of taking advantage of their countrymen to repent. In his rebuke he let them know how much he had invested in feeding people, the level of personal sacrifice he had made, and reminded them he had not exacted the amount of tribute he was due from them as their governor. His example of sacrificial service made his rebuke even more powerful.

A revitalizing pastor cannot be disconnected from his people or the work of ministry. Revitalization is a "roll up your sleeves and get your hands dirty" kind of ministry. It is impossible to revitalize a church without a lot of "sweat equity" from the pastor. An effective revitalizer can balance the demands of public ministry, private preparation, and family commitments, but none of those activities take care of themselves—they require time and effort. Anyone who experiences success in ministry will tell you it is not easy, but it is worth the effort. Your congregation will feed off of your energy and enthusiasm.

A Hopeful Spirit

When I was a child, my mother taught me to "always expect the worst, that way you will never be disappointed." In hindsight, that was a terrible thing to instill in a child. While I know my mom meant well, I must confess that her philosophy of life has messed me up at times. I can't tell you how many times I have had a great day only to start wondering what bad thing would happen as a result. It has taken me a long time to get to the place where I can truly enjoy blessings and endure hardship without wondering when the "other shoe is going to drop." Slowly but surely the Lord has taught me to have a hopeful spirit instead of a negative one.

I once read a newspaper column that addressed people with a negative attitude. The writer used vultures or buzzards to make his point. He talked about the fact that buzzards fly high above beautiful mountains and lush valleys but, instead of appreciating those majestic vistas, they look for a dead carcass to eat. He used that illustration to describe how people can get stuck in a pattern of negative or "stinking" thinking that keeps them from appreciating all the good things God has placed in their lives. He referred to those kind of people as having a "buzzard's eye view."

I believe pastors and laypeople can get into a pattern of thinking that causes us to focus on what is "wrong" with our lives, the people around us, and our church instead of seeing all the good God has placed in our lives. Let me encourage all of us to not allow "stinking thinking" to dominant our lives but instead become "captivated by hope." The Bible constantly reminds us of all the blessings we have because we know Christ, the benefits that are ours through that relationship, and the hope we have for our future. We have so much for which to be grateful and so much by which to be encouraged, so let's not allow Satan to rob us of the joy of the Lord which is our strength.

Negative thinking is devastating in revitalization. Unfortunately, you don't have to look very far to find things to discourage you as a revitalizer. Apathetic people, limited resources, crumbling buildings, and lack of hope are often a revitalizing pastor's reality. However, as I stated earlier, it is the Father's will that His church flourishes. We are not alone in this important work. The Sovereign God of the Universe is heavily invested in our ultimate success as revitalizers. That's a great truth to hold on to.

In Zechariah 9:12 we read, *"Return to your fortress, you **prisoners of hope**; even now I announce that I will restore twice as much to you."* (NIV, emphasis mine) Even though the children of Judah were in this midst of tough circumstances, God wanted them to know that better days were ahead and because of that truth they were prisoners of hope. Pastor/church leader, I hope you will join me in being "captured by hope" and "imprisoned by faith" to the point where no matter what happens around us, we remain positive and expectant. Persistent faith and confidence in God will be rewarded in the long run. Don't give up!

Are You Ready?

Pastor, as you reflect back on your life and ministry, examine your calling, and evaluate the current reality of your congregation; do you believe you are ready to lead your church to revitalize? Or better yet, do you believe God is leading you to initiate a revitalization effort within your church? If the answer is "yes," then get ready to see God do amazing things in your life and ministry. It will be hard work and there will be difficult days, but amid the trials you will discover the unlimited supply of blessings and resources God has for those who faithfully obey His calling. Stay strong in your faith and make sure you remain a prisoner of hope!

Chapter Three
Building Consensus Within Your Church for Revitalization and Renewal
(Guest Writer Steve Holt)

Church revitalization is not a solo journey for a pastor. It requires buy-in from the congregation as well as the investment of time, talent, and treasure to create a new day of health for the body. Whether you have just arrived on the field as a pastor or you have been there for years, you will need to bring your people along with you on the renewal pathway. Some will be willing and enthusiastic, many will be cautious and hesitant, and some will openly resist any effort to change the status quo. All of the members of the congregation will be looking to the pastor for direction as well as for cues that reveal your true motivation. Building consensus is a process that depends on a leader who makes people feel valued and who can project a genuine sense of hopefulness in the face of trying circumstances. As with so much of church revitalization, it is an "inside-out" process that begins in the heart and soul of the pastor.

Building Your Spiritual Core

Most fitness trainers stress the importance of having strong core muscles in one's abdominal area to be physically fit. Good core strength improves our posture, helps alleviate lower back pain, improves breathing, and makes it easier to do many physical activities. Good spiritual health works on a similar principle. We cultivate good spiritual core strength by maintaining our intimacy with God through prayer, obedience to God's Word, personal holiness, and daily discipline. We cannot effectively lead others spiritually unless we can lead ourselves toward greater spiritual health. Who would want to hire a personal fitness trainer who is overweight, a chain smoker, and never works out? Likewise, pastors should never ask their congregants to do anything they are not willing to do as well. Healthy spiritual leadership is essential in church revitalization.

Martin Luther is reported to have said, "I have so much to do that I shall spend the first three hours in prayer." The Bible commands us to pray without ceasing for a reason. We need to maintain a level of personal intimacy with our Heavenly Father to stay on the right track in life and prayer is our first line of access to Him. We often have trouble interpreting what is happening in the present much less predicting what the future will hold, so why would we not seek advice and counsel from the One who understands all things and holds the future in His Hands? Unfortunately, we frequently allow busyness and the stress of life to pull us away from time alone with God in prayer instead of driving us to Him. Consequently, we find ourselves drowning in the details of life and leadership with no clear direction or purpose. Our prayerlessness causes those we lead to suffer because we are unable to minister to them or lead them effectively. Revitalizers must make prayer a priority, not just for themselves, but for those they lead as well. Great things happen when we pray fervently and consistently.

Another vital component of building a strong spiritual core is time in God's Word. Pastors could easily substitute sermon preparation for personal bible study, but they are not the same. When I open the bible to do personal reflection and study, I want to encounter God and hear a word from Him to me, not my congregation. As a preacher, I am looking for ways to apply scriptural truth to the lives of the people who will hear my sermon. My primary focus is on their needs, not mine. There have been countless times in my life when I have opened God's Word in a moment of private devotion and the particular passage I was reading brought special clarity, conviction, confidence, or focus to whatever circumstance I was facing at that moment. I went to the Word just to be with the Father, but He had something more in mind that moment and it took me to a higher level of confidence and faith in Him. Effective pastors make time to be in the Word.

While reading the Bible is important, it is even more essential to obey it. Personal holiness and obedience to the Word are synonymous. Jesus told His disciples, *"If you love me, you will keep my commands."*9 Sounds easy enough, right? Our love for God and passion to serve Him should flow from our gratitude for His great salvation through Christ. Tragically, we are regularly bombarded with news stories about the moral failures of spiritual leaders, not to mention the countless failings about which we never hear. All these stories could be avoided if believers would take personal holiness and obedience more seriously. However, we all are subject to sin and temptation. Our enemy knows our weaknesses and how to exploit them in ways that distract us from our ultimate purpose of bringing God glory. That is why the personal disciplines of prayer, bible study, and holiness are essential to spiritual effectiveness.

As a revitalizer, you must build up your spiritual core through these daily disciplines. You must not let the demands of ministry rob you of your personal intimacy with the Father. Spiritual formation is not just a class we take in seminary to receive our degree. It is a lifelong, daily experience of living in constant awareness of the Presence of God and being overwhelmed by His love and grace. Our leadership should reflect that awareness and be colored by the humble gratitude of a person who has been given much. Never be guilty of serving God or His church out of a sense of duty or obligation. That mentality is devastating to your leadership and your spirit.

---

9 C.f. John 14:15.

Building Your Team of Encouragers

Still another aspect of building consensus within your church for church revitalization is creating an outside support network to keep you encouraged, focused, and accountable as you navigate through your renewal journey. Early in my ministry, I was encouraged to have three kinds of people in my life to keep me on track as a leader: a Barnabas, a Paul, and a Timothy. These biblical characters represent individuals at different stages of life and spiritual development. Each one contributes different things to my life and ministry and I can glean from them and they from me. Most of these people are not directly involved in my ministry, so they can speak frankly and objectively into my life. These three groups of people have made a real difference both in my development as a believer and as a leader. Let me describe them to you.

In my analogy, a Barnabas is someone who is farther along in the journey than I am, not necessarily older, but definitely more experienced. In the Book of Acts, we learn that Barnabas' actual name was Joseph, but he was given the nickname Barnabas which means "Son of Encouragement." He earned that name by consistently encouraging, mentoring, and networking with younger believers and leaders. Whether it was Saul of Tarsus, the young Church at Antioch, or his cousin, John Mark, Barnabas was always pouring himself into others. The encouragement of Barnabas becomes even more significant when you consider the fact that while he is not credited with writing a single word in the New Testament if you study his influence in the lives of the Apostle Paul and John Mark as well have their subsequent influence on Luke and Matthew a case can be made for the fact that Barnabas is indirectly responsible for over two-thirds of the New Testament! That is a tribute to the power of encouragement.

Who is encouraging you in that way? Is it a former pastor, professor, or significant influence from your childhood? Who do you call when you need a listening ear and an uplifting word? Throughout my life and ministry, God has placed people around me who loved me, prayed for me, and helped me fulfill God's purpose. I fear that many pastors don't have enough of those kinds of relationships. Consequently, many of us are running on an "encouragement deficit." Some of the greatest leaders I know give testimony to the Barnabas(s) in their lives. We need men and women who give wise counsel as well as words of encouragement and correction when needed. If you don't have people like that in your life, ask God to reveal some of them to you. I guarantee He has placed some around you.

When I think of the Apostle Paul, I am reminded of Hebrews 10:25, *"And let us watch out for one another to provoke love and good works."* The Greek word *paroxsmos* can be translated as "stimulate," "stir up," or "provoke." The sense is actively engaging with one another in ways that draw us closer to God and each other.10 Paul had a knack for "provoking" fellow workers and other believers to greater faithfulness and effectiveness. Whether it was one of the churches he sent an epistle, young Timothy and Titus, or his elders like Peter; Paul encouraged people but also held them accountable to the standard of God's Word. As a dedicated churchman, faithful friend, and a passionate Christ-follower, Paul maintained a high level of personal accountability for himself as well as those he served alongside. I am grateful for the people in my life who push me to be a better Christian, husband, father, and leader. I cannot say I always receive their words of challenge with joy, but I never doubt that they have my best interest at heart.

Do you have people like Paul in your life who "provoke" you to do greater things? Is there anyone who has permission

---

10 F. F. Bruce, *The Epistle to Hebrews, Revised Edition* (Grand Rapids: Wm. B. Eerdmans, 1990), pp. 256-257.

to speak words of truth to you and ask you hard questions? If you don't, you could be in danger of making serious errors in your life and leadership. We all need men like Paul, Samuel, Nathan, and the prophets of old who serve as God's messengers to us. However, we need to pursue those relationships and cultivate a level of trust and transparency within them to create an environment where true accountability can happen. Pastors don't let fear and insecurity keep you from having friends like Paul in your life.

In his book, *Reclaiming Glory: Revitalizing Dying Churches*, Mark Clifton makes a strong case for the importance of discipling young men as a part of revitalizing a church. He states that he has yet to find a dying or declining church that has a lot of young men who are actively involved in the church. He goes on to say revitalizing pastors need to be seeking young men to disciple and pour into their lives. Finally, he makes the bold statement that if you can't find and disciple at least one young man, you won't be able to revitalize your church.11 Those are strong words, but I believe they are true. Pastors need to be disciplers.

Paul had many people in his life who saw him as a mentor, but the most notable one was most likely Timothy. Paul referred to him as a "son in the faith," sent him to serve churches on his recommendation and wrote him two powerful letters of encouragement, counsel, instruction, and challenge. It is obvious that Paul loved Timothy and wanted him to succeed in life and ministry.

Do you have people in your life who you are pouring into regularly? There is a great need for discipleship in the North American church. I believe our lack of evangelistic effectiveness can be tied directly to our failure to effectively

---

11 Mark Clifton, *Reclaiming Glory: Revitalizing Dying Churches* (Nashville: B&H Books, 2016), pp. 54-58.

disciple new believers in what it means to be a follower of Jesus. Pastors must be role models in both evangelism and discipleship—especially in churches seeking revitalization. In our North American context, I believe women are more natural disciplers because they are more apt to seek out relationships with other women for support, encouragement, and accountability than are men. Pastor, I would challenge you to purposefully look for young men with whom you can build a discipling relationship. As our culture rapidly moves away from the biblical values of our past, young believers need mentors to guide them in how to live out their faith in an increasingly secular society. I believe you will find many younger men in your sphere of influence who would respond positively to being discipled.

Also, it has been my experience that such relationships are mutually beneficial to both parties. The younger believer gets the benefit of a Paul or Barnabas to instruct, encourage, and challenge him/her. The older believer gets the joy of seeing a younger Christian grow in faith and service as well as be challenged to stay personally engaged with the Lord to keep up with the enthusiasm and growth of the one being discipled. Younger believers ask great questions and provide unique insights that can stretch and challenge us as older Christ-followers. Ultimately, everyone wins when we take the time to be obedient to Christ's Great Commission to go and make disciples.

Building Your Message

Pastor Sam arrived on the field of his new church facing the daunting challenge of turning around a congregation that had been in steep decline for over ten years. While the church had seen years of positive growth and community impact, those years were definitely in the rearview mirror now. The people had become inwardly focused and no one could remember the last major outreach effort in their community. All their efforts were directed toward activities scheduled at church. He knew to reach the surrounding community he had to convince his church members to make time outside of activities at church to engage people with the gospel. He was also aware of the fact that most of them were already fatigued and stressed, so more activity would not be an easy sell. He realized he needed to have a clear, compelling message to motivate the kind of change needed to get the church moving in a new direction.

Pastors create messages on a weekly basis. We are in the communication "business." Some of us still prepare messages for Sunday morning, Sunday evening, and Wednesday—not to mention funerals, weekly bible studies, etc. We want them all to be clear, concise, compelling, and captivating. A person may spend weeks crafting an 18-minute TED talk, but pastors must produce at least one message every week. In addition to our weekly speaking responsibilities, we are tasked with the role of vision-caster and congregational leader. These roles require us to be able to have a clear, concise, and compelling message that helps our congregation understand and accept God's vision for our future as a church. Of all the messages we deliver, that one needs the most time and attention. All of our other messages will be impacted either directly or indirectly by our ability to cast a compelling "vision message."

Pastor Sam needed a message that would communicate the need to turn the church's collective focus toward impacting their surrounding community with the gospel. He knew this would require them to do a thorough examination of all their current activities to determine which ones no longer fit their mission, could be combined with other efforts or could be retooled for greater impact. Beyond the internal issues, the church faced was the issue of getting the congregation to see their community as a mission field full of opportunities to minister in Jesus' name and creating avenues for them to get involved. In short, Pastor Sam needed a stump speech.

The term "stump speech" originated in frontier days and refers to the practice of making political speeches to a group of citizens from the top of a sawed-off tree trunk. Politicians would go from village to village gathering people together in order to share the same message. His would hope that his message would resonate with the people, cause them to vote for him, and encourage their friends to do so as well. The speech would be short, repeated verbatim to each group, and end with a time for questions from the crowd. Even with the technology of the 21st century, the basic elements of political campaigning are essentially the same: develop a clear, concise message, repeat it over and over, and build a base of support.

Successful revitalizers know how to craft such a message for their churches and how to keep it constantly in front of their people. Pastor Sam began to formulate his message as he prayer walked his neighborhood and drove through his community. He made note of the closest schools, community centers, parks, and multi-family housing units to his church. He interviewed community leaders, school principals, and other area pastors to discover needs and what churches were already doing to meet those needs. He enlisted some of his key lay leaders to go with him on some of those interviews and do their own research as well. After several weeks of information gathering, he assembled his ministry staff, the lay leaders who had helped him, along with several other lay people to talk about what they had discovered. The result of that meeting was the identification of several key areas where Pastor Sam's church could focus their efforts within their community.

The first area of focus was the two closest schools to the church. Within a mile of the church there was an elementary and a middle school. While the children at Pastor Sam's church attended several different schools in the area, there were many who attended the two schools the task force identified. That meant there was already a high degree of connectivity with those campuses. After meeting with the principals of both schools, Pastor Sam and his team agreed to promote three specific outreach ministries to those schools. The first was to ask church members to volunteer some time to serve as tutors for at-risk kids. Second, they would engage the church in a ministry to provide food for some of the poorer children to take home in a backpack on Fridays. The principals told Pastor Sam that the meals those students received at school represented most of the food some of their students had during the week. They said sending backpacks with prepackaged, nutritious food items home with the students on weekends made a real difference for many of them. Third, the team decided to have an ongoing encouragement ministry to the teachers at both schools. They believed the church could provide lunch for the teachers at least once every six weeks and find other ways to minister to them as well. These efforts would require a good number of people and financial resources, but the task force felt the potential for effective ministry was well worth the investment.

The second area of focus was the city park just down the street from the church. The team believed it presented a tremendous opportunity to get church members out in the community in a very visible way as well as provide a platform to share the gospel. They envisioned ways to improve the park through "clean up" days, community block parties, and summer activities for children while they are out of school. Pastor Sam could see how having dozens of church members all wearing t-shirts emblazoned with the church's name doing ministry together in the park might help the people of the community become more familiar with who they were and what they were about. He also believed city officials would be happy to have a church working alongside them to make their park a better and more inviting place for families.

Finally, the task force identified the 200-unit apartment complex across the road from the church as their third focus area. Pastor Sam stated that people in multi-family housing are far less likely to attend church than those who live in single-family housing. The team also recognized that none of them knew of a single-family from the complex who currently attended their church. The group came up with several ideas about how the church could be more intentional in their outreach to their neighbors across the street. One of their ideas was to ask the apartment manager for permission to use the community room for a bible study and see if a ministry to kids would be a possibility during the summer. Someone even brought up the idea of asking a young couple from the church to move into the complex to serve as "missionaries" to the residents. The woman who made the suggestion also felt the church should pay that couple's rent as well. There was a lot of energy in the room around this proposal.

After their initial meeting, this informal task force covenanted to be in prayer for their church and these potential community ministries. Pastor Sam cautioned them all by emphasizing the reality that to mobilize enough of the membership to launch these new ministries, it would be necessary to take a hard look at the current ministries of the church and decide how to streamline them to create the capacity to do more outside the church building. A couple of people in the group volunteered to work with the staff to develop a plan for how those ministries could be restructured. Pastor Sam knew he had the content for his stump speech, but now he had to craft it into a message that would be used by the Lord to compel the people to make the sacrifices necessary to make the plan a reality. He knew

WHAT he needed to say. Next, he needed to figure out HOW to say it.

Crafting the Message

As he prayed about how best to share this vision with the congregation, Sam thought about how leaders communicated vision in the Bible. Whether it was Moses, Joshua, David, Nehemiah, or even Jesus; all the great leaders in Scripture faced the challenge of asking the people they led to make sacrifices to achieve God's perfect will for their future. All of them faced opposition and many of them had times of great doubt and internal struggle. Ultimately, they all found the strength and resolve to stay true to their calling as God granted them favor and the power to persevere. Pastor Sam knew that the changes needed to implement the team's vision for the future would not be made without opposition, but he knew the continued effectiveness of the church's ministry depended on making it happen. He just needed to be able to communicate the costs and benefits of those changes in a clear, concise, and compelling way.

He remembered God's challenge to Habakkuk regarding communicating vision, *"Write down this vision: clearly inscribe it on tablets so one may easily read it."*[12] He knew the vision message must be clear and easily understood. There was no doubt in Pastor Sam's mind what needed to happen to bring the vision to reality, but he was also aware that what he knew in his mind had to be communicated well for his congregation to understand it. He believed the vision came down to two things: what must be changed about the church's current ministries and the importance of the new ministries that needed to be started. The first part would be hard for many of the congregation to accept, because of their high degree of ownership and nostalgia regarding the existing ministries.

---

12 C.f. Habakkuk 2:2.

Besides any kind of change is hard to accept when it seems thrust upon you. The second part would require Pastor Sam and the other key leaders to be able to paint a mental picture of what the new ministries would look like, how the congregation could participate, and of all the benefits to the church and community that would result from their implementation. Pastor Sam went to work on putting such a message together.

Not only did the message have to be clear but it also needed to be concise—short enough so even the church member with the shortest attention span could hear it and understand what it meant. Sam wanted to come up with a slogan that could be easily remembered to use as a hook in his stump speech. The result was "Reclaiming Our Heritage to Reach Our Future." He sought to use the church's history of innovative ministry to build the case for making the needed changes to move the church forward. He read through minutes of past business meetings, a written account of the church's history compiled by a church member and talked with several longtime members to get a sense of how the church had grown in the past and what kind of changes had been made to facilitate that growth. He heard stories about tearing down buildings to create space for new ones, reorganizing the Sunday School by combining old classes and starting new ones, giving campaigns where people gave thousands of dollars to provide space for growth, etc. Over and over, he found story after story illustrating how the church had been willing to sacrifice in tangible ways to move the congregation forward. He believed those stories would help him build a clear message of how the church had always been willing to sacrifice when God's preferred future required it to do so.

Pastor Sam then went to work on making the case for why the church should adopt this vision for its future. A vision must be compelling and it has to have God's fingerprints all over it. As he prayed and sought the Lord, Sam became convinced this vision was not just the result of a brainstorming session with some church leaders. He believed God had used circumstances, scripture, and His people to lead Sam and his team to see the future from Heaven's point of view. While the overall vision was overwhelming to Pastor Sam given the church's current status, he knew it was birthed in the heart of God. He remembered the book, *Experiencing God*, and reading the following quote by Henry Blackaby, "I have come to the place in my life that, if the assignment I sense God is giving me is something I know I can handle, I know it probably is *not* from God. The kind of assignments God gives in the Bible are always God-sized. They are always beyond what people can do because He wants to demonstrate His nature, His strength, His provision, and His kindness to His people to a watching world. That is the only way the world will come to know Him."13 Blackaby's words along with his own sense of calling to reach beyond the circle of his church family drove Pastor Sam to push forward with his message of change and community engagement. He asked the Father to give him the words and the passion to communicate the vision to the church family in a compelling way.

One of Sam's mentors in ministry had once told him, "Your public ministry needs to project your private confidence in God's divine leadership." Consequently, he knew he had to get to a place in his own heart where his trust in God's power and provision was greater than his fear of failure. God told Joshua, "Haven't I commanded you: be strong and courageous? Do not be afraid or discouraged, for the Lord your God is with you wherever you go"14 So Sam

---

13 Henry Blackaby and Claude King, *Experiencing God: How to Live the Full Adventure of Knowing and Doing the Will of God* (Nashville: Broadman & Holman Publishers, 1994), p. 138.

14 C.f. Joshua 1:9.

knew he had to stop focusing on the obstacles and concentrate on the One who would be his Support and Sustainer. Making the necessary changes to accomplish God's vision would be difficult, would cause friction within the congregation, and might cause members to openly rebel or even leave. However, Pastor Sam rested in his confidence in God's direction as well as his faith in God's power to accomplish His will and purpose through Sam and the congregation.

Cascading the Message

Anyone who has watched the movie, *The Ten Commandments*, will remember the scene in which Moses, played by Charlton Heston, brings the stone tablets containing the Ten Commandments down from Mount Sinai. That is often the image that comes to mind when we think about vision casting. It is someone standing up in front of a mass of people boldly painting a picture of what the future needs to look like. However, Pastor Sam knew he was not Moses—or Charlton Heston for that matter. He also knew he was not a "top-down" type of leader, but a "consensus builder." He believed he could cascade the message out by sharing it with the staff, key influencers, lay leaders, and ultimately the entire congregation. He aimed to build consensus and momentum as he communicated the message in that manner. He envisioned the leaders with whom he conveyed the vision sharing it with others so that by the time it was formally introduced to the church, a good number of people would have already heard most of it. He saw it as an open secret to be disseminated individually or in clusters in order to create excitement, uncover unforeseen problems, and gain buy in. Initially, nothing would be set in stone, no slick promotion, just a clear message about how to move the church toward greater health and effectiveness communicated one-on-one or in small groups. With his communication strategy thus conceived, Pastor Sam started lining up meetings with his key leaders.

His first meeting was with all the members of his ministry staff. Pastor Sam was the "new kid on the block" at the church. All the other members of the ministry staff had been at the church for several years. While they had been very receptive and kind to him since his arrival on the field, Sam knew the changes he was envisioning would require a lot from them. The streamlining of the on-campus programming necessary to create the capacity to be more engaged with the community meant lots of hard work, sacrifice, and difficult conversations for the people on the ministry staff. All of them were passionate about the church and served the people out of love, but now they would be asked to adopt a new paradigm for how they approached their ministry.

Because all of them had been a part of the informal task force Pastor Sam had initially assembled, none of the plans he shared during this meeting were a surprise to them. However, now they knew he was serious about moving forward. As Sam shared, there were lots of questions about timing, the impact of several of the potential changes, and suggestions on how the changes might be better implemented. They knew the church needed to change to survive, so while there was a great deal of fear and even grief over some of the sacrifices the staff were being asked to make, almost all of them agreed to move forward. Pastor Sam listened to their concerns, made several changes based on their input, and promised to keep them in the loop as he met with the influencers and lay leaders to make the case for the new vision. They asked Sam to update them about what he was learning from those conversations during their weekly staff meetings.

Pastor Sam left the meeting feeling excited about the level of ownership for the vision he witnessed from the ministry staff. However, he was concerned by the demeanor of his discipleship pastor and his attitude about some of the potential changes. Sam had known this pastor would have the hardest time with the vision because it would impact his ministry more than any of the others. The discipleship pastor had been on staff at the church for many years and, while his time there had been fruitful for the most part, in recent years some of the steepest declines had been in the programs he oversaw. Pastor Sam sat down with this pastor later that day to have a private conversation with him. He assured him of his support and confidence, asked the discipleship pastor's support in return, and then gave the man a chance to share openly and honestly about how he was feeling. After about an hour of dialogue around the vision, both men promised to remain transparent with one another through the process. The discipleship pastor also committed his support to Pastor Sam and to the vision. This would not be the last heart-to-heart talk these two men would need to have about the subject of change, but it did establish a pattern of trust and transparency that would serve them well in the days to come.

After he met with the ministry staff, Pastor Sam took their suggestions and clarifications and worked them into his stump speech. He knew he was ready to take this new and improved message to the next level of leadership—the *Influencers*. The dictionary defines the word "influencer" as "one who exerts influence by inspiring or guiding the actions of other people." In the 21st Century, the term has also come to refer to individuals who influence people's behavior through social media. Sam knew there were a handful of long-term members at his church who carried a lot of influence among key groups of other church members. He believed having most if not all these influencers on board with the new direction of the church would go a long way toward helping the rest of the church to adopt it as well. Conversely, he knew if the influencers were critical of the plan it would be hard to get enough buy-in from the congregation to make it successful. Through the process of receiving his call to the church and his initial time there as pastor, Pastor Sam had identified at least five people whose opinion he believed carried significant weight with the membership of the church. He then began to look for opportunities to meet with them individually to share his message about the future.

When possible, he met them at their homes. He wanted them to be at ease and for the time to be unhurried and uninterrupted. Since all these folks had a long history with the church, he started each conversation by asking them to talk about the church, their time there, and tell stories of how they had seen God move in the past. These conversations were rich hours of celebration and even tears at times. All the influencers truly loved their church and were happy to share their stories and knowledge about what made it tick.

When he sensed an opening to begin to share his vision, Pastor Sam would share his concise, "Reclaiming Our Heritage to Reach Our Future" message. He would use the stories the person with whom he was talking had shared to show how the church had made changes and sacrifices in the past to grow. He would then move into the thought process behind the changes he was suggesting. After he finished, Sam asked all the influencers for feedback and questions. With only one exception, he believed everyone was at least open to the plan he described. One of the couples with whom he met took exception to the possible elimination of a popular children's ministry activity which they had been instrumental in starting. Sam knew it would take more conversation and convincing before they would support that decision.

Along with the conversations with the influencers, most of whom held no formal leadership positions in the church, Pastor Sam set up meetings with his key lay leaders. These were the men and women who served as the chairs of important teams and committees, led ministries within the church, or who taught large bible study classes. Sam followed a similar pattern in those conversations as in those he had with the influencers, but he was more intentional about how the vision might directly impact the leader's ministry or the committee they led. These conversations were some of the most fruitful and spirited Sam had through the entire process. These men and women were very passionate and had many great ideas about how to get the church moving in a positive direction. Sam came to realize that his church had lots of gifted people, but they needed someone to show them how their ministry could function more as a part of the church body and not like an island unto itself. They need a pastor who could help them work together to accomplish God's vision for their future.

A couple of months after the staff meeting where he had shared his plan, Pastor Sam gathered the informal task force together once again to share what he had learned and the adjustments he believed needed to be made to their initial implementation plan. The ministry staff distributed handouts giving details on adjustments they were prepared to make to move the plan forward. Everyone gave reports about conversations they had been having with members of the congregation about the potential plans for the future. All agreed that the mood of the church was positive and there was a sense of anticipation regarding the next steps. It was decided that the next step was to bring the entire congregation into the conversation about the future.

The group felt the best way to facilitate that kind of congregational involvement would be to gather as many as possible in "town hall" type meetings where the team could give the people the information and suggested next steps, then allow them to provide input and feedback. Pastor Sam recommended two such meetings. At the first, Pastor Sam would share his "stump speech," then the task force would give the rationale behind the need for change and the basic elements of what would be their next steps, and then end with a time of questions and answers. After a few weeks, they would gather everyone together again to talk more about the vision, get further input from the congregation, and end with a time of prayer. The goal was to involve the whole church in the plan to help them feel a part of it. While the heart of the vision would remain, everyone believed the congregation's input would make it even better.

The town hall meetings went very well. The members of the original task force met a few days after the second one to finalize their plans to present a proposal to the church at the next quarterly business meeting. It would come as a recommendation from the ministry staff. Several people commented on what a good job Pastor Sam had done in allowing the vision to bubble up through the congregation. Someone said there was no legitimate reason why anyone could say that he/she had not been allowed to hear about the plan or give input into it. Everyone felt confident the church would approve the proposed recommendations. Pastor Sam knew the Lord had given him the wisdom and skill he needed to lead the church through the process.

The Message Makes the Difference

The preceding story shows the great value of building consensus within the congregation by seeking the Lord, crafting a clear, concise, and compelling message, then communicating that message through cascading it throughout the congregation. This approach will take time and require the leader to be very patient and deliberate as he leads the people. Also, the leader will need to focus on building strong relationships throughout the church to help everyone feel they are a part of the process. But in the end, knowing God's fingerprints are all over that message will be the most satisfying part of it all.

Chapter Four
Building Your Initial Church Revitalization Team

Building a successful church revitalization team depends on forging a foundation of trust and harmony that allows for you as the church revitalization leader to stretch beyond what you can do alone into what your team can do together. If done correctly this style of team building allows you to expand far beyond your norms and into something blessed by the Lord for the purpose of revitalizing His church. The leader of revitalization still leads, but they are also the one who can inspire others, motivate the team as well as the entire congregation, and pursue with a godly passion the best for the renewing church. Church revitalization in today's world of declining churches is the David and Goliath story of old that still captures our attention. The comeback church is one that inspires all of us and yours can be another one of those churches. Building your team is a big first step in the effort. Teams work together whereas superstars work alone. You will be much more successful in revitalization if you build a team than if you go it alone. Great revitalizers know that a great revitalization team consists of solid relationships of mutual trust and comradery. Relationships on the team must be held in the highest of priorities. I believe that great revitalization teams have core competencies such as: ability to learn new skills; past perspective and future focused; willing to share ideas, concepts, and feelings; an unrelenting drive to achieve something significant; willingness to journey together; adaptable to the entire group; and a servant's heart.

While leading the Renovate Group, I have noticed that when putting together a *Church Revitalization Assistance Team (CRAT)* one should always start with participants who have the right stuff and then let it push out to the water's edge. You want a team that is quite able, well led, and displays the

72

right characteristics. Great renewal teams think collectively not individually. They own the process of renewal and are all in for the journey. "Team first for the good of the church" is a good moto to follow in leading the church revitalization team in your church. The question to ask is initially is simply, "Are we ready to begin the process of revitalizing our church?" We will see.

Ten Questions for Determining Your Readiness to Revitalize a Church

Some early questions should be considered when launching into any revitalization effort. How do you know if your church is ready to participate in Church Revitalization? Start with asking yourself these following ten questions. The more you and your church can answer these questions affirmatively, the more prepared you are to begin the church revitalization process. Here they are:

1) Do you and your people have a burden for lost people and a willingness to see your church revitalized and become healthy?

2) Has a leader surfaced to lead out the church revitalization effort?

3) Has your congregation shown a willingness to step out in faith and try new things?

4) Is the church open to the change required to see the church renewed?

5) Is your congregation spiritually mature and able to discern God's movement?

6) Has your congregation demonstrated a generous spirit?

7)   Are you willing to risk?

8)   Does your congregation have a genuine Kingdom mindset?

9)   Are you willing to invest resources (people & finances) towards renewing your church?

10) Do you have a vision for your city and region?

There are probably another ten questions that will be discovered along the way but these initial questions ought to be discussed and considered by those who are joining the church's revitalization team.

The Characteristics of Key Revitalization Team Members

In the selection of team members do not just make an announcement in church and accept all of those who volunteer. You must, as the pastor, select the right team and not become bogged down by those who either do not want the church to be revitalized and choose to be part of the team to disrupt the effort. Also, you must not allow some to serve on the team who are notorious in the church for not doing anything significant. These two types of individuals will destroy any real chance you have to revitalize one's church. The church revitalization teams which often fail are made up of individuals who lack a consistency to stay the course through the effort of revitalization. You are about to invest a minimum of one thousand days towards turning around your church and there are individuals which just cannot stay connected for that long. Choose your team carefully and wisely or you will regret the effort in the final analysis. Problems that arise on the renewal team often stem from not reflecting upon who should and who should not serve on the team. Do not get handed a group of people selected by someone besides the leader of the revitalization effort. When little thought is given to the characteristics for a successful revitalization team you will often have individuals with few if any skills necessary for the successful serving on the team. Here are some key member characteristics of the church revitalization assistance team:

Collaboration

The member's must be willing to work together and build the ability to work together as a unified core and not individual MVP's! When you fill your team with cooperative individuals who are committed to the goal of revitalizing one's church, you have a greater chance to see it come to fruition. Collaborators are your partners and teammates in the journey. They will be the ones who will encourage you and lift you up as you keep the throttle pressed forward and the pace of change continuing.

Dedication

If you cannot find individuals who possess the dedication for the renewal journey, do no place them on this team. Team members must be sold on the idea of revitalizing a church and be fully committed to the task. Placing people on the team will not convince them of the need to renew a work. You must have individuals who are willing to persevere in the process of turning around one's church. It is not a quick fix and it will take time. You must take the time, spend the time and endure the time it will take to bring about renewal to one's church. Loyalty to the process of revitalization and the particular church as it works hard to survive will be a key.

Evangelistic Fervor

To serve effectively on a church revitalization assistance team, individual members must believe in evangelism. If you have a group on the team that does not believe you must work to reach the lost for Christ Jesus, they will hurt every single effort to impact the culture you are trying to reach around the church. Evangelistic thinkers will have the passion needed to build the Kingdom by renewing churches into healthy bodies once again. Going after the lost ones of your community and reaching them for Christ is still a key to growing a church regardless if it is a plant, a healthy church, or a declining church which needs revitalization.

Optimism

The joy of the Lord is one's strength and nothing is more helpful to a church revitalizer building a team to assist in the revitalization effort than those who choose joy over depression regardless of the circumstances. Church revitalization is a challenging endeavor, so you do not want naysayers on your Church Revitalization Assistance Team. The best type of person to serve on this team are those who can discover the opportunities in the midst of obstacles. They are optimistic about the cause and refuse to fuss and feud over nonessential matters. There will be an intense effort by the status quo to place as many individuals onto team so they can control the outcome of the team's efforts. These type of efforts leads to even more decline because some of those in the church wanting renewal eventually see the big picture and do not want anything to do with the church anymore and leave because of this negativity towards change and renewal. In a church becoming renewed, there will be negative people because they will look at the new effort as giving up something which they hold dear. Stagnation is the thing they love. Yet such people cannot be allowed to come into this group or you are sunk.

Faith

The Church Revitalization Assistance Team must be people of faith! They must be willing to believe God for the impossible. They must be able to embrace a vision of what a revitalized church looks like. They must be willing to look beyond what is seen into the unseen. That takes great faith. The Bible says: *"Now faith is the assurance of things hoped for, the conviction of things not seen"* (Heb. 11:1).

Everybody has faith in something, even the most diehard skeptic. The question is whether or not that faith is in the right place and of the right amount. The revitalization team must be made up of people who believe in God for the impossible. They must believe in the person and work of the Lord Jesus. Throughout the Gospels, Jesus himself calls people to have faith in God. Many who run from the work of revitalization will in the end hear from the Savior, *"Oh, you of little faith."* We want this team to be faith-full and not faith-less. In Matthew's gospel, we are given five examples of little faith and an additional five examples of great faith. The difference could be summarized in these statements: Little faith is smothered by fear, while great faith is strengthened by boldness. Little faith pays attention on the material world, while great faith places one's emphases on the spiritual world. Little faith makes choices based on what is doable for individuals, while great faith makes decisions based on what is possible for God.

Church Revitalization Assistance Team Individual Member Gifts

As well as the previous characteristics which you will want in every single person on the team, additionally there are some specific gifts which should be displayed by various members. It goes without saying that members should enjoy working on teams. Not everyone needs all of gifts, but you should fill your team with individuals who possess these traits. It is wise to have at least one of each of these types of individuals on the team.

Strategic Thinking

You will need at least one strategic thinker on the team, someone who is adept at reasoning through a process. This person understands goals, objectives, plans, and strategic steps. Strategic thinkers typically ask penetrating questions. Someone has well stated that: *Thinking Strategically First Makes Strategic Planning Work.* Done well, a strategic plan provides a beneficial concentration that invigorates and transfers the church organizational structure toward its real mission of revitalizing the church. For the church revitalization effort, you need the kind of strategic thinker who can:

1.   Foresee the Needed Shifts the Church Must Make

2.   Think Diagnostically of the Circumstances in the Church Which Must be Addressed

3.   Translate the Changing Culture Around the Local Church

4.   Do Something and Stop Being Paralyzed by No Activity

5.   Align Others to the Cause of Revitalization

6.   Become a Lifelong Learner if Not One Already

I am sure there are others as well, but these will do to start you thinking strategically about what needs to happen for revitalization to have the best possible chance for success.

Institutional Memory

This historian type individual helps the church avoid repeating mistakes. A long tenured pastor or staff member is such a likely person. An individual who has been a positive long-term member can help the revitalization not to repeat past mistakes by providing past historical information at the appropriate time which could help newbies understand the past failures and take necessary actions to not repeat the past again.

Ministry Contribution

People who are active in the church's current ministries will contribute greatly to the team's effectiveness. Determine which groups would be most helpful and involve them as they are needed. Because they are already busy doing the work of ministry include them only when necessary. Having a large attendance is not your goal, revitalizing the church is the goal.

Creative Thinker

Every church in need of revitalization would like to have a battalion of creative thinkers, if it were not for the mess creative thinkers cause those stuck in outdated norms and functions. Creative thinkers are an asset to the *Church Revitalization Assistance Team*. Revitalizing a plateaued church is not a traditional endeavor. You will want people who see things a bit off center. I have learned from revitalizing churches, that people of habit do not have the ability to see other things. These types of creative team members will stretch the rest of the team. Creative people force others to break free from the confines of conventional wisdom. They help the rest of the team to clearly see new options and think clearly about the choices it makes. What is the difference between the words reactive and creative? Answer: It is how you arrange the letters. The same can be said about creative thinkers. They have the ability to rearrange the way we think for the betterment of the church.

During the days while Bill Gates led Microsoft, he realized that he did not have to know everything. He recognized that he had employees who did. But he appreciated the importance of taking the time to learn what they knew and absorb their creative thinking. He took time to listen to their ideas. He took time to think, to ponder the direction of Microsoft. The one who leads the church revitalization effort must be willing to spend the time listening to the creative in the group as they help bring the church out of its doldrums. Here is a great exercise to stimulate innovation and creativity for anyone who is going to lead the church revitalization effort of a local church:

1. Read with pen and notebook in hand; jot down any idea that comes into your consciousness.

2. Keep a notebook in which you can keep track of ideas, by your bed and in your car.

3. Write one idea down on a piece of paper and brainstorm any thought that comes from it: how to accomplish the idea, what to do about the idea, where to use the idea, who can help you implement the idea, and any other thought that enters your mind.

4. Read a non-fiction book every week. Read magazines, journals, online articles, all-the-time.

5. Clip articles and place them in a folder of related articles or ideas. Periodically, glance through the folder.

6.   Create "idea files" in most folders in your computer. Create an idea or to-do file in your email program. Add ideas as they come to you.

7.   Take time to stare out your window (if your setting deserves attention), play with a desk toy, and take a quiet walk.

8.   Do any rote activity that allows thoughts to swirl through your mind.

9.   Encourage your church revitalization assistance team to do all of the above and share ideas with each other at "think" or brainstorm sessions.

10. Schedule annual retreats or off-site meetings to plan and generate ideas.

11. Develop a church member idea box.

12. Schedule think weeks, think days, or think hours for yourself or your work group.

Thinking time and learning time are both critical to creativity and innovation. The old adage: "stop to smell the roses" is true for both your current ministry and your long-term ministry. Take time to cultivate and harvest the ideas that fuel your progress and success. Creative thinking reigns.

Leading the Church Revitalization Team

Who should lead the Church Revitalization Assistance Team? What is the Operative Team Size? I suggest that five to seven individuals serve on the Church Revitalization Assistance Team in order to accompany the Revitalization Leader. Here are some Church Revitalization Assistance Team

Responsibilities which should be considered. A Church Revitalization Assistance Teams will be responsible for at least the following actions:

- Identify and recruit intercessors who will pray for the revitalization project

- Communicate a biblical understanding of church revitalization to the congregation

- Develop a biblical understanding of the directive to become healthy again

- Create awareness of the process of change that awaits the congregation (A Missional Endeavor)

- Clarify relationships and mutual expectations with denominational leaders and with the church attempting revitalization

- Create a timeline for the project and identify critical milestones

These actions will help the church in the effort of renewal and keep you and your team on track. A Church Revitalization Team's purpose is to assist the church revitalizer in leading the church through the revitalization process. Understand that the team should not be an ongoing committee or team given a new assignment to serve as the revitalization assistance team. Their sole purpose is only to focus on the revitalization process for as long as it is required.

What Does Church Revitalization Mean?

Every place I go people ask me for a definition of church revitalization. Church Revitalization is a movement within protestant evangelicalism, which emphasizes the missional work of turning a plateau or rapidly declining church around and moving it back towards growth. It is lead through a Church Revitalization Initiative, which is when a local church begins to work on the renewal of the church with a concerted effort to see the ministry revitalized and the church become healthy. Church Revitalization means that the local church knew how, at one time previously, to renew, revitalize, and re-establish the health and vitality of the ministry. One of the challenges for the laity in the day in which we live is that they have lost the knowledge of church renewal and no longer want to cultivate the skill sets necessary to see their church experience revitalization. Even sadder is when a congregation does not have the corporate memory that there was a day when the local church was reaching people for Christ Jesus and active as evangelistic witnesses into their community.

Keys to Building a Qualified Revitalization Team

Your church revitalization team is critical to your success in the renewing of your church. This team is led by the pastor who serves as the church revitalizer with the single solitary purpose of working towards church renewal. How you build your team will either make you or break you. Here are some initial steps:

Seek the Lord About Your Selections

Going to the Father with a humble plea for revelation of the right members for your team is important. We are at war with the devil so begin with the one who has overcome the evil one. Take three weeks to pray over your list every day before making initial contacts with prospective individuals.

Decide the Structure of the Team

What you decide in your church might be different than what I do in my church revitalization effort. It is always wise to have a plan developed before you begin selecting those to serve on the team. What has been present earlier in this chapter has always worked well and worthy of your consideration.

Begin Selecting and Inviting Potential Members to Join the Team

Not everyone you have selected will be able to participate on the team so have a few individuals from the various types above will allow you to not lose momentum. Spiritual people serve best because revitalization is a spiritual journey first and foremost. If you could have some of your most spiritual and influential church members aboard that would go a long way. There must be a sense of unity so having harmonious people is a must. Look for those in your church who are busy but not too busy as well. This will take time so they must be able to invest in the effort. Be sure you have laid out the responsibilities ahead of time before you begin inviting others to join the team. Keep this in prayer as you make the invitations. Work on ways to get the team together so they begin building a bond with one another. We actually use our Biblical DiSC Assessment that allows us to know how each member on the team is wired.

Wrapping it Up!

The Church revitalizer must not only build a successful revitalization team they should also consider individuals which can work together without having to one up each other. That is never easy and often problematic. Creating a Church Revitalization Assistance Team necessitates the joining of people from different cultures and outlooks.

Further, it requires that the different revitalization skillsets you will need, be represented in your selections of members. Pastors and church revitalizers understand that once the team is formed it is always best to play to the strengths of the various participants. By doing so you get the best from everyone on the team. Allow them to do what they do best and the team will be stretched into a powerfully competent team. You are not the leader to referee squabbles. You are there to lead a team for the renewal of a local church. Create a win-win style emphasizing solutions over the problems. Remind the members of the team that you are there for them and you have their backs. That often means removal of the key obstacles that are causing decline in the church. Churches which have been successful in turning around declining churches in Church Revitalization and Renewal have revealed that it takes a singularly focused type of leader with unique revitalization skills to effectively construct great teams. Seeing a church revitalized is something which should be celebrated. It is usually a fleeting endeavor. Celebrate the win with the entire church and not just the team. Live in the moments of success for a while. The local church cannot make serious gains in renewal without a team that will guide the church towards health. Many a church revitalizer is looking for a magic bullet that will bring about renewal. The best church revitalization leaders are those who dare to practice quiet urgings given from the Lord in the moment of solitude. I can't tell you the number of times the Lord has spoken to me in the quiet of the night while the world slept. Boldness and courage are the necessary ingredients for revitalization leaders in today's ever-shifting, church. If you respond to His leading your church members who love the local church will want to give their best to the cause of renewal in your church.

Chapter Five
What Is the State of Your Church?
Assessing You and Your Church!

Because church revitalization takes some time you must begin to assess early with as much reality as possible, the current state of your church you pastor. I have worked with thousands of pastors and churches all across North America and it has amazed me just how many pastors and laity believe that they can revitalize a church in one hundred and eighty days or less. It just does not happen and yet many church leaders are seeking a quick fix turnkey solution that they can plug and play resulting in a glorious renewal without any sacrifice or repentance. Many nearsighted leaders believe it can be wrapped into a six-month period. In fact, I hear ministers who are accustomed to living and leading on peak-to-peak programing who consider giving more than six months a waste of time. While we are looking at the first one hundred and twenty days as you initiate your church renewal process, please understand that for real revitalization to last you must be willing to invest a minimum of 1000 days and if you are not willing to do this, you should not get into the effort of revitalization and renewal.

Every church at one time or another needs a little nudge. Each time I enter into another church revitalization project and begin working with a new church or set of churches, I think back to what I have affectionately called: "THE NUDGE LIST!"15 Remember when you were a kid and one of your parents gave you a gentle nudge to get you back to your homework assignment? Do you remember when one of

---

15 At the back of this book, in the conclusion, I have created *Your One Hundred Twenty Daily Nudges to Begin Revitalization*. It is a list that gives you one thing for each day of your first 120 days in renewal. These are designed to become starters or nudges as it were for you to get off running as a church revitalizer.

your parents came into your bedroom and gave you a soft word about the look of your room and how much better it would be if you cleaned it up? These were gentle nudges designed to get you to begin a task that was much needed. Churches that are falling back into becoming legacy churches often need the nudge in a similar way.

The Nudge List in Church Revitalization

So how do you create a Nudge List for church revitalization? Think about ideas and ways that will send a message to the community that you are doing new and exciting things. If you are the pastor think about ways you can share the dream using short-term, midterm, and long-range ideas and goals for renewal and revitalization. What would your church's nudge list look like as it begins the revitalization process?

A Suggested Nudge List Activity

Take a moment to gather a notepad and something to write with. Read Proverbs 27:23 *"Know the state of your flocks, and put your heart into caring for your herds."*[16] Please spend the next ten minutes thinking about some simple things (nudges as it is) you and your church can do to begin to lead it back to becoming a healthy church once more. Here are some suggestions that I have just Jens OK every year used and others as well have used to begin the gentle nudge of their church towards renewal and revitalization:

> Pastoral Dreams for the Church Shared
> Facility Improvements Begun (a little paint, rearranging the mess, cleaning up, etc.)
> Nursery Renovated (and shared as a positive)
> Discipleship Emphasized (and shared as a positive)

---

[16] Tyndale House Publishers, *Holy Bible: New Living Translation* (Carol Stream, IL: Tyndale House Publishers, 2015), Proverbs 27:23.

Music Team Revived (and shared as a positive)
Quarterly Church Fellowships launched to connect
members with prospects.
A New Young Adult Ministry Launched
Establishment of a Kids Ministry (and shared as a
positive step) such as kids church or other ministries like
Awana or Upward
Systematic Visiting of Every Church Member and
Prospect
Hosted Musical Events
New Member's Class Initiated
Church Signage Renovated
Laity Challenged and Enlisted for Service
Joining and Volunteering for Community
Celebrations as a Means of Evangelism
Developing Uniting Activities that Bring People
Together
Creating Evangelistic Projects and Events to Reach
into Community
New Things and New Plans Not Previously Tried
that Demonstrate a New Day
Home Groups and Discipleship Groups Emphasized
Preaching a Family Message Series
Your First 120 Days in Revitalization Drafted and
Designed

Every year as directed in the Constitution, the President
presents to Congress a "State of the Union" address. The
United States Constitution states that the president "shall
from time to time give to the Congress Information of the
State of the Union, and recommend to their Consideration
such measures as he shall judge necessary and expedient."17
According to the National Archives, George Washington first
fulfilled this particular presidential duty on January 8, 1790,
when he addressed the new Congress in the Senate Chamber

---

17 Article II, Section 3 of the U.S. Constitution.

of Federal Hall in New York City (then the U.S. capital).18 Similarly, the "State of the Church" address brings members up to date on how the church has progressed in the previous year in carrying out its mission. It also should give some direction for the church's ministry in the upcoming year. Keeping your focus on things that can help in renewing your church is a great way to utilize that annual message while leading a revitalization effort. A clear reality of where your church currently resides is important. Is it on the incline of growth, in a maintenance mentality, declining, or in a rapid period of decline? The pastor should prepare for this event and take it as an opportunity to unite the church towards revitalization and renewal. Many pastors choose to deliver their "State of the Church" address as a sermon during a worship service to impact a greater number of persons. Others use a more informal setting or a special service and a more targeted audience. Some pastors use charts or graphs to give visual representations of areas of growth or advance.

The Stages of Church Revitalization and Renewal

Like anyone who becomes ill there is a medical diagnosis that takes place in order to assess the situation. Three stages are:

> **Diagnosis** – Discovers reality and real issues or problems

> **Surgery** – Prepares the church to address the things which negatively affect the church

> **Recovery** – Seeks God's plans and develops God's new leaders

Perhaps the best way to begin the diagnosis of your church would be by looking at and considering your current

---

18 C.f. https://www.archives.gov/legislative/features/sotu

church realities. Make a list of the things you and your church are doing well. Then on a separate piece of paper list the areas in the church where there is the challenge of not achieving appropriate outcomes. By beginning to look at your current realities it prepares you to enter the church revitalization process with your eyes wide open. Consider items such as the number of new units you have begun in Bible Study or Home Groups. Listing of the new things that have been initiated over the past year would also be worth mentioning. I always acknowledged the number of new members and participants added over the previous year. If you are going to do that I suggest that you also acknowledge those who left the church or were deceased in that same time period. Addressing the church's plan for engaging the community culture in your area is a wise thing to include as well. The last three should intentionally be placed as you are moving towards the conclusion of your state of the church sermon. The first one most often presented near the end would be how the church is doing in reaching the lost and bringing them through believers' baptism. If you are increasing, plateaued or declining in this area it is best to acknowledge what has worked, what isn't working, or why it appears not to be working. The next item could be your state of the finances for the ministry. Are there some financial indicators for your church that you could emphasize? Lastly, some form of key factors for the revitalization of your church ought to be presented as a means of a challenge for everyone to jump aboard the effort for renewal. Closing out your "state of the church" message it would be good to demonstrate where you are at this point. Then share where you believe the Lord is calling the church to go from here and how we are going to get there. If there are changes that need to be made or key steps to be taken, presenting them at this time would be advised. Concluding with some quick initial steps you and the leaders are taking in the next thirty days would be a wonderful conclusion giving them hope and knowledge that both pastoral leadership and lay leadership have already been discussing, planning, and preparing for the days ahead. Be sure to share scripture throughout your message. The Bible has solutions for renewal so emphasize them.

Benchmarking A Church Revitalization and Renewal Strategic Planning Process

Do you not know that those who run in a race all run? And everyone who competes in the games exercises self-control in all things. They then do it to receive a perishable wreath, but we an imperishable. Therefore, I run in such a way, as not without aim; I box in such a way, as not beating the air (1 Cor. 9:24-26 NASB).

A common mistake made in declining churches is to be driven by their calendar and not compelled by critical benchmarks. Benchmark planning is one of the most important aspects of the renewal planning process, because project benchmarks are the most visible indicators of project progress. Benchmarks typically mark critical decision points, the completion of major project tasks, and the ends of various project phases. Benchmarks are tools used in project management to mark specific points along a revitalization project timeline. Essentially, you want to make the most important events of your revitalization project as benchmarks so that they are easily viewed and mapped by the church revitalization team. Benchmarks are given additional significance over tasks in a plan so that the revitalization team can track the tasks while the congregation can focus on forward progress.

What are Benchmarks?

Benchmarks are the results of actions. They identify the completed components of your projects. These benchmarks need to be written in the past tense as they show completed actions. Benchmarks measure progress in your project. In our Church Revitalization Boot Camps, one exercise we experience is when church leaders along with their pastor identify where they as a church is presently. Then they also define where the church needs to go in moving forward toward renewed health and vitality. Benchmarks are important because: they can tell you if your church is falling behind the needs of the community, allow you to refocus and catch up on your revitalization strategy, help your revitalization team to intercede at a moment's notice, and allow you to diagnose reoccurring issues that have yet to be resolved in the declining church. When Benchmarks are arranged in a logical sequence, and relationships between the benchmarks are established, a strategic plan has been outlined. Completed tasks are actions required to accomplish the benchmarks. A benchmark may be "four new Home Groups launched." What actions need to take place for that to happen? The actions might include, potential members identified, leaders enlisted and trained, meeting space secured, and materials ordered. Critical benchmarks must be achieved or the objective will not be attained and the church most likely will not move to the next desired level of growth. There may one hundred benchmarks to accomplish in the next twelve months, but only half a dozen would be critical benchmarks.

Characteristics of Effective Benchmarks

What are the characteristics of effective benchmarks? Effective benchmarks are consistent with vision, values, mission statement, and church system design; realistic in terms of time projections and sequence; enable a steady flow of relationships between benchmarks and are usually less than a dozen. In revitalization the development of benchmarks may be many but there will only be about twelve significant ones. Not everything is critical. There may be only ten to twelve critical benchmarks in a church revitalization process. Here are seven benchmarks towards success in your revitalization effort. They are:

Ask Yourself if There a Clear Vision for Renewal?

Every church member knows the objective of revitalization is to bring back renewed health and vitality to the congregation. Whatever the vision is it needs to be clearly and succinctly communicated in a memorable, easy to embrace way. This vision comes from God's leading, not man's invention, but *"without a vision the people perish."*

Ask yourself if there a Clear Strategy with Distinct Goals in Place?

There is a plan to achieve the vision for revitalization. Church leaders are operating with reasonable, attainable, measurable, and worthy goals. They have the resources in place to complete them.

Ask yourself if a Great Team has been Recruited?

You will spin your wheels and never have good traction if you fail to recruit a great team in your church. You simply can't do it alone. Consider this, because someone was a good fit yesterday doesn't mean they always will be. Church members are always the greatest asset, but they can also be the greatest hindrance to achieving success if they are the wrong people. Continually ask who the right players critical to the revitalization process are.

Ask yourself if the Tasks have been Divided Equitably?

I was naive early in my leadership as a pastor to believe everyone shared my work ethic. They don't. If a declining church is going to succeed, everyone must pull his or her weight. There can be no dawdlers. There is much hard work to be done.

Ask yourself if the Communication is Fluent and Frequent?

This is a tough one because as the church begins to grow again, people will naturally know less and less about everything. There's a danger of silos developing if people aren't continually engaged as a team. A huge challenge for any successful revitalization effort is effectively communicating throughout the entire congregation.

Ask yourself if there is a Resolve to Persevere and Endure?

I never knew how big this one was until I was in a church that was already in decline and I had come to restart it. There are some of the people which I thought were the most dedicated actually were not. That hurt the congregation. If a declining church wants to be successful in renewal, there must be a strong, committed core of people who are in it for the long-haul, regardless of the setbacks and disappointments, which will naturally come.

Ask yourself if there a Communal, Celebratory, and Fun Atmosphere?

People in revitalization need to have fun! There should be joy in the revitalization journey. Team members need to know they are valued, a part of something bigger than today, and they can laugh, cry, and do life together as a family would. The Revitalization team can easily lose its enthusiasm for the project and get bored quickly when renewal is not mixed with fun and celebration.

Wrapping it up!

By spending time in prayer and seeking the ideas of your fellow church leaders, both clergy and laity alike you are better prepared to clearly understand the state of your church. At the back of this book in the appendix, you will have various examples of assessments and surveys which you could use to understand the state of your church. There are additional action plan worksheets and a SWAT analysis worksheet that has proven helpful for many churches. A great question to ask yourself and your lay leadership team in your church is what time is it? Understanding the life and times of any church is fundamental for wise decisions. Too often, pastors and church leaders step into a church situation without understanding the specific moment the church is in. That is dangerous for the one leading in renewal. It is hard to make wise decisions that way. In his popular book, *The First 90 Days*, Michael Watkins connects one's understanding of the organization's situation to having the wisdom to make good decisions. "Matching your strategy to your situation requires a careful diagnosis of the business situation," he writes. "Only then can you be clearheaded, not just about the challenges, but also about the opportunities and resources available to you."19 Watkins sees four types of organizational "moments," which I think we can apply to a church setting.

1. The first is the **"start-up"** which could compare to a church plant; it involves getting the new project off the ground.
2. The second is the **"turnaround"** in which the church has declined precipitously and needs to implement significant changes to survive and grow.

---

19 Watkins, Michael D. *The First 90 Days: Proven Strategies for Getting Up to Speed Faster and Smarter.* Boston: MA Harvard Business Review Press, (2013). Quote can be found at: https://hbr.org/2009/01/picking-the-right-transition-strategy.

3. The third is **"realignment"** in which a church that is drifting into trouble or losing its focus needs revitalization.
4. The fourth is **"sustaining success"** when the church is healthy and needs a leader who can take the congregation to the next level.

You cannot understand where to take the church you are leading if you are unable to understand where it has been and just how the church got to where it is right now. By focusing on your church's spiritual health and vitality, attendance figures, membership rolls, number of individuals being discipled annually, and the state of evangelism in your church you are better prepared to begin your effort of revitalization and renewal. The number might be challenging and troubling but knowing this data will only prove helpful. Current realities considered leads to effective strategies for renewal. Do not miss the strategic key for these first one hundred and twenty days and that is becoming acquainted with the actual time it is in your church.

Chapter Six
What are the Critical Issues?
Facing Your Church?

This chapter will deal with the top seven most critical issues facing declining churches. If you get these corrected you have the best chance for turning around a struggling church. It is not a surprise to most church members today that the church of the western hemisphere is in grave trouble. There is a danger of church closure all around declining or dying churches. We are living in a day where everything around us is growing except for the majority of us, the church in which we attend. Our last census showed us that America is growing. Our schools are full of children and youth. Even in our colleges and universities, the attendance is on the rise. Yet our total church membership is down more than 22%[20], Sunday School attendance is down 24%[21], baptisms are down 28%[22], and the number of those joining the church by ways other than baptism is down 37%[23] over the past fifteen years! It is time for church revitalization and renewal!

The hard reality in North America is that most churches and most, if not all, denominations are in a state of decline. Huge numbers of congregations are now fighting for their survival, and many will close. Some experts predict that as many as two-thirds of the mainline congregations that exist today will close their doors over the coming two decades. The

---

20 https://news.gallup.com/poll/248837/church-membership-down-sharply-past-two-decades.aspx

21 https://kenbraddy.com/2016/09/07/25-reasons-why-sunday-school-is-declining-in-some-places-part-1/

22 https://www.baptistpress.com/resource-library/news/sbc-giving-increases-while-baptisms-continue-decline/

23 Ibid.

membership within these churches and denominations is plateauing and what used to pass for involvement and activity within churches is deteriorating. While all of this is happening, the rank and file of the church appear powerless to assemble the strength that is needed to get the churches growing again. Kevin Ezell, President of the North American Mission Board declares, "We must keep our denominations focused on the ministry of rebirth and redemption, not on the business of enforcing rules and rituals."

The need for training today's minister with the tools and skillsets necessary to combat this rampant plateau and decline is crucial. Most ministers coming out of our seminaries today lack preparation for the challenge of church revitalization and renewal. If the estimates are accurate that, at a minimum, eighty percent or more of our churches need revitalization, then it stands to reason that the majority of graduates from our seminaries are going to begin their ministries in the majority of these churches. Less than five percent of these graduates will actually be going to healthy churches. Existing ministers will pastor the healthy pool of churches that make up the twenty percent so the seminarian needs to prepare for the eventual challenge of revitalizing a plateaued or declining church. We need to begin the journey of revitalization right away.

The optimistic church revitalizer will recognize the enormous opportunity and potential for the local church and prayerfully seek the Lord in the effort of revitalization and renewal. If we take the time to understand the critical issues in church revitalization and renewal these could be our greatest days in "churchdom."

In Paul's letter to the Ephesians is says:

> *'When he ascended on high, he led captives in his train and gave gifts to men.' It was he who gave some to be apostles, some*

*to be prophets, some to be evangelists, and some to be pastors
and teachers, to prepare God's people for works of service, so
that the body of Christ may be built up until we all reach unity
in the faith and in the knowledge of the Son of God and become
mature, attaining to the whole measure of the fullness of Christ.
Then we will no longer be infants, tossed back and forth by the
waves, and blown here and there by every wind of teaching and
by the cunning and craftiness of men in their deceitful scheming.
Instead, speaking the truth in love, we will in all things grow up
into him who is the Head, that is, Christ. From him the whole
body, joined and held together by every supporting ligament,
grows and builds itself up in love, as each part does its
work."24*

There are a variety of issues identified as important
for church renewal and revitalization. In *Slaying the Dragon
of Church Revitalization: Dealing with the Critical Issues Which
are Hurting Your Church* I have identified seventeen. For
the purpose of your first 120 days in renewal, I want to
draw your attention to the critical few. These critical
seven are:

Leadership Development
Recruiting Volunteers
Worship
Evangelism
Relationships
Relevant Dynamic Structures
Stewardship & Financial

We will consider each one separately as we consider the
critical issues facing declining churches.

---

24 C.f. Ephesians 4:8, 11-16 NIV.

Leadership Development

Leadership is frequently a struggle, and yet most leaders refuse to talk about the difficulties for fear of appearing weak and seeming to lack the confidence a pastor/leader should possess. Many pastors unconsciously categorize the word "struggle" as a negative which makes dealing with struggle even more difficult than it needs to be. This can become especially problematic when pastors of revitalization efforts find themselves facing significant challenges. Let us face it; taking the lead in the revitalization of a declining or dying church is difficult. Some ministers are great preachers but terrible leaders. Some are great administrators but lack the skill sets to turn around the church. There are some who have the heart for revitalization but are unable to pull the trigger when it comes to leading the effort of revitalization. Leadership development is perplexing for those working in the field of revitalization. The reason is that many church members will fight the leader at every turn seeking to either stall the revitalization effort or to get the effort removed from consideration. Great leadership is the heart of great ministry and vision is the heart of great leadership. Vision inspires, attracts, builds, and sustains. Leaders must own the vision, protect the vision, and pray faithfully for the fulfillment of the vision.

Why did Christ give these gifted ones to the church? A common reading of these verses from the King James Version would outline the responsibility of these gifted servants as the ones who do each of the following ministries:

> For the perfecting of the saints,
> For the work of the ministry,
> For the edifying of the body of Christ.

A more helpful rendering is found in the New International Version which identifies the work of the gifted ones as *"to prepare God's people."* The result of their work is that God's people might do *"works of service."* As God's people do works of service, the result is *"that the body of Christ may be built up."* The building up of the church body is twofold:

> There are those within the body, they are continuing to become more mature and more stable in their faith—thus more Christ-like.

> Because of their growing character, the saints will do the works of service through ministry and witness, to those outside the church.

Many church revitalizers grieve the shortage of workers but at the same time fail to train new workers. One pastor told of this frustration. He looked out his study window and prayed, "God send me workers." He reported that God answered in an almost audible voice, "You have them but they are not in the clouds but in the crowds." He then complained to God that the people he had were not qualified or trained. God reminded him that when He began to use this pastor, he was not trained or qualified. His training and qualification came in the doing. A new pastor just after coming to the church complained to the associational missionary that the church planter left him no trained workers in the church. Every time they were together the pastor voiced the same complaint. After one year at the church, he began to express the same lament of no trained workers. The associational missionary stopped him and said, "For the first year, the lack of trained workers was your predecessor's fault. But now the lack of trained leaders is your responsibility and yours alone." Pastors should work hard at empowering and developing another believer for ministry. These leaders seek to assist church members to attain the spiritual potential God has for them. They invest a majority of time not in doing the work of ministry but in equipping supporting, motivating, delegating, and multiplying. They view their role as helping members identify their gifts and involve them in appropriate ministry. Here are the key questions to consider in developing leaders:

> Is the pastor seen as a minister or THE minister in the church?

> How can we work effectively to mobilize and equip God's people for the works of service?

> Are we expanding the core of leadership?

> What kind of leaders are we developing?

> What is our specific strategy for leadership development?

It takes a strong singularly focused leader who is unrelenting in the task to revitalize a church. Leading a turnaround process might even require you saying farewell to some of your membership only willing to live in the past and not interested in reach out for a new future. There are individuals within the church you are leading that because of their individual behavioral wiring they would rather see your church die than make the necessary changes required to revitalize or renew your church. According to my co-author Terry Rials in *The Nuts and Bolts of Church Revitalization,* "Virtually all experts agree that the primary responsibility for leading the church in revitalization falls upon the pastor." That is why it takes a huge focus on the task.

Recruiting Volunteers

The second critical issue facing your church as you begin working on revitalization and renewal is the recruiting of volunteers. Far too few pastors spend any appreciable time developing and recruiting volunteers. The volunteers in your church have the right to be treated as fellow workers and should be allowed to know as much about the church and its policies and procedures as possible. If a congregation is to reflect the community of Jesus and His disciples, if it is to really continue that community's mission, then it should act as a community. This means, that it must foster a spirit of trust and comradery. The things they volunteer for needs to be more than just the list of things that the pastoral staff decline to do. A volunteer needs to enjoy the work they have been recruited to carry out. If there is no joy in one's assignment the emotional drain will never cease and eventually burn the volunteer out. Volunteers have a right to assume that the congregation will take their abilities into consideration. One's talents should be appreciated for all that they do in the church. If you are going to recruit someone then they should also have some degree of training before you input them into the work of ministry. Enlist someone who will serve as a sounding board for the first six months of the new recruit's ministry. You can't overestimate the value of volunteers and you can't over appreciate them. Some churches don't like the word volunteer. Use the word that works best for you. A healthy benchmark to target is 50% - 80% of your adult worship attendance involved in some form of consistent service. The reason the percentage variable is so large is that the size of the church makes a significant difference.

There are many people in most churches that do not serve. Here are some of the most used answers as to their unwillingness to serve:

> No one has asked them.
> They have a fear of responsibility.
> They suffer from past burnout.
> They are intimidated by present workers.
> They are ignorant of the Biblical paradigm for ministry.

They are occupied with their personal agenda and
busyness.
They feel untrained, ill equipped, and ungifted.
They are unaware of the options available.
They do not "own" the cause.
They are selfish, lazy, and indifferent.

Remember to treat every ministry of the church as important
deserving the best group of leaders you can discover,
develop, and deploy. Treat every volunteer with respect.
Allow for differences in styles and mannerisms.

Worship

The Bible tells us in John 4 that God is seeking worshipers.
He is not seeking servants, learners, or soldiers. God seeks
worshipers. In other words, we are to gather together each
Lord's day for Him. Granted, a by-product of corporate
worship will be fellowship, learning, truth, encouragement,
and ministry. The primary reason for the gathering of God's
church together is that Jesus Christ is lifted up, God is
exalted, and the Holy Spirit is welcomed to do as He pleases.
The main thing is that you respond to Him. Worship is
something you do rather than sit through. Worship is active,
practical, and responsive. In a church, such responses will be
personal and diverse. Begin teaching that worship is finding
God and "getting in" on what He is saying and doing. Some
who come to worship will sit quietly in prayerful meditation.
Others will clap their hands to a praise-worthy chorus. Still,
others will say "Amen" to a sermon point that stirs their soul.
Yet there will be even others in some churches that will raise
their hands to the Lord in adoring praise. At times there will
be tears or laughter. Some will sing with all their heart while
others will sing quietly in stillness of soul. You see; it is not a
matter of how you worship. The mechanics of worship has
little to do with real worship actually! The issue is whether
you worship; is it not? Whatever is done must be done unto

the Lord. We are to honor Him. Never should worship celebration be done for show or worn as a spiritual merit badge to impress others. Neither should we ever condemn someone for the manner in which they respond to God in true worship.

Worship is our first or foundational ministry. It is not our only ministry, but the one that all other spheres of ministry should be built upon. As one peruses Scripture, the constant thread of worship runs through the lives of those that were intimate with their God and used mightily by Him. The Psalmist declares:

> *"As the deer pants for streams of water, so my soul pants for You, O God. My soul thirsts for God, for the living God. When can I go and meet with God?"*25

A desire to know God and to meet with Him is the key to Spirit-filled worship of God. Without this desire to stand in His presence, worship becomes a fruitless experience. Throughout the church today we can see a fruitless style of worship - worship without expectation, worship without the manifest presence of God. The apostle Paul tells us in 1 Corinthians 2:9 that *"Eye has not seen and ear has not heard, neither has it entered into the heart of man all that God has prepared for those who love Him."* Paul was speaking not only of our coming heavenly existence but also of our existence here and now!

Paul goes on to say that through God's Holy Spirit, we are able to enter into and know the deep things of God. Because the depths of God are without measure, we should never be satisfied with our knowledge of Him. There will always be more and more for us to know and experience. The life of the believer should be marked by a desire for an ever-expanding knowledge of God. We must come to the

---

25 Psalm 42:1-2.

realization that God by His Holy Spirit desires to lead us into His depths. We believe this because the Scripture tells us that we have within us the Spirit of God. Since this is true, we too can enter into the depths of God. Without this understanding, we approach God vainly, simply satisfied with the fragrance of God, and not God Himself. God wants us to enter freely and fully into His depths with the Holy Spirit as our guide. I have found that when we give ourselves over to Him - our mind, our emotions, our bodies, and our will - we not only have access to the deep things of God but to the very heart of God.

> *"Jesus answered, 'The foremost is, 'Hear, O Israel! The Lord our God is one Lord; and you shall love the Lord your God with all your heart, and with all your soul, and with all your mind, and with all your strength.'"*26

> *"But an hour is coming, and now is, when the true worshipers shall worship the Father in spirit and truth; for such people the Father seeks to be His worshipers. 'God is spirit, and those who worship Him must worship in spirit and truth.'"*27

Worship is best defined as meeting God. For some individuals, worship is tied to certain traditional experiences and external stimulation. One man from a liturgical background complained that he had difficulty feeling like he worshiped in a Baptist church, saying, "I miss the smells and the bells." Sometimes people equate worship with a certain style of music or preaching. If that style is not found, they may say, "I just cannot worship in that setting." Some persons equate worship with a certain personal emotional response that comes from a comfortable group experience. The comment after such an emotional encounter, "We

---

26 Mark 12:29, 30 NAS.

27 John 4:23, 24 NAS.

worshiped today!" The worship leader's responsibility is to facilitate people meeting God. Worship is critical to the life and vitality of a church. Worship should be viewed as one of the non-negotiable endeavors of a Christian's life. In today's culture, the church's corporate worship service is often the first point of contact for the majority of new people. A television commercial popularized the line; "You only get one time to make a first impression." For many people, the corporate worship service is that first impression. They may not understand what the "special" is but do they get the feeling that "there is something special here." Do they sense the church as friendly people? Do they see the church's worship services as relevant?

Ideally, in corporate worship, members join together for the highest experience of worship for the week. Are members taught that worship is only a corporate experience? Are they taught that worship is to be part of the daily, ongoing experience of believers, and what happens in the corporate setting is an overflow of the personal life experience? Are members trained in how to worship personally, as a nuclear family, and as a church family? Notice that Jesus said we are to love God with all our heart, soul, mind, and strength. Should not worship reflect all those capacities of a person? What are the aspects of worship that may differ with such things as traditions, regions, cultural or social groups, generations, personality types, personal preferences, and are not per se biblical or Christian issues? The church's worship leaders should help members understand and experience personal and family worship as well as corporate worship. Here are a few questions to consider relating to how your church does worship:

> The evaluation question is, "Did people meet God today?"

What are we doing to strengthen people's understanding of worship?

Whose issues and preferences are impacting our current worship style?

Are we regularly evaluating worship services?

Give worship preparation much prayer. Worship celebration is far too important to attempt without ample prayer and planning. God promised in His word that when we come together in His name, we could know that the spirit of God is already at work in the hearts of those gathered to worship. Seek to create an "at ease" environment. When people gather to worship, there needs to be a feeling of being at ease in the place of worship. Ask anyone who leaves a church as to why, and often it is either they felt unwelcome or not accepted in worship. Create a spiritual environment where our sins are forgiven. Worship should help us deal with our sins and feelings of inadequacy. Real worship does not seek to entertain, but balances celebration with a healthy fear of God. Worship sanctifies. Worship has a sense of wonder in it. Keep worship fairly simple. Since many worshipers lack musical aptitude today, it is helpful to keep your services fairly simple musically. When a worship celebration is too complex you take the personal experience away from the people. Sometimes a single instrument like a guitar is more effective in creating a refreshing moment of praise for the individual worshipers than a full orchestra. Worship should flow. Remind worshipers why they have come to church. Leaders of worship must help worshipers remember why they have come to worship and build a sense of community by establishing a collective goal. Statements like, "We have come to worship today the Lord our God. As part of our worship today we will see…" Take a few minutes to let those who have gathered hear what the morning's theme is and then explain it to them. Public worship is a participatory event. We love to worship God with outward expressions! Just watch young children and observe them react to worship favorably when it has chances for outward expression. A clap here and there goes a long way. On the other side, when worship is fashioned in liturgical inward self-reflection, people may long for the participatory nuances of worship that allow for outward expressions. The more people participate in the worship celebration, the more likely it is that part of them will open up to God.

Keep worship God-ward and non-mechanical. It is easy for those on the platform or at the front of the sanctuary to forget that our real ministry should be focused God-ward. Have you ever been in a service where it seemed that too much attention was focused on the worship leaders, or key changes and chord charts? All of us must strive to concentrate on God, so that part of our lives might open up to Him. Turning one's thoughts toward God alone takes effort. Worship must be authentic and not starchy. One of the hardest things today for any of us is to worship in such an authentic way that those who are participating do not view it as starchy and unfriendly. No worship celebration can be as effective and life-changing for the corporate body unless all those who have gathered are engaged. Reassure worshipers that it is all right to sing, pray, and respond to God. It has always amazed me that as worshipers we need to be assured that it is all right for us to pray, sing, and respond to God during the entire worship service. Permission often empowers the participants to experience God in a way that might not happen unless it is understood that God moves in His way throughout the celebration service. Creating the right worship environment allows participants the chance to interact with God as He works in each of our hearts specifically. Remember the attendees are sending you non-verbal messages describing what they hope will happen during the celebration service. Lead them to the throne and allow God to satisfy their individual need. Help them learn how to let

Him in. The divine priority is worship first and service is second.

Evangelism

In revitalizing a new church, the pastor must recognize that evangelism is not optional. The Bible declares:

> *"But you shall receive power when the Holy Spirit has come upon you; and you shall be My witnesses both in Jerusalem, and in all Judea and Samaria, and even to the remotest part of the earth."28*

> *"And on that day a great persecution arose against the church in Jerusalem; and they were all scattered throughout the regions of Judea and Samaria, except the apostles. Therefore, those who had been scattered went about preaching the word. And Philip went down to the city of Samaria and {began} proclaiming Christ to them."29*

> *"So, then those who were scattered because of the persecution that arose in connection with Stephen made their way to Phoenicia and Cyprus and Antioch, speaking the word to no one except to Jews alone. But there were some of them, men of Cyprus and Cyrene, who came to Antioch and {began} speaking to the Greeks also, preaching the Lord Jesus. And the hand of the Lord was with them, and a large number who believed turned to the Lord."30*

There are seven elements in a balanced church strategy for evangelism. The first element is prayer. The church needs an intentional strategy of praying for lost and unchurched

---

28 Acts 1:8 NAS.

29 Acts 8:1, 4-5 NAS.

30 Acts 11:19-21 NAS.

persons. It must be able to answer the question, "For whom are we praying that they might be saved?" The church must realize the truth of the statement that evangelism begins with talking to the Father about men before we talk to men about the Father. One resource a church might use is *Praying Your Friends to Christ.*31

Secondly, church revitalizers must model evangelism. There is significant truth in the statement that evangelism is more often caught than taught. The church revitalizer must evangelize and not just talk about evangelization. If the church is being renewed from the unchurched and unsaved population, those being saved will experience the revitalizer's modeling evangelism.

Thirdly, the church needs a process to identify, cultivate, and track prospects. How does a church prospect in a community? A well-used method with a variety of variations is the surveying method. Door-to-door, telephone, and random contacts in various settings are all designed to get information on persons who are lost and/or unchurched. A popular method of prospecting many churches use today is referred to as "fishing pool events." These events include interest meetings, block parties, concerts, etc. designed to get groups of people together. From these groups, the church seeks to identify the few of the group who are receptive to the gospel. In any evangelism strategy, a key element is tracking the persons who are identified as prospects for the church. After the person is identified with personal and spiritual data, a process of tracking the church's witnessing and ministering endeavors need to be utilized. The purpose of this is to have a timely, specific and intensive plan for evangelistic follow-up. There are several reasons for doing this. One reason for tracking is that people are not allowed to

---

31 https://www.sbcv.org/wp-content/uploads/Praying-Your-Friends-to-Christ-Manual.pdf.

fall through the cracks for lack of concern or contacts. Another reason is to make maximize activities and minimize duplication of work. The tracking is also a valuable tool to assist the church in building relationships so the assimilation begins to occur prior to the decision being made to receiving Jesus as Savior and Lord and joining the church.

Fourthly, the church must have a plan to mobilize members for the task of evangelism. Mobilizing members for evangelism is more than simply laying a guilt trip on church members to invite people to church or to "get serious about evangelism." It involves helping members see and accept the opportunities and calling of every believer to be witnesses for Jesus at whatever level of spiritual maturity and with whatever mix of gifts and talents they have been given.

Lastly, an ongoing plan to train members in evangelism is critical. The pastor might begin training by taking others with him and modeling evangelism.

Any effective evangelism strategy has a plan to deploy the trained members into the field. Evangelism is not an activity carried on primarily inside the walls of a church's building or during the times of a church's gathered meeting. It is carried on in the variety of setting that the members find themselves as they are scattered. In addition to helping members see and take advantage of the "as you are going" opportunities to evangelize, the church needs a well-planned strategy to deploy its members into every corner of its social, cultural, and geographic field of ministry. The church needs an effective plan to follow-up and disciple those who accept Jesus as Savior and Lord. The task of making disciples has only begun when a person accepts Jesus as Savior and Lord. Thus begins a lifelong process in which "*we are no longer to be children but we are to grow up in all aspects into Him, even Christ.*"*32*

---

32 Ephesians 4:14-15 NAS.

Relationships

The church is a social, relational organization. Sometimes pastors emphasize, "The church is a spiritual organization" to the exclusion of other aspects. Jesus said:

> *"And he answered and said, 'You shall love the Lord your God with all your heart, and with all your soul, and with all your strength, and with all your mind; and your neighbor as yourself.'"33*

> *"A new commandment I give to you, that you love one another, even as I have loved you, that you also love one another. By this all men will know that you are My disciples, if you have love for one another."34*

Every church needs to focus on some structure to assist people in developing and strengthening relationships. Some churches use Sunday School very effectively. Others are choosing to use small groups or cells that meet in homes during the week. One fact that must be recognized is that relationships are not built-in worship services. There must be other times and places for that to occur. The recurrent theme throughout the history of the church is that of creating a loving, caring community. People are in search of community. It has been charged that the church is willing to accept the pseudo community and not do the hard work of developing community. Those churches that fail to start new groups are churches that have decided to die. New people tend to join new groups. The by-product of healthy group life

---

33 Luke 10:27 NAS.

34 John 13:34, 35 NAS

is the multiplication of leadership. The multiplication of small groups makes possible the continual development of workers and leaders. Here are some questions worth responding to in light of beginning the process towards renewal:

How open are the circles of relationships?

What structures do we have in place to assist people to develop and strengthen relationships?

What new groups did we create last year?

What new groups do we plan to create this year?

When asked to define "fellowship" in this church, how would people define it and where would they say it occurs?

Do all members see our church as a loving, caring community?

How does the community reveal itself in the church?

Do we work at assimilation of new members?

Is the process effective?

Teddy Roosevelt once said, "The most important ingredient to the formula to success is knowing how to get along with people." That sounds great, but sometimes it is not always an easy task. Sometimes the most difficult days in our leadership would be concerning the fact of relationships that have become difficult in our lives. I love the story of the frog. A frog has a wonderful advantage in life; he can eat anything that bugs him. Romans 12:18, says: "*If possible, so far as it depends on you, be at peace with all men.*"

Relevant Dynamic Structures

The Bible does not give a specific structure for the church but uses many pictures to describe the church--the body, the army, a community, and a tree, a building. Often in design the statement is made, form follows function. Often in church, denominational tradition and culture dictate form. The structures exist to impact, not to impair ministry. The church's structure must serve it well and act as a launching pad for ministry. The effective congregation conserves its members' time by developing the most minimal and streamlined organizational structure possible so that people can be involved in the church's ministry.

> *"For even as the body is one and {yet} has many members, and all the members of the body, though they are many, are one body, so also is Christ."*[35]

> *"For the body is not one member, but many. If the foot should say, "Because I am not a hand, I am not {a part} of the body," it is not for this reason any the less {a part} of the body. And if the ear should say, "Because I am not an eye, I am not {a part} of the body," it is not for this reason any the less {a part} of the body. If the whole body were an eye, where would the hearing be? If the whole were hearing, where would the sense of smell be? But now God has placed the members, each one of them, in the body, just as He desired. And if they were all one member, where would the body be? But now there are many members, but one body."*[36]

---

35 1 Corinthians 12:12 NAS.

36 1 Corinthians 12: 14-20 NAS.

Here are some questions worth responding to relating to relevant structures in light of beginning the process towards renewal:

Did our structure develop by design or by default?

Does the structure serve our vision and values?

Does the structure fit our people and culture?

Are there some changes that need to be made?

Stewardship & Financial Practices

The final critical issue facing declining churches initially is the development of sound stewardship and financial practices. The Bible declares:

> "*A wise man thinks ahead; a fool doesn't and he even brags about it.*"37

> "*Any enterprise is built by wise planning, becomes strong through common sense, and profits wonderfully by keeping abreast of the facts.*"38

> "*Watch your business interests closely. Know the state of your flocks and herds.*"39

> "*For {it is} just like a man {about} to go on a journey, who called his own slaves, and entrusted his possessions to them....*

---

37 Proverbs 13:16 Living Bible.

38 Proverbs 24:3 LB.

39 Proverbs 27:23 LB.

Now after a long time the master of those slaves came and settled accounts with them."40

Normally two mistakes are made in relation to stewardship: it is ignored or dealt with only in terms of money (tithing) related to the church's budget. For a variety of reasons, many church planters fail to deal with the issue of stewardship. This failure can weaken or cripple a church for years to come. The principle, "Whatever you want at the end, build in at the beginning" also applies to stewardship and financial responsibility. Stewardship is a broad topic that includes many areas. Revitalizers who fail to teach stewardship are neglecting a major portion of Scripture. Review all the parables that Jesus taught about how a person relates to the opportunities and the material stuff of life. That is stewardship. Stewardship needs to be defined in terms of managing all the resources that have been entrusted to us by God. It is helpful to recognize that life management and stewardship are opposite sides of the same coin. The church needs a form of budgeting and accounting that inspires confidence in the church's financial dealings. Church leaders should communicate a sense of accountability in their handling of resources. Here are some questions worth responding to relating to the development of sound stewardship and financial practices in light of beginning the process towards renewal:

> What is our plan for developing strong stewards in this church?
>
> Does our budget reflect our church's vision and values?
>
> Are our financial policies reflective of our faith? Are they sound?

---

40 Matthew 25:14, 19 NAS.

Are they understandable?

Do members have an accurate understanding of the church's financial condition?

Wrapping it up!

Some leaders and some churches, like the Corinthians, find it hard to invest resources because they seem so deficient – feeling their commodities are about to run out. Good leaders and good churches see the same resources as sufficient seed to be sown - knowing the harvest will come and more will be created. We must guard life against poverty; we should give our lives because it is plentiful. All seven issues are important. Where are your strengths? Which areas need to be given special attention? How will you do that in the coming year?

Chapter Seven
The Number One Habit that Keeps You from Revitalizing Your Church

Revitalization is a layering endeavor that requires doing something every day. It is a series of tiny nudges until the ground is cultivated and ready for the initiation of the revitalization process. This is the stage where effort is required and procrastination results in stalled efforts. "Hi, I am Tom and I am a formerly world-class procrastinator." That was my mantra all through high school and for the first few years of college until I began to realize just how detrimental such a habit was towards my success and advancement. When I was in my second year of college, I had come to realize I was settling into an outstanding pattern of procrastination. Often, I would put off an assignment only to find myself slammed the few days before it was due because of other assignments and commitments. By the time I got through my second year of college, I had outgrown my procrastination posture. Because I was a good student, I was able to fake it and jump into crisis mode to get the book reports, projects, and other assignments completed. I hid my self-imposed form of laziness until it snowballed and almost cost me my opportunity to attend college. Procrastination has been labeled as the thief of time. I was involved in a lot of functions but seemed to seldom find time for the real study required to excel. There are many churches led today by similar procrastinators and if you are one of these please do not pass by this chapter. It could be the most important thing you could consider when it comes to revitalizing your church. Are you a procrastinator? Are you an all-pro procrastinator? Would you say your play in the procrastination league is in the minor or major leagues?

Procrastination is usually one of the top habits if not the number one habit that keeps you as the revitalization leader from revitalizing your church. To be fair, most of us are procrastinators sometimes. Procrastination is one of the main barriers blocking church leaders from getting up, making the right decisions, and living the dream of a revitalized vibrant church. Maybe some pastors are programmed to procrastinate. Being attracted to conflict, people most likely – perhaps even subconsciously – put off things because they are always in desperate need of a distraction from the ultimate destination achievement. The word procrastination comes from the Latin word *procrastinus*. Its definition comes is of Latin origins meaning to *belonging to tomorrow*. It also has a root meaning of *putting things off intentionally or habitually*. The noun form of the word refers to the action of delaying or postponing something. The plural noun form is demonstrated as an action or strategy designed to defer or postpone something in order to gain an advantage for oneself. Recent studies have revealed that people, in general regret more the things they have not completed rather than the things they have finished. Feelings of regret and guilt resulting from missed opportunities tend to stay with people much longer. Sometimes all our opportunities seem to at our fingertips, but we cannot seem to reach them. When you procrastinate, you waste time that you could be investing in something meaningful. If you can overcome this fierce enemy, you will be able to accomplish more and in doing so better utilize the potential that life has to offer. Your ministry will blossom. Granted we all have those officially declared procrastination days. These are usually signaling that we need a little rest and recuperation. Yet, while we waste our time hesitating, vacillating, and postponing as revitalization pastors, the chances of successful renewal begins slipping away. Learning how to overcome procrastination is one of the most important skills you can ever learn as a revitalization leader. It is often the difference between a coasting church and a growing church. Because revitalization takes a minimal effort of one thousand days, how you begin your initial one hundred and twenty of them will point in a direction either towards renewal or further decline.

I will never forget in high school a lesson my father taught me while working on his construction site one summer. He had asked me to bring two large stacks of two-by-fours up to the ninth floor of a condo he was building. He told me on Monday he did not need them until Friday up there but if I could work it into my schedule, he could give me two other workers to help. I was setting scaffolding around the outside of the construction project so I put it off thinking I had plenty of time and that the other workers and I could make quick work of the task. Thursday came and a big shipment of doors and shelving came in for the previous condo on the other side of the property. Now my extra helpers were moved over to the more pressing task and I was faced with carrying up nine floors all of these two-by-fours. Because I procrastinated, it fell to me to do the job all by myself. That Thursday I faced the reality of my procrastination and began the long hard job of carrying seven two by fours each time up the stairs to the top floor so they could be used to build the walls on that level. That was the beginning of me facing my propensity towards procrastination. It was late into the night when I finished and drove home. The house was quiet and my brothers were asleep. I showered and fell into bed wishing and promising to stop this vicious problem of putting things off.

Churches sometimes are much like my high school and early college lifestyle. They too can begin to stand out in the area of procrastination. Many a church needs to do something and they need to do it right away only to discover that by the time they eventually get to it, the opportunity to make a transformation has come and gone, and the opportunity is squandered.

What Procrastination is Not

Realize that procrastination is not another word for laziness. While procrastinators often put off doing things, leave them to the very last moment, or sometimes even spend their time staring at the wall, it is not because they are lazy. There are lazy minsters all around the world. One must be careful not to label procrastination as a synonym for being lazy. Lazy people simply do not do anything and they are just fine with it. Procrastinators, on the other hand, have the desire to actually do something but cannot force themselves to get started. It's a good idea to start using the word procrastination instead of using the terms laziness or putting things off. It provides a much more accurate description of your situation. Only by giving the right name to your problem can you begin working on it.

While many a church member might label procrastination this way, relaxation is not procrastination. Do not confuse procrastination with relaxation either. Relaxing recharges you with energy. In stark contrast, procrastination drains it from you. The less energy you have, the more stressed or even depressed you might have become, and the higher the chances of you putting off your responsibilities as the church leader. The opposite of procrastination is actually getting things done and then being able to relax. If you will deal with your workload well you will be happier in the long term.

As pastor leaders, our reasons for putting off pressing action are as extensive as our aptitude for creative thoughts, but some of the more common excuses are:

We need to just get ourselves out of debt at church first

May I challenge briefly each of these excuses and perhaps offer some words that will dispel the power of these ideas that often paralyze the local church:

> Well, a little debt actually will not hurt most churches today! Most often if the debt is tied to the financing of something that helps the church grow it is a safe investment. But take notice of this; if your church fellowship is in a death dive as far as its regular attendance, it would be unwise to invest in this way. When you are not sure of the future income base for the local church it could further cripple the church beyond any chance of recovery. As pastor leaders, our reasons for putting off pressing action are as extensive as our capacity for creative thoughts, but some of the more common excuses are: Our church needs to place all of our energy on a building campaign and the funding of this facility. Many new church buildings do not yield anything more than help the church get further in debt. Far better would be working aggressively to draw new people toward the work. If you build a new building new people seldom come as the result, unless you had them coming to begin with. Something that is challenging the mainline churches today is that in building gyms, pastor housing, youth buildings, and other things while they seem helpful and they sound good, I have come to see and know that these facilities will probably not advance the cause of Christ in that local church and its mission. As pastor leaders, our reasons for putting off pressing action are as extensive as our aptitude for creative thoughts.

Our church needs to work first at doing a better job of pastoral care for its own existing membership

Pastoral care no matter how good or how bad it is a poor excuse for procrastinating in the area of revitalization. We are choosing to put off new ministry forever if not for a very long time. The idea that the local church should focus on efficiency in Pastoral Care while neglecting the evangelistic outreach of the church is an idea marked by the devil's darkness and Satan's infection into the local church. Since no matter how good pastoral care is in a church it will never be enough for some, so this becomes a perfect tool for ministry procrastination and avoidance of outreach. Our church really does not have sufficient workers and volunteers for the things we are attempting to achieve right now. Granted, inadequate numbers of workers or volunteers is a serious matter, yet it is not a valid motive for benching advancements in the church's ministry. Most church growth advances happen as a result of a newly trained and deployed leadership base. It would help all of us as ministers to stop thinking about those who are currently volunteering as potential volunteers for new causes and ministries. Look for the new individuals who could lead out in new endeavors. As pastor leaders, our reasons for putting off pressing action are as extensive as our aptitude for creative thoughts.

Our church needs to grow our current ministries first before we expand ourselves out into new ministries and spread ourselves too thin

It is always a challenge when a church takes an inward focus before launching out into something new such as renewal. Often ministries that have been part of the local church for a long-time experience the ebb and flow of success as it relates to attendance peaks and plateaus. But if your church's ministry attendance is stuck or in a decline, it is urgent that the church start something new as quickly as possible. Often it is the new things that spark the entire church's growth momentum and get it going again. One of the Tom Cheyney-isms that you will often hear from me is that you must try new things and do something every day, almost anything. These daily little nudges have an amazing way of beginning to move a declining or dying church off stuck. They are part of the layering process for renewal. Little steps lead to bigger steps and forward steps towards revitalization and renewal.

Our church needs to help our aging pastor get to retirement first before we add new ministries to the work

A real challenge to the local declining church is that if you are five years or more away from the retirement of a present pastor and you are hesitant to help your church start something new because you are feeling tired or unable to accomplish the task, then in all seriousness is not the church already a retired church and its leader already in retirement? If you find yourself as the church revitalizer in this situation you would serve your present church better by stepping into a new pastorate that demands a less hands-on and industrious energetic leader! Many churches today are helping pastors who still desire pulpit ministry to discover other avenues while at the same time developing younger leadership staff that could continue to lead the church in new and exciting ways.

Our church needs to wait until our brand-new pastor gets settled and the honeymoon period is over

We do not want to make major changes too fast. While most pastoral books say to go slow during your first year, the chances of your church's transformation being accomplished diminish if you wait during your initial year to make strategic changes while you can. In revitalization, while you must go more slowly than you would in a new church plant, still you must begin steering the ship in a new direction right away. The majority of churches that squander the initial years of a new minister's ministry generally fall back into a plateaued, declining, or stuck church unable to make any advancement. Most revitalization efforts that are successful begin during the first year of the starting of a revitalization effort. While in years 3 or 5 it sometimes happens most successful revitalization efforts begin right away. A pastor's honeymoon should be a window to make the right changes while everyone still loves you. A few key changes are what we are talking about here. It sends a signal of a bright future. Revitalization leaders cannot squander their initial years in revitalization doing nothing just to make a group of church members on sabbatical happy.

I think our church needs to spend a year or so researching this issue

Many churches needing renewal want to study the issue first. That translates from the Greek to mean: If we get the leader focused on the nuisances of renewal and not doing renewal, we can keep the status quo going until we go to glory. Many will say that they need to clearly define their mission first. The number of times I have gone to a church in need of renewal and discovered that the membership was happily willing to kill their Lord's church until they passed on into heaven is staggering. It is as if there is an unspoken covenant with long time members that the last one alive would turn the light off. In the Old Testament, the children of Israel spent forty years in the wilderness offered the world its first church mission, vision, and values discernment process. That did not work out to well. The children of Israel walked around the desert for an entire generation and then died in the dust and dryness of the desert. Here is the point: Running from the past and scared of its future is never the best for any church. We can think strategically for a long long time and still kill any momentum.

I will wait until the membership is ready to grow the church

Guess what you will discover? Most churches never reach the place where they are to grow again by accident. They must be led to grow once more. Also, understand that godly vision does not fall on the masses but on the individual leader. It is the job of the masses to confirm the vision but not to create it. Paralyzed churches can study forever and gain nothing in the end. But hear one thing also. Even growing churches can study as well and still gain nothing. The longer it takes your church to get moving the less chance you have of actually sustaining renewal in your church. A practical place to start is to begin reading the Book of Acts and seek God in what He wants you to do. That is faster and more biblical. As pastor leaders, our reasons for putting off pressing actions are as extensive as our aptitude for creative thoughts.

Our church really needs for Sister Satisfied and Brother Bewildered to die first because they are not in favor of the church growing

My personal favorite, though extremely sad, is this one. It amazes me how those who hinder the advancement of the gospel are in such good health and may outlive the chance for growth and renewal. I know you probably have not thought about this but most of us will live to be somewhere around 95 years of age before we go to the Father. Have you thought about that? Do you really want to wait that long before you take the necessary steps to get your church growing again? Do not rush past this. Stop for a moment to think about this question and answer it.

Our church is excited about the planned senior center going in behind our church on the adjacent property

I know a church in which we were once members who put all of their hopes on the Senior Center that was being built directly behind the church. They even made a sidewalk so those who were living there could walk across to the church. The church membership stated that they could wait until they first sought to minister to these seniors before they tried other things. The senior center has been built and the end result was very few if any attended the church. Yet they misspent more than five years waiting for something that never materialized. You know, I would be a wealthy minister if I had a nickel for every time a church told me they were waiting for the "new group" to arrive that was supposed to becoming. Here is the point church revitalizer, they do not come. You have to go get them. I do not read in the Bible of any time that God ever said to not go and keep on advancing for the cause of Christ. He always says go. Serve the populace you can find to serve right now. Stop investing in tomorrow's dreams and start ministering in today's realities. You might get the chance to realize your dreams later but it will start with your effort in the here and now first.

Understand the Myth

I hear it all the time in the students I teach at two institutions I teach doctoral seminars for in church revitalization. Here is the Myth: We Work Better Under Pressure. It is not true. I discovered in my journey away from being a procrastinator that I was no longer on edge because something was not completed in a timely manner. Where in the past I was nervous because I was pushing things right up until the deadline, since I got past being a chronic procrastinator, my grades went up and my ministries were more successful. A lot of the time we hear the excuse that people often love leaving things to the last minute. They justify their actions by claiming that they are most productive under pressure. However, scientific studies show that the opposite is true. Putting things off until the very last moment creates fertile ground for stress, guilt, and ineffectiveness. Excellence is hard to achieve in a last-minute sprint while it comes from a disciplined commitment of practice and training. "Don't put off till tomorrow what you can do today" This old saying really hits the nail on the head. Here are some suggestions for you as the church revitalizer:

Avoid Decision Paralysis

The number of opportunities that today's church offer is staggering. We live in a day of freedom where we are able to try new things. New ministries make us happy and the church content. So then why aren't church members today significantly happier than in the past? Because with more freedom to make our own decisions and to perform our own actions, we have become easily confused about what is a priority for the local church, what is essential and what is not, and with what is right and wrong, and therefore we have become demotivated to do anything at all. We need to set straight our values and visions and to cultivate our positive habits. This is the essential thing that can help us overcome procrastination in a church body.

Stop Ignoring the Value of Time

We were all born and unfortunately at some point will all die as well. The time we spend on earth is both limited and finite. In light of these facts, time is the most valuable commodity you have in your ministry pastor. Every single second you waste is gone forever, never to be reclaimed. Churches that sit around wasting time cannot reclaim the time they lost because it is gone forever. The mere realization that life and ministry are finite leads pastors to begin managing their time more carefully. It makes you think about how you would ideally like to spend your time on earth doing the ministries that you love.

Work on Your Lack of Self-Discipline

None of us want to admit it but often we lack the discipline necessary to see something worthy come into being. You can imagine self-discipline or self-control as a moment when you give yourself directions, but you are having a difficult time following them. Lacking self-discipline is not the cause of procrastination. This is an important thought to consider. To be disciplined, you need to have the correct type of motivation and learn to maintain and work on positive habits that will allow you to become more effective as a minister. For instance, I grew to understand that if I got up and got at it every morning early when those unseen challenges came my way and I had to stop and deal with them, it did not sidetrack the things that were needing to be achieved that day. I still had ample time to get the non-scheduled requirement of my time accomplished and then had sufficient time left in my day to achieve the things that would help the work of ministry for my church. Another way I found more time in my day and being less of a procrastinator was handling everyday responsibilities as few times as possible. For instance, I have had many conversations with ministers who handle their emails all day long as soon as they come in and they are left with a feeling of not accomplishing anything significant for the day. I get a lot of emails between my two primary responsibilities as a minister. It is not uncommon to have north of a thousand but usually around eight hundred each day. Instead of becoming a handcuffed to emails, I have chosen to handle emails at 6:30 a.m. in the morning, 1:30 p.m. in the afternoon right after lunch, and 5:30 p.m. in the evening. If not, I could be just getting started in sermon preparation or a project creation and get sideswiped by the mundane.

Stop Goal Setting and Start Getting Your Goals Done

A little bit of goal setting daily is probably wise but if you spend more time thinking about goal setting than achieving the accomplishment of a task needing your attention, then what have you really achieved? You have achieved little or nothing because you have lost the time. You are like the rest of us. When we do things, we don't want to do, we are less happy, and our brains release less dopamine. Doing a list for the sake of a list every day will become less productive in the long run. Develop a simple set of goals for the week and then proceed. Daily lists will wear you out but simple ones will allow you the time to achieve your plan. If you have time to work hard on your goals rather than thinking about goals in general, sooner or later, you will indeed achieve them. When that finally does happen, a one-time dose of dopamine is released, resulting in an intense emotion of joy. Yet unless you are pressing onward and upward through your week and your goal list by the end of that week you will replace that feeling of accomplishment with the sense of what now. Because your goals are built around your vision for renewal it becomes quite satisfying when you take a big step forward through your actions. Intrinsically you are motivated to press onward. Remember, revitalization and renewal is a journey and not a sprint. Your achievement is in the journey and not in a final destination.

Wrapping it up!

Procrastination is part of many people's lives. Each person has a different reason for procrastinating. We all need to work at not taking on too many tasks as we enter into the revitalization process. Begin by motivating yourself into action. Staying motivated is the key to avoiding the procrastination cycle. If you will declutter a little it will help. Procrastination is a comfortable cloak but a terrible uniform for working in ministry. Procrastination causes you to eventually become less productive and effective. If you are not regularly able to distinguish between the things needing your attention now and the things that could require your attention in the future, you are locked more in the realm of the procrastinator than you realize. Not everything we do in ministry has the same weight or value. The wise revitalizer knows the difference between things I get to eventually and the things I must get to today. Successful church revitalizers might want to be procrastinators for a day, but they press on because success for the renewing church is right around the corner and they do not want to miss the opportunity and see it pass them as the leader and the church in general by. Some of the best tools to help you stop being overcome by that procrastinating onslaught are:

Development of Your Personal Vision as a Church Revitalizer

A primary tool for pastors in revitalization is vision casting and individual vision. Personal vision is one of the fundamental tools for renewal pastors. It helps you understand your skills and priorities, and by creating your own personal vision for revitalization, you will never feel confused about what is it that you desire to do with your ministry. The personal vision helps you to focus your effort on the right activities and set priorities to avoid continually switching between actions. Understand what motivates you, and you will be able to maintain your discipline and make the most out of each day as the revitalization pastor.

Tonight, Develop Your To-Do List for Tomorrow

Every night before I go to bed, I develop my to-do list for the next day. Those who know me have heard me say that the Lord throughout the night takes that list and orders it in the way He would have me go. I wake up with incredible clarity the next day and proceed in carrying out the things the Lord desires of me. I also, feel more empowered by the Lord and competent to meet the needs He has for me. It does not take a long time and yet it often saves me many hours if not half of my day. My tonight thinking allows me to develop a funneling effect and get at only the most important stuff for revitalization and renewal. Small things are like rabbits and keep multiplying so tackle the big things and let the rabbits run free. The trivial of the many can kill your efforts towards renewal so keep that To-Do list short and sweet. When you have not developed such a list, it is easy to run around for a large portion of the day trying to figure out what you should really be doing with your day. If you make too big of a list you will be prone to procrastinate because of the size of the list. A large list causes many of us to give up rather than go up. John Maxwell taught me this when I was in my early thirties and I have been doing it ever since. I wake up each morning with clarity and direction that allows me to be my best and get things done, as the Lord desires. By knowing what is important and what is not, I am able to be more effective daily. I am also not as worn out as I once was because achieving my goals is energizing and exciting.

Learn Something New or Perhaps Two

As you learn a new productive habit as a church revitalizer determine to practice it for the next thirty days every day. Habits become cemented into our being once they have been allowed to grow over an extended period. When you learn something new try to add another one as well. The power of two new things can propel you toward greatness as a church revitalizer. We grow when we take on new habits that will be beneficial to our life's work. We develop as the leader and once it is ingrown it will be part of who we are and how we lead. Learning new habits is, extremely important. New habits for ministry motivate us further and further towards the goal of revitalizing the church.

Hey Tom, It's Tom, How Are You Doing?

I enjoy what I call my "Hey Tom Times." It is so very simple to get started this way. You could begin this tomorrow morning if you wanted. My personal meeting with the bald one is something that no one can interrupt. It is God fashioning, forming, focusing me on me and allowing me to think about myself for a while. What do I sense God telling me to do next is a big part of my meetings? How do I feel is another one? Am I running too fast and need to slow down or am I coasting along and need to kick it into a higher gear? These "Hey Tom" meetings allow me to think with the Lord about the long-haul stuff while also thinking about the urgent stuff. I think upon my three core tasks as a leader of my organization: the planting of healthy New Testament churches, the revitalization of the declining churches wanting to be revitalized, and the development of new and existing leaders for the work of the ministry. Everything else can be put on the sideline until these core tasks are developed. What may I ask are your three core tasks that will move your church forward? Progression is moving forward focusing on the worthy things of God. Regression is what got many a church in trouble so as a leader in revitalization I want to be thoughtful about solutions. It also helps me grow as a leader.

My personal advice is to start getting up early so you have more time in your day. As soon as coffee, prayer, and personal needs are taken care of get to work. I rise every day around 4:30 a.m. within minutes without an alarm clock. Because I work better in the early morning I get up. You ought to see me at night. I am praying on my couch by 8:30 p.m. in the evening with my wife laughing. Be time conscious and be focused. Practice what I suggested above. Exercise well and stay away from junk food that saps your creativity. Practice times where you are not to be interrupted. We had a study room at one of my churches called Miami. If we were studying to prepare for something our assistants said we were in Miami. Stop allowing others to give you tasks that you don't need to do as the pastor. You are being run over because you allow them to run over you. Declining church leaders procrastinate for a number of reasons. One is a lack of resources. People also procrastinate because they have more important things to do, perhaps because they have bigger problems to solve. Other times, people procrastinate out of dread, as well. They choose not to do something because they don't want to do it, or because the process or perhaps the effect of doing it is not so pleasurable or something they want to do. Some of you are anxious procrastinators because what is required of you for the day makes you uneasy. Others are fun procrastinators. They make a choice to do a fun thing over a fruitful thing. This was me in college as I was the *plenty of time procrastinator* thinking I could do it later until later ran out. There are even *perfectionist procrastinators* who keep from releasing a project because they can keep making it better. By the way, once a project reaches the eighty percent perfection line let it go because the return on the additional investment of time will not be equal to the time you keep working on it to make it perfect. Realize that your church just like mine is not getting any younger. It will be harder to accomplish tomorrow what you need to accomplish today. Jesus said, *"Follow me."* It was not a call for some time later but a call for today and right now. Choose life in your church over death. Choose community over isolation. Choose fun over drudgery. Choose being bold over being mild. Choose a frontier mentality over a fortress mentality. Today there is a higher degree of spiritual discussion by the lost than in previous times. Get into the conversation and tell them your story and His story!

Start something new!

Start something soon!

Choose now over later!

Chapter Eight
Components that Encumber Church Revitalization

In most churches in need of church revitalization or one of the other Pillars of Church Revitalization there are some elements, ingredients, or instruments that become components that are either already encumbering, impeding, or hampering the church's efforts to revitalize its ministry. Once a church becomes burdened with the need to begin its renewal efforts a careful look at some of the possible components that hinder most churches would be helpful. So, what are the usual things that encumber the success of your church? Many churches fear being led into a new day because they will lose the comfortable feel of remaining in the status quo. Yet, being anchored to the status quo is a church sentence that thrusts it towards closure at lightning speed. Declining churches fear losing their long-time identity and are often willing to risk destruction just to keep the well familiar around. Many churches and people within these churches engage in behavior that torpedoes the church's success and they do not understand why. Many church members are unwilling to acknowledge what they might gain if the church became successful once again. There is an ongoing struggle to reconcile the joy which remaining in the comfortable sweater of the status quo brings with the mandate to go into all the world and reach the lost for Christ Jesus. So, they practice as a church full of comfortable members, a self-defeating behavior which indicates a fear of losing an essential part of who they are as a church. Let me give some examples.

The Feeling of One Close-Knit Church Family

Many churches filled to the top with older and elderly members have a strong pull of the familial bond with each other that makes it hard for them to truly welcome the revitalization and saving of God's church. Giving up the "tiny

136

church feeling" and replacing it with an "everyone come feeling" is something that the older members dread. These members feel like they are losing the emotional attachment that has been developed over the many years of decline. The "we are in this together" feeling gets replaced with we will not know everyone as we have in the past feeling.

When the Church Family Expectations Clash with the Church Revitalizer's Aspirations

Though the church called their pastor to come and bring about renewal the family expectations of the church actually clash with the personal aspirations of the one called to renew the church. Because they implied they wanted to save their church and did what was necessary to get a new pastor, now they are clashing with the goals of the church revitalizer. What happens many times is the pastor retreats into a "don't rock the boat" mentality while the members retreat into "let's avoid the issue of renewal for as long as we can mentality" and all the time the church losses more members and continues to drift into rapid decline.

Getting the Church Moving Forward

The longer a church waits in neutral not tackling the issue of revitalization and renewal the greater the tension of deciding to get started. There becomes a sense of a stalemate as the church keeps doing church but is not really ready to advance. The membership and the pastor both understand that they cannot save the church and remain the same. The expectations to grow and the passivity to allow the church to die are in direct conflict with members and church leaders. The pastor and key lay leaders have come to realize that an unreflective, knee-jerk rejection of the church's legacy would be detrimental to the church's future. Loyalty to the past must be honored and yet a church needing renewal must not lock itself in former days. Honoring the past is part of moving into the future. But you can't stay in the past.

The Components that Encumber

What do you think are the primary components that encumber, burden, and hinder most churches from becoming revitalized or engaged in effective ministry and evangelism? Let's take a look:

Number One – A We Can't Do It Mentality

I have seen far too many churches and church leaders today in need of renewal who have a mentality that says they are not up to the task of revitalization or simply not willing to stretch themselves in order to become ready for the journey. Some church leaders and some churches for that matter have a very insecure view of who they are and what it is that God desires for them to accomplish. This low self-esteem by either the pastor leader on the congregation as a whole is a huge component that will encumber any church's revitalization efforts. When the members of a congregation are the ones who demonstrate this challenge, it will be extremely difficult to turn the church around if not impossible to do so. God can do all things I know for sure and yet it is usually the people of the church that God chooses to work through so if they have a defeatist mentality and low esteem it will encumber the possibilities of a great renewal work.

Number Two - A Church Membership Unwilling to Work Hard

If you are going to begin the task of church revitalization there is a large commitment that must be made to the work necessary. I tell most, if not all, of my churches I consult with, that if they are not willing to work hard and commit a minimum of at least one thousand days then they should not try to turn around their church! When a church membership desires to let the church just slide further and further into desperation and decline it is saying that it is unwilling to do the hard work needed to get it growing again. I have even seen some church memberships that see nothing wrong with letting a church die if all of the original members have passed away. Their thinking is almost never expressed verbally in a crowd but to a few that since we are all dying while you do our individual funerals, pastor would you do the churches as well. Now what type of God called minister wants to do that? Yet some might not say it but they coast week after week into poisonous patterns that demonstrate they are fine with it. Church Revitalization takes hard work by both the laity and the leadership! Anything less is not what the Lord had in mind for the New Testament Church.

Number Three - Pastors Who Do Not Lead

Closely interconnected to number two above is when a pastor refuses to lead the church towards church renewal. If the leader is unwilling to lead in the church's revitalization efforts perhaps it is time to get a new leader! In fact, my experience has revealed that there is a higher degree of these leaders out there than we would like to admit. About 30% of the 100% of the churches that need to be revitalized will be revitalized by its present leader. With that in mind, it is not a surprise that there are leaders who simply refuse to lead a church into a renewal effort. If you have heard me speak to seminaries before on this subject you now know why I say that training our young future pastors in church revitalization techniques and principles is a must since most of them will be going into churches in need of revitalizing and need an energetic leader to lead them. Only about 5% of these seminarians will be going into healthy vital churches so let's change the challenge by preparing these young leaders for future successes in ministry areas God has not abandoned.

Number Four - A Church Closed to "Outsiders" and Visitors

If you have ever visited a church where you knew from the first moment you entered the facility that you were an outsider and were less than welcome, you know what I mean by this phrase. Many churches have never been taught how to be a visitor-friendly church and the result is that most visitors feel a sense of coldness and anything but welcomed when they visit these churches. You take a church that desperately needs to be revitalized or renewed and often you will discover a church that has become unwelcoming to those who just might be part of the solution to revitalizing the work. One church we visited as a family a few years ago was so locked up with only the rank and file that even our kids said to us when we finally got back in the car and began talking about our experiences, "That was the worse church we have ever been to Daddy!" What they meant by this was they were not even welcomed in the youth departments and that is usually the one place that everyone feels welcomed. When a church essentially closes itself to outsiders it is hurting any potential of turning the church around. If you want to begin one of the little nudges towards revitalizing the church, begin by leading your people to discover the importance of opening the church to outsiders and visitors.

Number Five – An "Us versus Them" Attitude

Matriarchs and patriarchs in churches easily can fall into an "Us versus Them" type of attitude. As a Patriarch. you have guided and actively participated in the various functions of the church. As a Matriarch, you have similarly invested in the life of the church usually by following the stronger desires of those serving as active patriarchs. When a church begins to get engaged in the process of church revitalization, often the very first group of participants in the church who feel threatened are the Patriarchs and Matriarchs! It is often hard for people who have served diligently for many years to begin to include new people in the leadership decisions of a church. Part of that is that they feel new people are saying that what they did was not good or right and part of it is the insecurity that once you commence into the process of revitalization and begin dealing with all of the unknowns it is just hard for them to handle. Part of renewing any church usually includes widening the circle of influence and participation and a wise revitalization leader would do well to share that kindly often and without apology.

Number Six – No Vision for the Future

Church Revitalization is something that most pastors and young seminarians have not been trained in! It is quite difficult to lead a congregation into revitalization if you have not first been trained or presently have a revitalization coach helping you navigate the path towards renewal. Creating a healthy compelling vision for a church in need of revitalization is a bit more difficult than it is for the healthy church or even the new church plant. Part of this is because there have been so many visions offered in the past that were not finished or did not come to fruition that the rank and file, no matter how small it is now, have become callous towards any "God-given vision" due to past performances. Therefore, it is difficult to get people to rally around a new vision when they are experiencing "Vision Fatigue" from all of the previous visions that did get carried out. Any church revitalization pastor would do well to receive a little coaching in this area before he rolls out the next plan that most laity will receive less than enthusiastically.

Number Seven - Fear of Change and Taking Risks

New churches love taking risks because they are new and everything is a risk. Young churches that have been around for periods longer than twelve years have often become entrenched a little. Still, older churches that are twenty years old or more have a fear that develops mostly out of comfort with the previous state of affairs in the church and are often challenged when it comes to renewal and revitalization. People of habit and churches of habit do not respond well to change and often have problems seeing a new or possible reality. Usually, it is the catalytic types who thrive on change while the rest are struggling with various degrees towards change. Churches of habit cannot see other possibilities. Change often frightens people. People do not relax well in the midst of change. It makes them anxious. Realize you are trapped in a routine. Become aware of what you have tried in the past that has not worked. Become willing to let go of what has not worked while honoring previous attempts.

Number Eight - Power Cliques within the Church

"Not in my Church!" the elder might say. "We have been doing it this way for forty years now and I see no reason the stop doing it the way we have always done it" another might say. Another component that often encumbers the process of church revitalization is when power brokers and power cliques begin to operate within the church. New ideas and new methodologies are often squelched in these types of churches simply because the power brokers did not think them up. I often say to the churches I am coaching in revitalization: "If you are not willing to invest a minimum of 3-5 years in the process, don't seek to revitalize your church!" Part of that is because I know it will take time to gain the trust and cooperation of the power brokers within the church. Cliques usually follow tenured leaders that have little to do with the real leadership of the church. Winning these individuals will take some wins under your belt before they give you their approvals.

Number Nine – Lack of Finances and Consistent Church Stewardship

A big hindrance to church revitalization is the lack of financial resources necessary to begin to turn the church around towards a growth and health mentality. Many a church that was once vital and had consistent resources necessary to see the work advance, now by the time it considers the concept of church revitalization, is strapped with the inability to provide the necessary resources needed to move the church towards renewal. Be careful not to wait until the very last moment of the church's life before you make the decision to restart and revitalize the church. If you do, you might discover you have few resources needed to move into the process and see the church advance once more.

Number Ten – Apathy and Church Burnout

Ministers can become burned out and churches can find themselves that way also. Apathy in a fellowship is a very dangerous component that encumbers church revitalization. Have you ever been to a church that was spiritually exhausted? I have. In these churches, there is so much effort placed on trying to ride from one peak to another peak of activity, that the church never takes a moment to catch its breath and eventually it wears the laity out and they need a rest. That rest will come in one of three ways:

Recharging of Their Batteries

The first way it will come is through a wise church revitalization leader seeing the early signs of burnout in the laity and taking the necessary steps to allow it time to recharge its batteries. If you are always pushing hard as a leader it will either take a constantly renewing number of volunteers replacing those who you have burned out or it will

143

take a slowing down for a few months to allow your hard charges to catch their breath! Many a leader in renewal and revitalization efforts understands the Law of the Ninety Day Push. Here is the idea in brief. Work hard with your laity for three months and then slack off a bit (about a month) and get ready for the next ninety-day push. Most churches can facilitate three well thought out evangelistic pushes per year without burning out your leaders and causing apathy to become rampant.

A Sabbatical from Service

Another way is for the people to take a sabbatical from service. When you have worked and worked and worked it is easy to get burned out a little and become apathetic. Even while the Holy Spirit is energizing you our human frailty can cause us to grow weary. When a church needs to begin the renewal process having a worn-out group of volunteers can mean trouble. Active members who are the strength of the work will often seek to impose an in-service sabbatical just so they can refuel their batteries. That usually means that the leader has done a poor job in developing, enlisting, and apprenticing new leaders that could come alongside of the present leaders and give them a few weeks or months to catch their breath.

Departure from the Church

Lastly a departure from the church by key laity who have served faithfully is a sign of burnout and apathy. Burnout on the volunteers and apathy on the leaders to hear the call and do something about it! Usually, there will be a clarion call for some time off from the deeply committed to recharge their batteries. When it is not heard, volunteers feel trapped and think they are faced with only one last option, that of leaving the church. A wise church revitalization leader understands that the rank and file may all actually be a little burnt out and that it necessitates the apprenticing of eventually lay leaders who will either start new things of ministry or take over those things that are presently going on.

These are some of the components that encumber church revitalization. If attention is not given to these areas it will hamper the possibilities of future success and renewal. Such impediments can halt your efforts for renewal and revitalization keeping the church from engaging in effective evangelism and healthy ministry.

What Are the Things That Can Hinder Your Success?

In order for our churches to succeed in renewal, we as their leaders need to have an optimistic mentality to achieve our goals and allow the church to become its best version of revitalization it can be. It can be easy to dream and set goals but making them successful can be difficult sometimes. It takes working on and in revitalization each and every day. There can be numerous interruptions, distractions, and disturbances that can serve as obstructions in achieving the strengthening of the church we want. That's why it is important to know what are the things that can hinder a church's success. Traveling the road of revitalization is not an easy trek. There can be some bumps and rough roads before you reach your destination. Here are some of the things that can feasibly hinder your church from moving towards revitalization success:

Failure to Act

There is a high degree of fear in churches that have waited too long before they began to consider the revitalization of their church. Even the words "failure to act" conger up an uneasy feeling for church leaders. Church leaders which wait too long before they get working on revitalization can become locked into not being able to take action. They talk about what they need to do but they are unable to pull the trigger and act. If church leaders become frozen into doing nothing negativity will surface in the membership. In some churches needing renewal, failure to act can become a vital steppingstone towards success. Jerry Falwell taught many of us that often failure is the back door to eventual success. If we fail and get back up we will begin to learn what works and what will not. Pastors are often motivated when things don't work to try something else. Thomas Edison tried over 10,000 times to make a light bulb. He only needed one successful experiment to change the world.

Excuses Offered Early and Often

Perhaps the biggest roadblock is when church leaders, both clergy and laity, offer up a series of excuses why they have not been successful. Instead of taking actions to achieve their goals, they keep on making excuses such as:

"I am not gifted of doing something like this."

"I am not yet prepared for renewal."

"I am not experienced enough."

"I don't have the assets needed."

"I can't do it."

There is the rub. It is much easier to throw one's hands in the air and declare the negative. Such excuses are not conducive to success. Excuse making must be eliminated in a church seeking renewal. If your church is to be saved negative talk must be jettisoned. Everyone who leads often finds themselves out of their comfort zones. That is usually when the Lord can do His greatest miracle for the church. Begin praying positively. Begin speaking positively. Begin believing positively. Begin risking positively. Churches have a greater chance to rebound and renew if the negative is removed.

Perfectionism Isn't a Character Quality of a Church Revitalizer

Perfectionism will defeat a church's chances for revitalization because things will never be good enough nor will the time be right. If there was a Declining Churches Twelve Step program for recovering perfectionists, how many pastors of declining churches would be there? I can hear them now, "Hi I am Pastor Lead Feet and I am a recovering perfectionist." Perfectionism keeps you stuck. It is filled with self-doubt. It keeps you from moving forward toward your dreams of revitalization in any meaningful way. It is not something we should glorify or gloss over. It's not a strength. The most dangerous way we sabotage our declining churches is by waiting for the perfect moment to begin. Do not let perfectionism become an excuse for never getting started. Pastors and church leaders are not perfect people. We all make mistakes sometimes.

Forgetting to Take Little Steps

In revitalization, it is often three steps forward two steps back sort of thing. Yet we gain one step. That initial step towards renewal is the beginning of your first one hundred and twenty days in the revitalization process and your minimal investment of a one-thousand-day journey. Revitalization is a process and takes time. To fully revitalize a church, you just can't believe you are going to achieve it in a few days. Take your steps with great care. Planning of your steps is best. Patience is part of revitalization so be careful. Do not jump over critical steps because you will lose your footing and often have to start over again. Enjoy the ride and don't try to rush things.

Procrastinating and Dawdling

Are you a dawdler? Have you caught yourself procrastinating? In church revitalization these two traits are one of the most common causes of church leaders failing to accomplish their goals. In Chapter Sixteen we deal with the concept of procrastination and its effects on church revitalization so only a small portion will be addressed here. Needless to say, if you are a dawdler or a procrastinator you really ought to let these go. Now is the time for revitalization so get to work. By beginning today rather than tomorrow you will come closer to your goal of successful renewal and revitalization.

Lack of Consistency

Consistency is one trait of successful church revitalizers that makes them different from pastors who are stuck in a maintenance mentality. Unswerving leadership from the pastor is needed in renewal and it is a part of achieving your dreams for a growing church. One of the reasons I often say you must do something each day for revitalization, almost anything, is to emphasize the point that you must be about it every day. Growth habits are developed this way.

Lack of Self-esteem

Church Revitalizer's who believe in themselves are more likely to be successful in turning around their church. God has wired you for the task so watch how the Lord will utilize your abilities. Revitalization is a layering discipline as well as a stretching discipline. You can do more than you give yourself credit. Stop walking the defeated stroll just because you are pastoring a declining church. Start today and get at it, believe in your abilities, lack action, and watch the dream of renewal come to life. One's potential is developed in the hard stuff, not the easy stuff.

Stop Looking Out the Window of Greener Church Pastures

Distractions to revitalization are often found when you are looking at the greener church pastures out your window. Interruptions of our own choosing often get in our way. Doubt comes upon us as the church revitalizer when we are straining to see the better church down the road. It also sucks all of the hope from what you are doing if you let it into your life. Looking down the road is a temptress at least and dangerous for sure to what God wants to do through you in the church your serve. This temptress will affect your eyesight and cause your focus to wander aimlessly.

Wrapping it Up!

Avoiding these components which encumber church revitalization is a great first step. Keep your eyes on the prize of renewal is critical. Develop your plan and set your goals. Understand that distractions will come your way but press on nevertheless. Believe in who you are and whose you are. Take firm steps and don't stumble off the path for renewal. Revitalization is a worthwhile ministry for pastors. Keep on keeping on and never give up.

Chapter Nine
Practical Steps for Leading a Church off the Plateau

The second decade of the twenty-first century has ushered in with perhaps more uncertainty for the plateaued church than any other time in our religious history. We have all had to learn how to do church in different settings such as online, drive-in, venues, multiple days of the week, and multiple times on the Lord's day. The fundamental issue for plateaued or declining churches in the second decade of this century is not growth but the salvation of the church in general. Certainly, all of us desire growth in our churches and yet in plateaued churches that is a secondary question. Most plateaued churches are asking the wrong question when they ask: What are the things that will make our church flourish? The real question we should be asking is: What are the things that is keeping our church from flourishing? Plateaued churches often seek a quick fix to a difficult situation. By focusing on how to flourish once more is not going to get the plateaued church off of the stuckness it is experiencing. Getting the membership healthy first will allow the church the best chance of flourishing. Innumerable churches drift along each and every year in a state of plateau and refuse to do anything about it. They are content to live out the church's remaining life of the eternal drift of plateau. Somehow, they have come to believe one of Satan's lies about churches and that is that it is perfectly all right to be stuck and stagnate all the way until the church closes its doors. It is as if they have a covenant with one another that the last one left alive would turn the lights off. Getting off of stuck and the proverbial treadmill of plateau is a choice and too few churches in the western hemisphere want to make that choice today. They lock themselves into a plateau that eventually leads to decline which eventually leads to rapid decline with eventually leads to a dying church which leads to a church closure and someone turns the lights out. Because the church and its leaders failed to embrace change, they began to lose ground a little at a time until there was no more ground to lose. North America is full of plateaued churches and there are large numbers who closed their doors last Sunday for the very last time.

Understanding Your Church's Ground Zero

Do you remember where you were on September 11, 2001? I was at work getting ready to enter a staff meeting with our team. Someone had just turned on the television in the conference room because our cell phones began to light up with news reports that there had been a disaster at the World Trade Center in New York City. Quickly the site was named by many as ground zero. Ground Zero is where New York City's famous landscape changed forever after the 9/11 attacks. The world trade center was a complex of seven buildings, all of which were destroyed when the skyscrapers collapsed from airplanes crashing into them. Nearly three thousand people died that day as the result of that crash. It all just came crashing down that day as we watched it on the TV in our conference room. After the collapse of the World Trade Center people began referring to the site as Ground Zero. We know where ground zero is in south Manhattan.

Your Church Leadership Needs to Know Where You Have Come From

Churches that are plateaued have a ground zero as well. Your church if it is plateaued has a ground zero and so does mine. What do you do when it all comes crashing down and your church is left in a pile of rubble? In order to get to where you want to go you must know first where you have come from. You need to discover your church's ground zero! Understanding where you are currently, will help you pray and plan for a preferred future that with God's blessings can be bright. That is the first obstacle so many pastors usually blow because they are not honest with themselves as to where the church actually is. They are usually much more positive than reality actual portrays. You must become a historian of your church's past so you do not repeat its past mistakes and you can honor that past so you can move into the future. If the leadership of a church wants to lead it forward, that leadership must get in touch with that church's history.

Ground Zero Questions

I have said it for a long time that if you desire to lead your church through revitalization and renewal you must be willing to know where you have been and where you are desiring to go. While you are going you must honor the past if you hope to see a preferred future of renewal. Here are some ground zero questions pastors and church leaders must seek answers to:

Where has the church been?

What has the church done in areas of achievements?

What has the church done in areas of disasters?

What kind of direction has the church experienced?

What traumas has the church suffered?

Where is the church right now?

Your initial one hundred and twenty days will find yourself asking these types of questions seeking to get the complete picture of how, when, and why the church has become plateaued. But where do you go to get these answers? I always began by sitting down with long time members having coffee and picking their memories. By sitting down and talking to older members asking about their favorite memories and the worst thing that ever happened to the church, you can begin to understand your church's ground zero. Old worship guides or bulletins are another good place to find key items referencing some form of decline. Community newspapers often will have an article when a long-time pastor departs or significant change in a church has occurred. The last place I usually go is to the church clerk's business meeting notes that are stored in a church file cabinet somewhere. Very revealing are these minutes of meetings as written from the hand of a church member. Listening and reading about the church cannot be overemphasized in setting the stage for healthy church revitalization. Once you have discovered where your church's past has been you will be better able to move it forward into a better future.

Develop Areas of Healing from Past Dealings

Many churches try to hide or cover up their past that has led to strained relationships or broken relationships that impact the entire church today. So many churches suffer from failure to seek confession and repentance in dark areas that were simply covered up and not dealt with. Here are some things you can learn relating to areas where healing was not sought:

Problems Solved by a Firing

The number of churches I have worked with that were not willing to deal with challenging issues of clergy and church member differences would astonish you. Far too many churches in need of revitalization seek to solve their problems by firing and hiring pastors. They believe that if they fire the present guy and get the new guy then their troubled days are over. That seldom works due to a church's failure to deal with past issues. What they discover is that after three years of the new pastor the same issues have arisen and they start the same process over and over again. In fact, the rank-and-file membership actually wonder why things do not get better but are only getting worse.

Self-Destruction Due to Strained Relationships Within Membership

Churches often self-destruct once relationships are severed because a place of worship which once was so much fun, now has become a place of no fun. There is tension each and every week that visitors can see clearly causing them to choose to not come back. Because the membership is so close, they are often blind to what prospects see from the strain in the church. When the relationship strain causes the church to be no fun decline will surface and cause a defeatist attitude. Think about the scripture. Jesus was fun or the children would have never come unto Him. Most people do not want to hang out with people who are no fun. Most churches have within them an escalating number of strained relationships that if left un-confronted will eventually become part of the decline within the church.

Confronting Unrepentant Members

One of the first difficult things a leader will find himself doing in church revitalization is confronting some longtime members about their unacceptable behavior. The way they gossip about others and the way they do not honor the man of God nor the sanctuary of the Lord. Tip toeing around your church's problems will only give you as the leader sore feet. Do you have anyone within your fellowship that uses anger to get their way on things? Have the rank and file stopped coming up with new ideas for ministry? This might be because they are afraid of setting this person off again and experiencing their rage. The result is the church loses the potential for community impact!

When Mr. or Mrs. Crankie Thrive in your Church

Grouchy church members are a complete turnoff to potential new members so be warned. New people begin leaving your church once they have had one or two tastes of Mr. or Mrs. C's rage because the new member suggested an idea for saving the church. Nothing silences the Crankies in a church like members who are full of gratitude. Crankies are ungrateful and bellyache all the time. They are the sour and dour crowd. Remember, it is these new people who are offering new ideas for new ministries that might have been part of the leading the church out of the decline. Church Revitalizer listen to me here for a moment. Do you realize that many non-threatened long-time members wonder regularly why you as a leader can't keep these new people? They have missed the point that the Crankies are chasing away these new prospects faster than you can find them, develop them, and deploy them. Often these are the long-term protectors of the status quo. If that fits where you minister, try having a healing service where past behaviors are confessed and laid on the altar of forgiveness. I realize that most members do not care for confrontation. But if you are going to truly be the leader you must learn the art of positive healthy confrontation. Your willingness to confront negative unhealthy behavior in the church is a sign of leadership!

It takes courage mixed with much prayer and a daily exercise of bold faith demonstrated in a deep love for the church to actually confront people in the church who are damaging the church by their unhealthy hurtful behavior. Keep your confrontations in private meeting but never conduct these meetings without a lay leader with you. This will keep you from being misunderstood, misquoted, and most importantly misrepresented. Always go to a confrontation with at least one witness who has credibility in the church.

Allow the Reputation that You as the Leader Will Confront Inappropriate Behavior

Think about this for a moment: Just as problem people get reputations in the church around their inappropriate behavior, a revitalization leader willing to confront problems and people also quickly gets a reputation. Once people begin to understand this type of behavior will not be tolerated, such behavior will quickly cease or these problem people will attach themselves on to another church. Be sure to remove them from every leadership responsibility once they have departed. Far too many pastors miss the opportunity to remove one who has kept the church from advancing. They often will be back so be sure to detach them from power through position.

Embrace Your Elderly and Lead Them Through Revitalization

Begin acting as the change agent. Embrace the entire congregation not just the ones who think you are cool. Running away the longtime member not only makes you the adversary, it also makes you appear foolish to most of the members. Some revitalization leaders make the mistake of seeing these veterans as the enemy. While some individuals do become negative and disruptive, they are still God's people who have given sacrificially to often launch, expand, build and grow the church. The goal is not to get rid of them but to get them so committed to being like Jesus that they are willing to sacrifice what they love to reach those whom God loves. Most churches seem to be just days or hours from being put on life support before they realize they are dying. There is no such thing as holding your own and waiting to consider revitalization at a later time.

Most churches like each one of us as individuals are aging and death is growing closer every day. The church must know it is dying before it can be revived. Most churches in need of revitalization are in denial. The only place to start is at the beginning. Groundwork for revitalization is not much fun. Preparing the soil and pulling the weeds is the most difficult and demanding work for renewal. Do not allow yourself to take any short cuts because there aren't any. Now it is time to get started!

Steps to Turning Around the Plateaued Church

One of the rudimentary laws of physics is that it is much simpler to keep a body in motion than it is to reverse the motion of a moving object. The healthy growing church seems to have a momentum of its own that enables it to continue growing. The plateaued church, on the other hand, tends to become a declining church, and the declining church has a negative momentum that must be reversed if the church is to begin to flourish once more. Growing churches have, in a sense, a drive that propels them through each and every challenge with little or no hesitation. Plateaued churches though, lack such drive and will get sidetracked in a struggle to convince the membership that it needs to grow and grow now. There are practical steps the church revitalizer and the church revitalization team can take to begin to move the church off of the plateau of stuckness. Here are some of the most important you can use during your first one hundred and twenty days:

Church Renewal Advances on its Knees

Renewal growth begins with an increased emphasis on prayer. Mobilize a prayer coalition to begin praying for church renewal and revitalization. It is amazing how often this is done as an afterthought or as an add on after everything else has been decided. Keeping prayer first and foremost is essential. Any revitalizing church moves forward only on its knees. When the membership gets serious about prayer God can do amazing things. My friend and fellow Church Revitalization leader Tracy Jaggers says, "This is not the final straw, but rather the vital conduit for inviting the presence and power of God into the revitalization process." When God begins to renew a Church, it is a miraculously supernatural event. Real revitalization blessed by the Holy One begins with and is fueled by focused prayer on renewing of the local body. Pastor realize this, prayer is the issue not the stuff.

Repentance Leads to Holiness, Holiness Leads to Spiritual Maturity

Somewhere along the way declining churches have lose their way and are plateaued. One of the basic areas that help churches begin the journey is to emphasize individual repentance, corporate repentance, and God's holiness with leads to spiritual maturity. God's formula for renewal is that as churches become more holy and spiritually grow, there seems to be a direct correlation to a renewed membership. As the congregation matures in the faith, the church will have a deeper resolve to fulfill the Great Commission. The mature believer is more likely to obediently *"go into the highways and byways and compel them to come in."* Renewal growth begins with renewed vision. Many plateaued and declining churches have lost their vision for the future. The best way to renew is to rediscover God's purpose and mission for the church. Renewal growth requires that the pastor generate enthusiasm for accomplishing the God-given vision.

The Membership Must Be Willing to Change

Without change it is impossible to revitalize a plateaued church. Your members' willingness to embrace change is a beginning place for renewal and revitalization. Change is seen in new things that help jump start the effort of renewal. Things such as: new priorities, changes in the building, and a movement away from ineffective, unbiblical traditions may be needed. Over ninety percent of the plateaued churches which have been renewed have experienced the eagerness to change first. You as the pastor are the change agent so do not shy away from the task in which you are called.41

Understanding Community and Culture is Paramount

Most plateaued churches have stopped understanding who lives in their community and the cultures represented around the church. Renewing churches know themselves first, the community second, and the culture third. One church I was working with towards

---

41 Available from Renovate Publishing Group is the book: *The Church Revitalizer as Change Agent* by Tom Cheyney. It is a book designed to help the pastor become better at leading a church through the necessary changes required to bring back church health.

renewal totally missed understanding their community and surrounding cultures. They had in their mind that the community was made up of seniors because the church was made up of seniors. I had done the demographic work before I met with them and knew that was not the case. During our discussion I asked how many of those present lived less than two miles from the church. Only the pastor raised his hand. I then asked if they had lived around the church at one time and most of the hands were raised. What had happened over the years was that the church had become a commuter church where people drove in on Sunday to worship. What they were surprised to discover was that the community did not look like them. The community was much younger and more ethnically diverse than those present. All of the ideas coming from the laity were fashioned around who they saw on Sunday and not on who lived around the church. The pastor is then allowed to envision and launch ministries and outreach activities designed to reach the community and its cultures.

Goals for Renewal Must Be Set

Not until the church begins to set a series of goals towards renewal does it have the chance of being renewed. Setting goals requires the church seeking renewal to look to and plan for the future. Goals established by the laity under the direction of the pastor will motivate the church to plan for the fulfillment of those goals. At the least, set goals for an increase in Sunday School and baptisms. Once the goals are adopted by the church, they should be given adequate publicity. Do a few things well but not everything poorly. Revitalization of a plateaued church requires a series of gentle nudges and not a canon blast of thirty things to be done yesterday. By producing a few wins initially, the membership will be more willing to follow you long term. Learn to celebrate even the tiniest of victories together. A series of small wins is better than failing in a big one initially. Allow the Lord time to prepare you as the leader and the church as the followers for a larger victory when the time is right.

Get Back to Doing Evangelism and Visitation

Far too many plateaued churches think that people are longing to come back to your church. They are not so you must go after them. Revitalizing churches place a greater focus on outreach and evangelism. When people begin to see the results of evangelistic visitation, they become aware of the supernatural work of the Holy Spirit. The pastor can provide motivation for visitation by leading the way through increased personal visitation. Renewal growth occurred in more than sixty percent of the churches where pastors and staff made more than five prospect visits in a week.

Embrace Sunday School or Small Groups

Leading a church off of the plateau and beginning to be renewed requires that the church re-embrace Sunday School or Small Groups. Sunday School or Bible Study is the church organized for ministry. It is the pull of the people and the anchor in times of transition. Seventy-eight percent of Renewal churches reported an increased emphasis on Sunday School.

Boast in the Lord

Far too much boasting in church is about everything that has little to do with the church. Church revitalization and renewal is best aided by a series of positive rumors. Talk about the good things that are happening in the church and stop talking about giving up. The plateaued or declining church often has been the topic of community conversation, but it often has been negative. Start a good rumor about a positive experience in your church and begin to publicize it.

My Quick List of Big Things Not to Forget

The above steps are solid launching points for leading the church off of a plateau. The list I offer below is my quick list for the busy pastor trying to renew their church:

- Cast a gripping vision of what the church could become.
- You must see the vision as a possibility and then lead your people to see it as a possibility as well. The groundwork to achieve the vision must be done.
- Build relationships as early and often as possible.
- Train staff and laity.
- Keep vision casting.
- Pep up the music just a little.
- Keep growing the prayer ministry.
- Help new members fit in, create new ministries that will facilitate growth.
- Preach and Teach on what it takes to be a healthy growing church.
- Change the perception that everyone is a minister at this church.
- Renew, reinvent, and refresh your mission statement so that everyone can catch it.
- Develop a working strategy for present, near future, and long-term growth.
- Connect the laity to the work of ministry.
- Work on ways to accommodate growth
- Add services

- Make reaching people the new priority
- Allow God to provide for the financial resources needed for the church.
- Keep personal evangelism on the front burner and lead lost people to Christ.
- Light a candle when some gets saved.
- Remember the responsibility for keeping evangelism a priority in the lead pastor revitalizer and no one else. Keep your commitment to evangelism public.
- Disciple those who are won to Christ.
- Share the plan of salvation in your new member's class.
- Give your fellowship handles for doing evangelism.
- Conduct Special Evangelistic Events that will create awareness of your churches love for the community.
- Use the natural seasons for events.
- Become known as a church of compassion for its community.
- Utilize the media to help you share your story.
- Openly and outwardly display to your community your love in specific and practical ways that demonstrate this love.
- Within your organization structure to begin new classes and programs to meet new needs.

If you cannot implement all of these steps, begin where you can and then plan for the future. Work hard to include all age groups in evangelism. Allow evangelism to become the driving force in revitalizing your church! When it becomes the top priority, new life will surge into your fellowship. Keep evangelism the driving force.

Key Reasons Churches Face Plateau and Decline in Church Revitalization

Churches facing plateau or decline often struggle with various challenges which can cause a church to stall beyond its ability to regain it health and vitality. Here are some key reasons:

Spiritual Illness

There begins to surface a spiritual illness that is not addressed which leads to stagnation, plateau or decline. Like the church in the Book of Revelation which lost its first love, these church's faith questions are discontinued as comfort becomes the new norm. Within these hurting churches participants are not able to be candid with each other because the truth is just too painful. Declining churches lack a passion for knowing God, for becoming what God wants them to become, and for doing what God wants them to do.

Blatant Refusal to Change

There is a powerful negativity towards change which left to its own doing will result in a church's inability to make the changes necessary to turn it around. Many churches founded before 1980 will struggle with plateau and decline as their membership disappears. Because the church failed to replace aging members with younger ones the plateau often pushes over into decline rapidly. Change is part of the new world and younger individuals adapt quickly to change as older people do not. The longer the church resists change and making the necessary changes in programs and ministries, the more difficult the changes will become as the culture moves forward at an increasing rate of speed. A high amount of conflict has risen within the church which is often connected to its unwillingness to move forward. There are usually incidents where a pastor or staff member has been dismissed, finances have been utilized improperly, or legal issues dragging the church down.

Structured for Comfort Not Advancement

Many plateaued churches have an organizational structure designed more for comfort than reaching the unchurched. Poor structure handcuffs pastors who are trying to lead a renewal effort. Lay leaders are either blind to this confinement or just don't care enough about saving their church to change structure. Most churches today are structured with a model that is well over 100 years old. They are trying to drive a Model T in a lane where a Mustang is required. They are organized in a way to protect the status quo over against ministries designed to effectively reach people. Church revitalizers are vision casters but even that is not enough unless there are those around them who can make the vision a reality.

Pastors Who Are Not Trained in Revitalization

We are living in a time where most pastors are unsure of their individual abilities to turn a church back towards health and revitalization. They neither have led strong churches nor are they individuals which are driven towards growth and advancement. Some leaders have no attainable vision for growth which renders them unable to lead. The needed leader is a church revitalizer which has a strong deep driven capacity to lead and reinforce a powerful vision which God's people can buy in to. Most church maintainers are pastors who lack a driven focus which can compel followers to pursue the vision of God. Pastors with an inadequate skill set in compelling followers to pursue the vision for renewal will have lay leaders within their ministry which are unable to compel others as well.

Lay Leadership Which Repels Members from Being Involved

Even though most lay leaders of plateaued or declining churches will not admit it, they are a big part of the reason other members refuse to get involved. They refuse to accept the responsibility for decline in a local church. Laity which possesses and present negative attitudes and outlooks towards the responsibility they hold in this situation are unwilling to face the real issues which keep their church from growing. Sometimes healthy pastoral leaders simply leave a church because the laity are cantankerous and unwilling to follow. This usually happens when the historical heritage of a church is more important to the present membership than reaching others in the community for Jesus. Sometimes the present membership within a church is so selfish that God cannot work towards revitalization because new people are a threat to the current leadership.

Meeting Felt Needs Overreaching Others for Jesus

A local church which has become locked in an inward focus is more concerned about meeting felt needs of the present membership than reaching out to those who need Jesus. When seventy percent of your time and energy as a pastor is spent on an inward focus of attendees a church will eventually face severe decline. It has been said that a true sense of biblical mission moves a church beyond demographic changes, generational differences, and cultural challenges to see the big picture from God's perspective. Churches which are able to move past decline today see themselves more as missional outposts rather than a church for us. Missional outposts think more of developing a church for others which are not currently part of the church.

Wrapping it up!

Plateaued, declining and dying churches will exhibit a vast majority of the following traits. They will: lack a vision for God's mission for the church, misunderstand evangelism and disciple-making. not be able to handle regular conflict, allows the insignificant to become critical and stuck in board verses body struggles. The church staff displays an inability to work together as a team and a laity which can't follow their leaders. The result is they become polarized because of church organization and structure. The laity, which are not equipped nor in ministry often have a large degree of unconfessed and unrepented sin. There is corporate sin throughout and a high degree of refusal to deal with it. Members are prone to explain away their sin like explaining why they bought their new car over another one. Their refusal to be obedient to scripture allows for Satan to get a strong hold in the church. Often these churches have fired one or more of their past pastors and have lied about it to their present one. The lay leadership have become repeat offenders of firing the shepherd of God. These kinds of church boards seek power for themselves and want an errand boy for their pastor rather than a leader of the pack.

In church revitalization and renewal most of the long-term advancements towards growth is accomplished through those on the outside. Usually, a smaller group of insiders realize they need help and will work with and through the local Director of Missions to enlist a church revitalizer to begin about change. A church revitalizer has the giftedness, leadership qualities, and skill sets necessary to embrace the challenges and opportunities a dying church need. They are called to be a church revitalizer and are not looking for a place to preach in the later years of their ministry. As Paul requires of Titus to *"set things in order"* (Titus 1:5), a church revitalizer must bring a firm stance and action plan to set the ministry on a course towards renewal. This church revitalizer is a provider of hope to a group which does not have much hope. This revitalizer is a provider of hope to those who are weakened with pessimism due to a high degree of decline. The rank and file of the church are in a state of hurt and in need of a revitalizer which can bring hope, love, passion for growth, and godly direction. They must be able to see things others cannot see, solve the unseen, provide other options through a compelling vision. A church revitalizer has a unique innate ability and skill set to be more vision driven rather than history driven. Tradition is not something which compels others to join a renewing church so his emphasis on the new vision takes greater precedence over a historical past focused on an individual church's heritage. They are able to risk in the following areas so that vibrant Christian experience is renewed within the church: 1) Improve your quality of worship, 2) Be responsive to the spiritual needs of the people, and 3) Increase the level of output of the church staff. Remember that your church can grow! Jesus promised that He would build His church. Allow Him to build His church through you.

Chapter Ten
Factors that Impede Church Revitalization

No one likes to admit that most of our churches are struggling to keep their heads above the water in this new century. If you ask one thousand pastors of declining churches what are the biggest factors that are hindering your growth, you will get many responses. We did just that for an entire year during our Renovate National Church Revitalization Conferences and the results were interesting. If you are going to begin the work of revitalization in your church, then how you address many of these factors during your initial one hundred and twenty days will be important. Before we tackle these factors we first need to observe those things which often trip us up at the initial stage of revitalization and then we fight or wrestle with them for the rest of the journey. I call these things the stumbling blocks to revitalizing your church.

Stumbling Blocks to Revitalization Church Revitalization

There are many stumbling blocks to church revitalization. To be perfectly honest with you if the work of a church revitalizer was easy, we would have more ministers committed to doing the work of church strengthening and renewal. It is a difficult thing and often hard grueling work that gets messy at times. At the heart of most of this is that people and churches are not all that interested in change. Let's face it, most of your church members are more in love with the bygone days of their church than they are in the upcoming days of their church. They place their historical church heredity as much more important than they place leaving the church in good shape for the generations which follow. Churches get accustomed to the general environment of how the church functions and are unwilling to try new things to reach a new crowd. The result is a paralysis of outreach and an unwillingness towards reaching new prospects. Churches which love their traditions much more then they love lost people getting to heaven because someone shared Jesus with them, stumble all over themselves when they try to begin working on church renewal. This is often a clear sign that your members (and perhaps even you) are more in love with past days of the church than they are in its future ones. I see it all over North America where churches are museums to the 1960's. What year is your church functioning in is a big question the church leader needs to ask. If you focused on the past the chances of you reaching the new generations coming on the scene fades greatly. The renewal economy for churches working towards revitalization is made up of two critical activities: 1) They get the church to move forward and 2) they find ways to transform the old "no longer useful traditions" into new and useful ones. In opposite to the renewal economy is the death economy of many churches. These dying churches are focused on two dangerous activities: 1) They work hard to keep the church right where it is and 2) they work hard as protectors of the status quo. There are positive factors which become additives as it is, towards renewal and vitality. There are negative factors which become detriments, stumbling blocks, towards any form of renewal. Here are some stumbling blocks often revealed in church revitalization:

Stakeholder Symmetry

We have all seen it in churches where a select few members own everything that is going on in the church and make all of the decisions. If they are not in favor of it then there will be no action. Pastors move to these churches all the time believing that the search committee is being honest with them that they really do want to see their church renewed. Only to discover later that these stakeholders who usually sit on the peripheral of the church and wield strong influence were never consulted and now that the pastor has arrived and want to begin to renew the church, they are not in favor of it and will often work against seeing the church revitalized.

Pardon Me You Are Sitting in My Seat

It sounds almost humorous if it were not for the truth behind this stumbling block. Many new people come to a church only to find it hard to actually find a place to sit that is not already reserved for those who come each and every week. The feeling of being welcomed goes out the door and so does the prospect.

Poor Theology

Many struggling churches are so desperate for new blood that it is open to include those who are not theologically aligned with where the church is going theologically. Then it wonders why it is hard to get anything moving because there are just too many factions all pulling the nucleus in different directions. Know who you are as a church and stop trying to be one church with eight different denominational influences fighting for the right to be heard.

Confusing Worship

Another stumbling block is when a church has a worship program that is confusing to all of those who are not a regular part of the weekly experience. Standing up, sitting down on a que that is not given but assumed is a big turnoff to first time guests. Singing the familiar "our song" in worship that visitors would not know and is not in the bulletin or on the screen is hard for guest since some of our words in songs are strange to the unchurched ear. Another area that hurts the renewing church is worship quality or lack of it. The quality of the worship experience is more important even than its style. If the service itself seems slapped together,

incoherent or unable to be embraced, then it will not provide
the traction needed for ongoing growth. The better that
service is at helping people connect with God, the more
people it will attract. The weekend service is the front door of
the church. It is where we "win" or "lose" people. Begin
looking at your service through the eyes of someone far from
God and deeply unchurched. Would this draw or repel
people from your church service?

Reciting Various Creeds, Themes or Prayers

While it is usually a big thing to many pastors reciting
something that only the "regulars" know is a gigantic turn off
to those seeking to discover if they might fit in to your
church.

Apprehensive Leadership

When pastors are afraid to make changes because of the
consequences the apprehensive leader becomes a stumbling
block to revitalization. If negative responses can cause you to
abandon revitalization efforts stop now. Not only is the
church not ready to be revitalized, you are not ready to be the
revitalization leader. Abandonment prematurely of changes
will hurt the momentum toward renewal and keep it from
ever considering the subject again. Then the church just
withers and dies a slow and agonizing death all the time
mocking Jesus Christ to a community that needs Him.

Fear of the Unknown Future

If it is hard for you to look towards a future that is much
different than your present situation, then the fear of the
unknown will keep you from proceeding. Your church's past,
the known past and the covered-up past, will affect this fear
of future as well.

Membership That is Fearful of New Things

If the church membership and pastor are fearful of new changes and new things that might be done for advancing the church and getting it back on the road to recovery, renewal will be hard. Most laity fear that there is change all around their lives and are unable to cope with it. They are unable to cope with things like their changing health, physical vigor, and aging.

Looking at the Present State of Affairs at Church as the Safe-Place

Older members want a safe place to worship. For many seniors, growth and evangelism are not as important as it once was. The familiar is more important than new things. Ritual over creativity is a comfort. Any change could shake or anger older members.

I'll Take My Toys and Go Play Somewhere Else

I am always was amused with my wife and her excitement when someone would join our church from another church in the area. We would discuss it after the service at lunch and she often would question my lack of enthusiasm. The reason was they didn't like the changes at their church and wanted to make a statement to the pastor and staff of the previous church. The end result is they will eventually not like what I do and will make the same exodus.

People of Habit Cannot See Other Things

Many members are comfortable in the routine. They like the same old same old no matter how un-appealing it may be. While things are changing all around them, they opt for remaining the same.

Inability to Change the Basic Thinking of the Majority of Church Members and Leaders

If pressed most church people want to keep things the status quo. That is why we often hear things such as doing what we are already doing better, more frequently, or with new leadership.

Unaware of What a Revitalized Church Looks Like

Since many ministers and church members grew up in unhealthy churches, they are not able or aware of what a healthy revitalized church looks like. The result is that these churches keep the same level of dysfunction that they have always had.

Your Church's Strength Can Also Be Its Weakness

What is it that you do well? Often for revitalization our strength can be part of the problem because we are unable to move on past that one thing we do well. Those who are seeking a church today are interested in options over conformity.

Bylaws and Constitution that Keeps the Church from Growing

It is amazing how often people who never follow the church constitution will use it as a club towards anything or anyone who is trying to do something new with the church! Many church bylaws keep things from happening. There are too many rules and regulations for members to follow that eventually the new member will say: "Farewell and keep your rules while you die." Declining and dying churches are more ministers of the "NO" over becoming the ministers of the "Yes." If all you do is say no all the time, you are part of killing your church. Jesus died for that church and others like it so watch out.

The Mistrust and Resentment Most Members Have Towards Pastoral Leadership

It is not a personal thing so hear me clearly on this. It is more towards any leader even if you have proven yourself. In one of my churches, I experienced this even after the Lord was using my ministry to turn the church totally around. Even with a proven track record right there before their eyes, I was still not trusted because of a former minister.

Do you want a church revitalization lesson? Here it is:

> Any changes made in the church must have at their heart the design to facilitate ministry and make it easier for the church to follow its God-given vision and reach more people with the good news. Revitalization is less about things the church does and more about who the church really is. You must work towards changing the church's personality if you are going to bring about renewal. If your church is hard to get along with, exclusive, grace-less, and hateful you will struggle towards renewal and revitalization.

The change in the personality of the church happens only when the church experiences healing of broken relationships and forgiveness of past hurts. Tension has to be released before a true welcoming atmosphere can prevail in a church. Healing must have taken place before warmth and love must just ooze out of the pores of the church. Conflict is inevitable. Managing conflict is a basic skill needed in living life, and especially in renewal and revitalizing a church. Do not change just for change sake. Change has a high risk for stirring up some already troubled waters, so do not bother causing conflict without it yielding a strong return on the effort. Understand that congregations change only as the people who are the congregation change.

Factors that Impede Church Revitalization

There are some primary factors which keep your church from growing. Many these are the very thing which is hold a church back. You might be reading this and sailing along when suddenly you have crashed with the onslaught of certainty that this is one of the factors hold your church back. If that happens stop, get out a pad of paper, and begin to write everything that come to your head about that factor. Why has it hindered your church? What are you going to do about it? When are you going to begin addressing this factor? What do you think are the primary factors that most impede churches from becoming revitalized and engaged in effective ministry and evangelism? With that in mind, let's consider the factors that impede church revitalization and renewal in the local church:

A Lack of Vision for Doing the Will of God

When a church and its leadership lack vision, it is hard to revitalize a church. Because of the laity and the pastor's diminished faith it is difficult to get the church started off well in renewal. Church leaders will simply stop believing that God can turn the church around. Pastors and lay leaders all across the country are losing their faith that their church will ever be able to be revitalized. When you as the leader has no vision for the future the church is in trouble. Discouragement is the breeding ground for complacency and maintenance. As a leader, you may remain faithful, but without any fire. The church revitalizer must find their fire if they are going to be part of renewing a church. It's all too common that a leader can lose heart and slide into discouragement. This is the enemy's strategy. Vision is then lost. When the leader loses vision, it's not long before growth slows or stops. Fight for your faith. Fight to believe again. Who do you know that believes in you? Get some time with them. Borrow their faith in you. Reflect back on when you believed in yourself and remember that God is with you. It is His Church, it is His idea, and what you are doing matters.

Low Congregational Self-esteem

When a congregation lives out of fear rather than faith their self-esteem begins to drain and declines with every passing event in which they were unsuccessful. They live in an inward focus which is defeating. No church begins being inward focused. If you want to reach people, you can't be self-focused. A church turns inward from a good thing that has gone bad. When a church continues down that path it becomes a habit and not only will it become inward focused, it will also develop patterns of low self-esteem. Things done inside of the church become the priority focus for the church as it falls out of touch with the very community it is called to serve. Evangelism inevitably drops off while the programming becomes all about what the believer's inside the church want for themselves, and the worship service begins to be accommodating only to those within that local body of Christ. The scary thing is that all churches drift in that direction. All churches drift inward without the purposeful and deliberate effort to keep an outward focus on those who are far from God. The leaders of the church must agree and align with a ministry that intentionally commits time, resources, effort and energy to reach out. Too many churches are focused on their wants, preferences and perceived needs. They are self-focused societies and become self-focused saints. It should be no surprise that outsiders never feel welcomed, valued, accepted, embraced or integrated into the fellowship of that type of church.

A Church Closed to "Outsiders" and Visitors

Have you ever been to a church that was closed to outsiders? I have. In fact, my family went to a church when we first moved to the Atlanta area that was close to our house and we thought it would become our church home. We went to the Sunday School class the first week and were less than warmly treated. Believing it was a bad week we went back the second week with little changing from the previous week. The third week we tried another class and had the same experience as the first two weeks. Then we picked up our children and went and found another friendly church where we could grow and make friends. The former church was more interested in longtime members only and was closed to visitors. The pastor was doing everything he could to turn around that church but was defeated at every turn by a membership that was unwilling to embrace newcomers. A cold shoulder towards outsiders while being exclusive instead of being inclusive will kill your church.

Fear of Change and Taking Risks

Declining churches often get that way because they fear changing from the status quo. In fact, they are quite comfortable with the status quo. These churches usually cannot see themselves taking risks in order to draw new prospects into the church fellowship. It is interesting if you think about this, the favor of God prospers us and prosperity makes us comfortable. As we get comfortable, we realize we have more to lose so we are less likely to risk it all for the cause of Christ. Minimizing risk becomes paramount and is a large impediment to church revitalization. Many stalled churches are afraid to risk what they have for the sake of what might be. Let's face it, at least you have got something going for you. You are paying the bills. You at least have a certain amount of people. And if you have had any modicum of success recently, you are going to be hesitant to risk what is for what could be. The greatest enemy of your future success in renewal is your current success though it might be minute. When you are perpetually afraid to risk what is for the sake of what might be, you might as well cue the funeral music now. Never be afraid to risk what is for the sake of what could be. Declining churches refuse to chart uncharted territory and reach new people which need the Lord. While the status Quo seeks to wear out well-worn roads, Church Revitalizers are interested in fashioning new roads. Take a risk. Follow the voice of the Holy Spirit as He leads you into uncharted waters. Status Quo temperaments do not rebuild the declining church. I run into a surprising number of leaders and church members who love their church but cannot figure out why no one else does. Well, those churches are on their way to soon having not much more than a small club for the already convinced status quo.

An "Us Versus Them" Attitude

Another factor that impedes church revitalization is the development of the we verse all of you attitude. There are many declining churches where you can actually go in and see that on the left of the church is the "Us-s." Then look to the far right and you will see the "Them-s." These two groups are always at one another fighting, bickering, and just hurting the remaining portion of the congregation until the soft middle gets fed up and departs the church leaving the pastor with just the two polarized remaining. To be fair to the middle, they waited on you pastor to deal with this, but you turned a blind eye to all of this so you left them no other option then to take flight and make a quick exit from the church. That group you had hope to revitalize the church with, got tired of your inaction so they took action.

A Church Membership Unwilling to Work Hard

When a church stops developing leaders and workers it is all but finished. When a church allows underdeveloped workers to take on key responsibilities without adequate training decline is right around the corner. Without more and better trained leaders, your renewing church cannot continue to flourish. If your vision for renewal is big and bold, it requires more leaders to help realize that vision. These leaders need to be developed and empowered. Your leaders need continuing training, personal development, and encouragement to keep rising to their potential as well as remain aligned with the vision of the church.

Power Cliques within the Church that Leads to Conflict

There are many power cliques in churches that meet weekly to argue with one another instead of worshiping the Lord. More often than not the pastor is stuck in the middle trying to keep his head down so it does not get chopped off. Visitors are turned off each and every week by those within the church that gather to bicker not worship. We were in one church where it was so awful, I told my wife that at the first "everyone bows your heads" type prayer we were each to gather up a child and meet out in the parking lot. The power cliques were waging war between one another and not only was the church losing out the pastor was also. If you are constantly bickering and arguing, why would any new people stay? It is not that Christians shouldn't have conflict, but we should be the best in the world at handling it. The New Testament is a virtual manual of conflict resolution, but so many of us prefer gossip, non-confrontation and dealing with anyone but the party involved. Dying churches fight one another within the fellowship. Growing churches handle conflict biblically, humbly and healthily.

Pastors Who Do Not Lead

Ministers are not immune to challenges in declining churches. They are some certainly who long to lead and the laity will not let them. Yet, there are pastors that refuse to lead and hide their heads in the sand hoping that they will not be challenged and asked to decide. Many pastors all over the country have the title of Pastor but have not been given the authority to lead the church. The consequences of this lack of leadership at the local church level are too devastating to ignore. John Maxwell has declared it well: "everything rises and falls on leadership." Perhaps a more accurate way of putting it would be that no church will rise above the level of its leadership. Too many pastors of declining or dying churches forfeit their leadership responsibility. In some churches it is taken from the pastor while other is it given away not realizing the harm that is done long term. When your lay governance has more say in a church than the pastor, not only is it wrong but it sends the sinful picture that the Lord's anointed one is weak and pathetic as a leader. Stop letting someone lead you beside the Lord Himself. Also, there are pastors who want everything to be voted upon so they are not placed in the middle of a decision. Stop it. Some pastors are blindsided by staff members who will lead in the absence of the pastor being willing to do so. Pastors get run over when the staff leads and the one who should lead becomes a nobody. It is our calling to lead. You just cannot sit by and wander in a status quo setting - "lead your church pastor!"

The church grows only in proportion to its leadership. If the leaders do not grow, neither will the church. One thing that kills church growth is the refusal of its leaders to grow. If you fail at this task the church loses. If the church wants to lose, then shake the dust off your feet and move on. Do not ignore that when you lead there may be fireworks but if you are still standing at the end of the deliberation, the Kingdom wins. A group rarely rises above its leadership, and in the church, this is true as well.

Lack of Finances and Consistent Church Stewardship

An early sign of a church in trouble is when the finances begin to be strained due to the number of individuals who have left the church. Usually, the leadership fails to act promptly and there begins to be a snowballing effect towards decline. When the stewardship levels of the church dwindle to the point where you cannot keep doing what you are doing something drastic must be done. Declining churches often get here when they see the barometers out on the horizon yet refuse to deal with it. For instance, a church is losing money quickly yet it wants to keep staff on just because they have been around for a long time. The membership is sealing their fate by not wanting to deal with these issues. One church I recently worked with kept doing this until they were totally out of money and then asked if I could find them a church which would give them fifty members. I guess that was so they could do it again and avoid the eventual outcome of a dying church. Keeping staff on that you cannot afford is unwise and it leads the church down a path that most are not able to reverse.

Apathy and Church Burnout

Churches burnout and become apathetic. Members become burned out when they see little or no fruit from the harvest fields. Churches which formerly saw people placing their faith in the Lord Jesus and joining the church, become apathetic and unwilling to serve when they think there is little or no hope. They become churches which are slipping from relevance into irrelevance. Change is essential. The message of Jesus never changes but our methods, style, and approach must always adapt to the needs of the current culture. The longer a church goes without change the less relevant it becomes. In more extreme cases, when entering an outdated church environment, it is like walking into a time warp. It causes those who visit to question if the leadership understands how to navigate current culture. There has never been a greater time or higher need for innovation in the church. Talk with people who do not attend church and brainstorm new ideas. What needs to be done to remain salt and light in your community?

Frequent Obstacles Church Revitalization Leaders Face

Here is my quick list of six additional obstacles church revitalization leaders face that I see more than not:

> A defeatist attitude draining energy from people
> Church members attached to old ways and ideas
> Inflexible older church members
> Inadequate or rundown facilities
> Low levels of faith and commitment
> A survival mentality

Wrapping it up!

Church renewal often begins its journey focused on the leader of the effort because they are the initial driving force. Yet, it cannot stay that way. The leader must expand the group and add revitalization team members who can begin to lighten the leader's load. Though the leader often possesses a high degree of entrepreneurship, they cannot do it all alone. It will burn them out. Also, in order to achieve success, the church revitalizer needs the right kind of people on board. If the staff is not on board for the effort of revitalization it would be wise to let them go immediately. Ensure everyone in your ministry team is competent, effective and aligned towards renewal. The longer one waits the greater damage they can do to the church. Think about your church organizational structure for a moment. Its customs, traditions, values and beliefs, will either contribute to the church's growth or the churches non-growth. God's people must become more enthusiastic about who God is and what he is doing in your midst. The church must become a praying church. The church's structure needs to change to facilitate ministry taking place. The lead pastor role must evolve and the laity needs to comprehend this evolution. The major role of the church must move from doing maintenance ministries to doing and becoming on mission. A church that does not grow will eventually die. If your church is stockpiling financial resources in the bank for a rainy day, let it be released for the work of the ministry. Failure to do so means your church will close with a large bank account and few people. Both are a misunderstanding of the biblical mandate to reach the lost.

Chapter Eleven
Developing the Commitment of the Laity to Stay in Renewal:
How to Become Part of Saving Your Church!

God creates churches to live "in community" and to be the Christ-like example for the residents of a geographical locale. We were created for community and never was it the Lord's design that we walk alone. When either a singular church or a singular individual begins to walk alone you can be assured that trials, tribulations, and tidal waves of destruction will come your way. So, I want us to consider how to become part of saving your church! Any church facing rapid decline is to some degree facing this reality. Will the church be saved and turned around towards new life and vitality or will it be allowed to falter and continue to decline until what is left is such a drastic depiction of a church that has failed to remain in touch with its ever-changing community it has been called to serve? Leading a church through church revitalization and renewal becomes impossible if the church's leadership is unclear about the actual mission and vision of the church. At the opposite end of the spectrum, the church working towards revitalization is dramatically increased and empowered when a majority of the church members join the leader in pursuing the mission or vision of the church. The sad reality is that today this does not happen very often. This partially due to the church of the west believing that the professional minister is the one called to do everything for the church. No wonder churches decline. It is not surprising that they begin to die as the laity begin to do less and not take on their portion of responsibility for the growth and life of the church. One of the hardest aspects of leading a church is getting people to become involved. I have yet to meet a church that considers itself to have sufficient member involvement. That's why we have put together some ideas to help you get your members to be more active in the church.

It is vital to realize as a pastor working in renewal and revitalization that you are not in the leadership role to police the petty squabbles that take place at church. As leaders, we are there to keep the church on track, to understand and sense from the Lord God that you are doing what He has called you to do, to reach those who need Christ, and then to provide a way for these new believers to become fully functioning followers of Christ! Sounds simple does it not? Perhaps. Is it that easy? Not really. Bringing about church revitalization is not easy, but we must be extremely careful not to make it more complex than it needs to be.

The church is designed for those in it to bear one another's burden. We should hold our individual churches in high esteem. We should do everything we can to keep it growing and remaining a healthy viable gospel expression to our community. Even if that means that what we like most might be of lesser value if it means the lost of the area will be led to Christ by adapting our styles, structures, and systems to reach those without Jesus in our community. Many church members they look at the task of saving one's church as something terrible. They would rather allow it to remain stuck and stagnant a little longer. At least until they have passed away or are no longer healthy enough to attend. The worst thing can become the best thing if you will allow the Lord to begin something new within the body of Christ.

Someone must lead the church! It is better if you as the pastor take on that task. Your laity must be able to see clearly where the church is and should be going. You must be the visionary leader who hears from the Lord God and shares it with your people. If you choose not to hear and then share what God is telling you, your people will have an unclear and unstable view of the future under your leadership. Chaos becomes the eventual norm instead of a vision that people can buy in to. Keep your people working with you in developing a vision and watch a greater number of participants follow willingly and joyfully towards a healthy future. Others discover the vision for the church and then give it to the people. Sometimes that works very well and sometimes it does not. You will know if that would work best in your situation. It matters less how you as a church discover your vision and more about them knowing they have one to follow. It is much wiser to get moving in revitalization than spending a large number of hours trying to define what church revitalization actually looks like. Let the revitalization process shape your "go" as the congregation grows in its acceptance of the process.

A Revitalization Lesson

May I give you a lesson that Church Revitalizers must understand? It is simply this: Not everyone in your church is supposed to be happy in your revitalization process. That is a huge misconception that many dying churches hold as truth. I would challenge you in this area when I suggest that it is not your job to make everyone happy but to get the church growing once more. Today's church can be rather confusing. In a place where the Christian community is supposed to exist often there is no community. The authenticity of the church body has been sacrificed for formats that no longer work. Grace to try something new is disbanded for the dogma structures of a one-hundred-year-old model. What we are often left with is a poor taste for one's community and a despondency to seek something new.

Does Your Church Have C.A.D.D.

How many churches do you know that have C.A.D.D.? CADD stands for the **C**hurch **A**ttention **D**eficit **D**isorder. That is when a church bounces from ministry project to ministry project each month. Pastors can do this as well as they bounce from church to church. Sometimes the local church in need of revitalization needs a little love and encouragement because often it is paralyzed into doing nothing. They are afraid to do anything and by doing nothing, the comatose effect takes place and lifelessness begins to be the church's new identity. A sense of passionless plight takes effect when a new day advancement must take place. There are many traits of a dying church. Here are some you might want to consider:

Worn Out People Unwilling to Remain Engaged

Many members of declining churches are so overworked and so totally worn out that they have little ability to remain engaged in the congregation. When the laity become so overworked that all they can do is to simply show up and sit passively in the church pews, you know that the church of the past burdened a few and let the many coast.

Disillusioned with the church scene

When the rank and file of a local church become so disenchanted with the things going on at church, it is easy for the membership to begin to drift and decline to take on the laity's responsibility for doing the work of the ministry. They simply become disillusioned with the church scene.

Hurting individuals who have become sequestered

Another trait of a dying church is when there is a high degree of hurting individuals within the church that have never been ministered to nor helped. Some of it has to do with the feeling within the laity that no one will understand what they are feeling so it is best to remain silent. At times it has more to do with clergy barriers which have been established that pushes hurting laity into a small bubble and keeps them isolated from the staff. A sequestered laity is a laity unwilling to serve the church and pushes back when the pastoral leadership challenges them to become committed to the work. Revitalization will not happen unless the laity embrace their biblical responsibility of committing to ministry.

Burn each other at the stake if you do not see things as they do

Within many declining churches that eventually become dying churches, there is a philosophy by some lay leaders that if you do not see things the way I see things then you are my adversary and not my ally. Far too many churches have members who get bent out of shape if everyone does not see things as they do. The result is that they start hurting one another. New members feel this the most in declining churches because they are part of the new beginning that some former long-time members want to destroy. Burning new members who join the church at the stake is not only wrong, it keeps the church from receiving the blessings that God could provide. Why would the Lord desire to bless a church that is nothing but a fight waiting to happen?

God is the scapegoat for people leaving

Have you considered why people are leaving your church? Often the Lord becomes the scapegoat for people leaving when in reality they do not want to see the church become something new again. If the passive-aggressive members can't keep the church from being revitalized, then they will up and leave because they were not able to have their own way. I am so amazed that I have never heard one of those types of individuals actually declare that the Lord told them to destroy His church. Yet they up and leave a declining church once they realize that the pastor is serious about saving the church through renewal.

Status Quo Lobbyists

Those who want the church to slowly decline until it dies are often found becoming status quo lobbyists. There are groups of cliques in these churches which desire so much to not change that they will lobby for the status quo. They have no desire to embrace a new vision nor begin reaching the community with a new strategy for renewal. The sense of reaching their community is quite foreign to these individuals. Understand that there are individuals in your community which need your church and it is up to you to reach them. When the status quo twists the truth in order to avoid doing the things which would invite new prospects and help grow the church, it is not only hurting the community but also hurting those in the church who are working hard and want to see the church be renewed. Then there will come a time where those who want to do nothing win, but actually lose. Within a matter of weeks, the committed will take flight and leave the SQL's with the mess they have created.

Passive Pew Sitters Comfortable with Merely Being There

Those timid individuals who are withdrawn in your church and lack any desire to serve the Lord. If you have the majority of church members who have little or no yearning to serve the Lord it will be hard to revitalize your church. Showing up is not the same as giving out in acts of service. I asked a lady in my church one time what her spiritual gift was and she replied, "I am here every Sunday." She was there every week unless family came to town or company was coming over for Sunday dinner. Just being there is killing so many churches today.

Staying in a church which seems to not care about what could be done to renew itself is difficult. The easy thing that so many do after they have created all of the intense turmoil is to leave the church. I wonder how many new churches have been started because someone in the originating church leadership did not see things the same way as those who split the church. Sometimes saving a church means that you must be able to overlook the cruelty and bitterness which will be thrown your way. Even Christians often repay your willingness to revitalize their church with a bitter spirit as they stubbornly seek to spread hurt and venom all around. Dietrich Bonhoeffer has said: "Every church member serves the whole body, either to its health or to its destruction. This is no mere theory, it is a spiritual reality."42 R. Paul Stevens says that the roles of clergy and laity should not be separated; rather, clergy and laity should be one body of believers functioning together.43 Sue Mallory in her work the *Equipping Church: Serving Together to Transform Lives*, states: "Many congregations do an admirable job identifying potential lay ministers; however, when not encouraged to serve, laity end up feeling disappointed and discouraged, and the gap widens."44

---

42 Dietrich Bonhoeffer, *Life Together: The Classic Exploration of Christian Community* (New York: Harper & Row Publishers, 1954), 89.

43 R. Paul Stevens, *The Other Six Days.* (Vancouver: Regent College, 1999), 185.

44 Sue Mallory, *The Equipping Church: Serving Together to Transform Lives.* (Grand Rapids: Zondervan, 2001), 37.

During your initial one hundred and twenty days in church renewal, it would be wise to discuss the ministry model where pastors and laity work together serving in various forms of ministry. It is the biblical and historical model certainly. Many in the church might erroneously believe that the traditional ministry model where the pastor is paid by the church to do all of the ministries and the laity sit back and watch them burn themselves out is the biblical pattern. In principle for these types of churches, the pastor is the manufacturer, and the congregation is the customer. This model of ministry, which is entrenched within many churches all across North America, hinders the amount and quality of ministry that can take place. Declining churches can easily fall into this pattern.

The biblical prototype for ministry is one where the pastor/leader encourages, equips, and empowers the laity to serve in ministry. Revitalizing churches strategically become lay releasing congregations. As a church revitalizer one can no longer settle for individuals who are willing to merely sit in your pews unwilling to do the work of ministry in their church. Revitalization is not a sideline sport. If your church is going to be revitalized you must get your members to do more than attend and give weekly. You must teach them or reteach them how to share their faith with everyone they meet. Pastors which have the gift of gospel presentation make wonderful church revitalizers while those who refuse to share their faith will struggle to renew their church.

Rick Warren observes the need for pastors to release their laity into ministry. He says: "The greatest need in evangelical churches is the release of members for ministry. A Gallup poll discovered that only 10% of American church members are active in any kind of personal ministry and that 50% of all church members have no interest in serving in any ministry. The encouraging news that Gallup uncovered is this:

40% of all members have expressed an interest in having a ministry, but they have never been asked or they don't know how."45 The traditional leadership model that many churches follow where the pastor serves as the single solitary contributor towards ministry and the primary minister of the congregation is not a new struggle for the Church. No sooner had the church been established in Acts 6 we find their leaders dealing with the plentiful responsibilities that come with leading a church. As you study Acts 6 the releasing of the laity to do the work of the Lord solves the challenge. The New Testament model of ministry in Acts 6 is a lay-releasing and lay-empowering one. In Acts 6 Luke the physician and writer of Acts records the model that released first-century believers into ministry:

> *In those days when the number of disciples was increasing, the Grecian Jews among them complained against the Hebraic Jews because their widows were being overlooked in the daily distribution of food. So the Twelve gathered all the disciples together and said, "It would not be right for us to neglect the ministry of the word of God in order to wait on tables. Brothers choose seven men from among you who are known to be full of the Spirit and wisdom. We will turn this responsibility over to them and will give our attention to prayer and the ministry of the word." This proposal pleased the whole group. They chose Stephen, a man full of faith and of the Holy Spirit; also Philip, Procorus, Nicanor, Timon, Parmenas, and Nicolas from Antioch, a convert to Judaism. They presented these men to the apostles, who prayed and laid their hands on them. So the word of God spread. The number of disciples in Jerusalem increased rapidly, and a large number of priests became obedient to the faith. These leaders knew that they alone could not meet the needs of the church. They acknowledged that neglecting the ministry in order to "wait on tables" was not the best use of*

---

45 Warren, Rick. *The Purpose Driven Church.* (Grand Rapids: Zondervan, 1995), (365-66).

their gifts or time. The twelve delegated the ministry to those who were capable, and Luke goes on to say that "the disciples in Jerusalem increased rapidly."46

When your church's laity are released to do the work of the ministry it allows pastors to do that which they are called to do including encouraging, equipping, and empowering the saints. The pastor's time is freed up so they can concentrate on the work they are called to accomplish and lead the church towards renewal. Pastors must realize that guiding a church to release laity for ministry is a long-term project with long-term benefits. The church revitalizer who will take the time to equip their laity will see their congregations begin to be renewed.

The great apostle charges the early church leaders to prepare the laity to serve the kingdom. In Ephesians 4:11-13 Paul gives a basis for the equipping of the laity. He declares they are to be released into the work of the ministry. Paul says:

It was He who gave some to be apostles, some to be prophets, some to be evangelists, and some to be pastors and teachers, to prepare God's people for works of service, so that the body of Christ may be built up until we all reach unity in the faith and in the knowledge of the Son of God and become mature, attaining to the whole measure of the fullness of Christ.47

Paul makes this New Testament prototype clear when he says that prophets, evangelists, pastors, and teachers are not given to do the ministry of the Church; rather, these Church leaders are to equip the laity to do the work of the ministry. When today's pastor leader does not follow the biblical

---

46 Acts 6:1-7.

47 Ephesians 4:11-13.

mandate, it is no wonder their church is not growing. They simply do not have the time to do the work of a minister and do the member's work as well. The early church in the Book of Acts and also the book of Ephesians makes it clear that the release of the laity to do the work of ministry is non-negotiable. The New Testament teaches that all believers are ministers and all ministers are called to serve. Churches who are equipping their laity for ministry experience the benefits of following this biblical model. Alvin Lindgren and Norman Shawchuck declare: "When the laity discover that they have a role to play in the kingdom and clergy have more time to focus on their areas of strength. The key to a growing, vital church is the empowerment of laity with laity and clergy becoming active coworkers, as God's people."48 Wayne Cordeiro says that the era of the "Lone Ranger" pastor leading an effective church is over. A team approach to ministry may be new to many local congregations, but if churches are going to make a difference in the twenty-first century, they must adapt to doing ministry this way.49

A Practical Question Worth Considering

In church revitalization and renewal there is a question which a church's leadership team ought to consider. This question is worth spending time on at your next deacons or elders meeting. It would be great to wrestle with it with those of your church that serve in the various organizations. Here is the question:

---

48 Lindgren, Alvin J., and Norman Shawchuck. *Let My People Go.* (Nashville: Abingdon, 1980), 13.

49 Cordeiro, Wayne. *Doing Church as a Team.* (Ventura, CA: Regal, 2001), 176.

Do we love God's churches as much as Christ loves the church?

That is a very revealing question I believe. Do we love God's churches as much as Christ loves the church? If so, we must work at recovering those who have left despondently and left their first love the church. Jesus loves the church and because of that, we should do everything within our power to love it as well. While many disillusioned believers feel that leaving the church is the only answer to the challenge of an unwilling stagnant leadership, the right answer is to remain and begin again doing the things that the Lord Jesus would want us to do and have us to do. The hard truth of revitalization and renewal is that if your place of worship no longer desires the divine presence of the Lord then get out. If the church refuses to sense the divine and faithfully follow Jesus, then leave. If saving the future generations of lost people who need Jesus is no longer what that church is about, move on. If your worship center is more highly honored than an individual's soul, drop out. But before you make that decision, let's journey on. In the Gospel of John, we see that:

> Swarms of people came to him. He sat down and taught them. The religion scholars and Pharisees led in a woman who had been caught in an act of adultery. They stood her in plain sight of everyone and said, "Teacher, this woman was caught red-handed in the act of adultery. Moses, in the Law, gives orders to stone such persons. What do you say?" They were trying to trap him into saying something incriminating so they could bring charges against him. Jesus bent down and wrote with his finger in the dirt. They kept at him, badgering him. He straightened up and said, "The sinless one among you, go first: Throw the stone." Bending down again, he wrote some more in the dirt. Hearing that, they walked away, one after another, beginning with the

oldest. The woman was left alone. Jesus stood up and spoke to her. "Woman, where are they? Does no one condemn you?" "No one, Master." "Neither do I," said Jesus. "Go on your way. From now on, don't sin."50

The Laity's Manifesto for Ministering in a Dying Church

There are some critical declarations I would suggest for you to consider in talking to new members who have chosen to join you in the effort to revitalize your church. If you are going to have them stay then they ought to consider these manifestos. Here they are:

Overcome your frustrations regarding the current status of the church.

Work on ways to keep your church relevant.

Seek to Glorify Christ above one's own expectations and likes.

Develop daily compassion for seeing your church renewed and work with others within the fellowship to achieve such revitalization.

Help keep others intact within the church when they are overwhelmed and worn out.

Show them that a hasty exit is not the best way.

Sick churches do not get well unless healthy leaders look after them.

---

50 Eugene H. Peterson, *The Message: The Bible in Contemporary Language* (Colorado Springs, CO: NavPress, 2005), John 8:2–11.

Become more intentional in your actions at church for the good of the future.

Stay the course and keep keeping on.

Love God with your heart, mind, and soul.

Love the unlovely at church even if it is hard work.

This list is just a basic one but I am sure you get the idea. The word manifesto has Latin origins. As a noun, "Manifesto" is related to manifest, which occurs in English as a noun, verb, and adjective. Of these, the adjective, which means "readily perceived by the senses" or "easily recognized," is the oldest, dating to the 14th century. Both manifest and manifesto derive ultimately from the Latin noun *manus* ("hand") and -*festus*, a combining form that is related to the Latin adjective *infestus*, meaning "hostile." Something manifest is easy to perceive or recognize, and a manifesto is a statement in which someone makes his or her intentions or views easy for people to ascertain. The Laity's Manifesto for Ministering in a Dying Church is a way to make those of your members who desire to see the church revitalized clearly presented to any and all. You are saying here is what we will do to see this church revitalized.

How to Become Part of Saving Your Church

God desires that His churches be salvaged from the decline they are experiencing. If you are to lead the effort during those initial one hundred and twenty days there are some things that everyone participating in the renewal effort must agree to. Here are some items you will want to be sure everyone is clear about how you are going to lead out in the revitalization effort:

Stop Stoning the Ungodliness of Others and Remember We All Have Sinned

Every one of us as the Lord's children is at times unlovely. We are all simply sinners saved by grace. In your church just like mine, there will be individuals which actually seek to hurt the church and those who desire renewal simply because the price for renewal in their eyes is too high. There will be too much for these individuals to give up. Stop stoning these members and start loving on them. There is much which can be accomplished through a kind word and a loving heart. Besides, there are always those who are late adopters and after all of the hard work of revitalization is completed, they will jump back on the bandwagon and proceed like they were never a thorn to the effort. That is all right so stop holding a grudge because they were negative towards everything. They are back supporting the church so embrace them.

Throwing Rocks Does the Church No Good

Remember the old adage written by Alexander William Kinglake, "Sticks and stones will break my bones, but words will never hurt me." It is reported to have appeared in *The Christian Recorder* of March 1862, a publication of the African Methodist Episcopal Church, where it is presented as an "old adage" in the form above.51 In like manner to throw verbal rocks at those in the church who are less excited about church renewal will do the effort no good. Remember that they haven't left and are still with you. Allow them time to wrestle with the new changes and ideas coming upon them. Once they see the effort working, many if not all, will realign towards the new effort and health of the church.

---

51 https://en.wikipedia.org/wiki/Sticks_and_Stones.

Messed Up People Take Time to Fix, So Begin Loving and Ministering to Them

If our idiosyncrasies could be fixed in an instant they would have already been done so. The best way to fix messed up people in the church is to show them Jesus and to love on them while ministering to them. Just like revitalization and renewal cannot be accomplished overnight, neither can the creation of new creations in Christ Jesus. We all take a little time to fix so be patient and keep moving the revitalization effort down the road.

Lead Them Gently and Graciously

You cannot run over those who are less excited about the renewal of the church and its new vision and all of the changes which go with it. Those who are slow to respond must be led gently. You must be a gracious leader allowing them to vent now and then. But it is not your place to allow their lamenting to move into grumbling and griping. Do you know what to grumble means? It means: To murmur or mutter with discontent; to make ill-natured complaints in a low voice and a surly manner. As in a grumbling, discontented disposition. It is the Hebrew word *"ragan"* which means to murmur, whisper, or slander. It has the connotation of being a rebel again the Lord God. Our grumbling and complaining do not change a thing. Paul said in Philippians, *"Do all things without grumbling or disputing, that you may be blameless and innocent, children of God without blemish in the midst of a crooked and twisted generation, among whom you shine as lights in the world."*[52]

---

52 Philippians 2:15.

Speak the Truth Lovingly

Renewal is a process of turning the church around and great care should be taken to not offend your members who do not agree with you. Lovingly directing the church towards revitalization takes care and kindness to your entire congregation. In the Book of Hebrews, Paul challenges us when he says: *"Let's see how inventive we can be in encouraging love and helping out, not avoiding worshiping together as some do but spurring each other on, especially as we see the big Day approaching."53*

Model for Others the Correct Way to Live One's Faith in Community Biblically

If you want to set a preferred practice for how the church will function begin by modeling the preferred behavior. When abusive church members begin to understand that non-biblical behavior will not be tolerated in the renewal process, they will usually either leave the church because they do not want to embrace a new norm or they will confess such sinful behavior and align themselves towards the new process of renewal. Many declining churches allow negative sinful behavior to exist within the fellowship because they are afraid of confronting inappropriate behavior. They need to understand that this type of behavior actually repels prospects rather than drawing prospects to the church. Leaders must model the correct way to live one's faith in a church community biblically. By modeling preferred practices, you are able to demonstrate a life lived out in order to forgive others.

---

53 Eugene H. Peterson, *The Message: The Bible in Contemporary Language* (Colorado Springs, CO: NavPress, 2005), Hebrews 10:24-25.

Rev-Up Your Passion and Go Full Throttle for the Church: Make Belonging Count Again

If you are not excited about the opportunities available for revitalization in your church who will be? You must be passionate about what the Lord is going to do and tell everyone about the chances God is giving your church to be revitalized. You must not only paint the new dream for all to see but you must also provide the guide through your leadership to take them there. Churches, where the Lord is bringing renewal, are churches that others want to be a part of and will readily align themselves towards the new future. On the cautious side, church revitalizers need to stop wanting to renew a church that does not want to be renewed and move on. If the church is going to fight you at every turn then seek one that wants life, not death. You need to go full throttle in church revitalization so begin by sharing your passion, proceed by leading your people and plan your next one hundred and twenty days to bring about the beginnings of a new day for your church.

Don't Seek Position in a Church: Seek Influence

There are too many pastors out there that have positional authority over influential authority. Church revitalizers must be influencers of the congregation and lead members to embrace their opportunity for renewal. Influence is fundamental if you want to lead others. Leadership is not about your title as pastor. In fact, influence cannot be bestowed, appointed, or dispersed. It must be earned. Proof of your leadership ability in revitalization is uncovered in the followers that have bought into the dream of saving the church. The true measure of leadership is influence and nothing more nor nothing less.

Draw People to Jesus First Not a Cause Regardless if it is Positive or Negative

It will do your church little good if you draw people to anything else but Jesus first. Challenging the masses to consider renewal in your church is not the initial attraction but seeing people receive Christ as their Savior and Lord. Most renewal efforts have people getting saved and confessing a personal relationship with the Lord before the real work of renewal begins. Nothing is sweeter than seeing individuals ask the Lord Jesus into the hearts. Members get excited about that and then they will get excited about your ideal of renewal.

Stop Searching for Another Church and Content Oneself with the One God has Placed You In

If you want to see the church renewed you must challenge your members to commit to stay the course and be part of bringing renewal to the church. Members need to stop shopping for a new church once they are called upon to begin doing the work of ministry. They need to get happy with theirs and be part of rolling up their sleeves to get involved in the ministries that will be required to revitalize the church. God has placed you in the church so start working to renew it.

Hold a Candle Up for Making Friends with the Old and New Alike, Display Unity to Others

I love this idea and did this in every one of my churches. Bring everybody along with your efforts to revitalize your church. Members must work hand in hand and arm in arm to transform the church. Developing events where new members get to know long time members is vital. Allowing environments where they can discover some commonalities is a must. Unity comes to a church when they discover each other is a blessing and not a curse.

Go Deep with the Authentic and Allow the Others Time to Catch Up

There will be authentic members who want renewal now and not later. Start with that group and then allow those which are unsure time to catch up. Not everyone needs to be all in the day you launch renewal efforts. Allow them room to adjust and align as the Lord begins to rebuild the house of God.

Decide to Work Towards the Best of the Church Over Your Own Personal Desires and Agendas

As pastors we all have dreams and desires. We must be careful not to place our own desires above those things which are best for the church. We must be careful not to set agendas which are not possible for the majority of the membership to embrace.

Understand, when we build a "leave the church" argument, in reality, we are questioning the authority of scripture and might be stepping outside of the Bible's clearly marked guidelines. The result is that the Lord is never pleased with that argument!

A Prayer of Repentance and Restoration Initiated

There must begin with a prayer for repentance and restoration in any church once it decides that they wish to be restored and get growing again. David in Psalm 51 declares:

> *Generous in love—God, give grace! Huge in mercy—wipe out my bad record. Scrub away my guilt, soak out my sins in your laundry. I know how bad I've been; my sins are staring me*

down. You're the One I've violated, and you've seen it all, seen the full extent of my evil. You have all the facts before you; whatever you decide about me is fair. I've been out of step with you for a long time, in the wrong since before I was born. What you're after is truth from the inside out. Enter me, then; conceive a new, true life.[54]

Without individual repentance and then corporate repentance following, the church will not be able to do anything on its own to bring renewal. Churches can't try to seek renewal by the ways of man and the ways of the world. True revitalization only comes from the loving and generous hand of God. Here are some of the points that arise from these passages.

- Displaying and demonstration of the regret over lack of devotion
- Longing for the Lord to renew a right spirit within you for Him
- Overflowing with a desire to become a servant
- Requesting a closer form of worship with the Father

Ask yourself who are the individuals within your church you must embrace? I am sure there are names which come to mind and pictures of these members you must embrace. Some will be quite easy while others will be very difficult. Ask the Lord to give you what you need in order to be able to carry out the task.

---

[54] Eugene H. Peterson, *The Message: The Bible in Contemporary Language* (Colorado Springs, CO: NavPress, 2005), Ps 51:1–6. Further encouragement is found throughout the chapter from verses:7-19.

When to Consider Leaving a Church as a Lay Leader

Sometimes you will as a lay leader need to leave a church. While that is never easy and always with some degree of regret, there are times when it is the only thing you can do. Many dying churches are faced with this regularly because there has developed an entrenchment philosophy in the congregation and renewal is given nothing more than lip service. Here are a few signs that it might be time to leave the church you presently are attending:

- You are throwing pearls before swine
- It is destroying you and your family
- Your thoughts must be fully aligned with the majority or you are blacklisted
- Threats are being thrown your way most of the time
- Leadership is un-repentant of sin
- Bible is not the final authority
- The Holy Spirit is moving you to leave

Sadly, these are some factors you must take into consideration regarding the church you dearly love. It even hurts you to think about leaving the church. But before you do here are a few questions to consider before you leave:

- Is the move related to the heat of the moment?
- Have you done enough or am I part of the problem?
- Is your exodus related to pettiness on my part?
- Have you loved these individuals enough?
- Do you pray over those who have hurt me?
- Are you bitter and bewildered right now?
- Have you slandered those who have hurt you?
- Do you look at yourself as an elitist and the rest as sinful?
- Is confession of your own sins part of this?

- What have your advisors and coaches said about your leaving?
- Is God calling you to stay but you are avoiding that call on your life?

How to Keep Your Church Members Engaged

As a church revitalization leader, you can impact your membership's engagement in simple but profound ways. Here are 5 tips to help you get started:

Define Realistic Engagement Goals in Every Day Easy to Understand Terms

By making lofty objectives meaningful to your church members' daily experiences, it enables you to give them anchors to embrace. Weave your engagements into your weekly interactions and activities with you people.

Find Ways to Connect with Active and Inactive Church Members Individually

One of the workshops that the Renovate Group continues to sell out every time we offer it is our Reclaiming Inactive Church Members. A large portion of the workshop deals with ways churches can reconnect with those who have opted out of the church. Not only do the leadership teams of laity and clergy need to reconnect with former members but they need to keep connecting with those who are regular participants. Especially in light of our Post Covid-19 pandemic, we are all realizing that a certain percentage of our memberships are unlikely to return. Here are some facts to keep in mind:

- Young adult members at the beginning of their causing them to be less engaged.

- Older adults tend to be more engaged but want church usually on their terms.
- Those in the middle of their careers are very engaged and are usually the working force behind what the church can achieve.
- Millennials are the most likely to say that they will leave if you do not make the necessary changes to remain relevant (The 9- & 12-Month Rule).
- Women as a whole have slightly higher overall engagement than men.

As a Pastor, Show You Care About Your Members' Lives, Family, and Work

This is especially important for the Baby Boomer generation within your church. They are a big group of people within most churches and displaying care and concern is critical. Boomers are great drifters so if you are unwilling to keeping the lines of communication open, they will question whether the church values their participation. They will question if the leadership cares.

Focus on and Develop Your Church Member's Strengths

By building on members' strengths, it is far more effective than trying to improve their weaknesses and it will boost engagement.'

Extend and Intensify the Engagement Level of New Church Members

New church members are as engaged as they will ever be during the first six months of their tenure at a church. To increase this level early on, consider pairing a new church member up with a committed church member who is all in for the renewal of the church. There is one great way to increase church attendance and that is getting your people engaged in the work of the ministry. It is the key to addressing your attendance struggles because no one is going to bother to attend something week after week when they are not engaged in it. If you've decided the status quo isn't working and something needs to change, your leadership team needs to initiate that change. You need to create a church culture that embraces healthy changes, and that means making changes often. Innovation is the key to engagement. This means being willing to try new things and make a series of changes until you find the ones that help you reach your goals. Engagement can come in many forms, and you cannot expect every person to engage in the same way. Here are some practical reasons why church members of healthy churches engage:

- To be part of a community of people they want to be with
- To feel inspired and express themselves creatively
- To be able to share their talents with others
- To be able to give back to a cause they believe in
- To serve others and feel the sense of accomplishment that comes with it
- To feel good about themselves
- To meet new people and develop friendships
- To feel valued and useful
- To do something that helps them grow
- To do something that makes them feel happy, peaceful, loved, etc.
- To do something that brings meaning to their lives
- To experience something new and exciting
- To gain respect or status
- To do something they enjoy
- To develop themselves spiritually, mentally, emotionally, or physically

- To help their children or loved ones overcome their struggles

Ultimately, your members who show up week after week do so because they are gaining some kind of value that goes far beyond just sitting and listening to a sermon. That value makes them engage in your church community in whatever way makes sense for them, and that engagement keeps them coming back. Make sure your current and future members know about all the different ways they can engage. Stop focusing on how to increase your church's attendance and start focusing on how to get your members engaged in the work of ministry. My friends Gary McIntosh and Charles Arn recently released a delightful book, *What Every Pastor Should Know*. I love the data and research within this book. One of my favorite sections dealt with the retention of members. Two of the most critical findings were:

- Of all the members who drop out of the church, eighty-two percent leave in the first year of their membership.

- Retention efforts are thus critical in the first twelve months after a member joins a church.

The pattern of dropout is not random. Most leave close to their six-month tenure or close to their twelve-month tenure. It appears that church members seem to give new churches a "test" at both six months and twelve months. If the church passes the test at six months, the member will stay for another six months. If the church passes the test at the one-year mark, the member is likely to become fully assimilated into the church. The first "test" consists of three questions. Though the church member may not ask these questions specifically, he or she is evaluating three critical issues to determine if it's time to move or stay. These are the issues around the six-month point:

Have I made friends in this church?

New members who remained active in the church made an average of seven new friends in these first six months. The dropouts had an average of fewer than two friends. The first "test" consists of three questions. Though the church member may not ask these questions specifically, he or she is evaluating three critical issues to determine if it's time to move or stay. These are the issues around the six-month point.

Is there a place in the church where I fit?

The critically important answer to this question is whether or not the new member is in a group or class.

Does this church really want me?

Are the members still as friendly as they were when I first joined? Am I being invited or encouraged to participate in ministries in the church?

Assuming the new member feels good about these first three questions, he or she is likely to stay another six months or so. At roughly the twelve-month point, the new member then evaluates the church on three more issues.

Are my new friends as good as my old friends?

The members begin to assess the quality of their relationships.

Does the group meet my needs?

By the time the new member has been involved in a group for more than six months, he or she is asking if the investment of time in the group is really worth it.

Is my contribution important?

Everyone wants to be a part of something significant, something greater than themselves. Church members join a church with those expectations. Near the end of the first year, they begin to evaluate that issue and their contributions to the overall mission of the church.

Though there are no great surprises in these six issues, what is new in the study by McIntosh and Arn is the timing issue. Most of those who will drop out will do so before the end of their first year. And at six months and twelve months respectively, new members will intuitively ask themselves six questions. How they respond to those questions ultimately determines if they will stay or leave. How do you and your church sit as you evaluate these six questions? What can your church do to prevent members from dropping out? One of the hardest aspects of managing a church is getting people to become involved. Many church members are caught in the gap between attending church and being part of it. They are spectators at best, birthed into a consumer-driven culture, unwittingly pressuring churches to be consumer-driven, too. I have yet to meet a church that considers itself to have sufficient member involvement. The future of church renewal effort depends on your ability to engage the people in it. Peter Drucker's management advice holds true for church leaders. You can't expect your church to "get more engaged" if you don't know how engaged they are now. Likewise, if you're not measuring engagement, you won't know how effective your efforts are (and you won't know which efforts *are not* working). That's why we have put together some ideas to help you get your members to be more active in the church.

Practical Suggestions for Anchoring Your Members to the Ministry of the Church

The anchoring of your church members to the great things the Lord is doing in and through the church is important. The last seven months dealing with the pandemic has taught all of us how important this is. Here are some suggestions for anchoring your members to the worthy things God is doing through your church's ministry:

Present Your Church's Vision with Excitement and Vitality

This is the core of every successful attempt to get people involved in the life of your church. All the gimmicks and all the systems in the world can't do anything if your members never say to themselves, "I want to be a part of that." But, if you dream big and share that dream with your members, you give them something to latch onto (anchor if you will) and something they can unite behind. Of course, you also have to accept that not everyone wants to dream big. You are going to have some members who prefer to show up on Sundays and go home without any other involvement or commitments. You cannot fall into the trap of catering to these people. You have to dream big and share your vision despite of those who don't want to be involved. On those hard days, just remember that dreams are viral. You may not get a lot of response at first, but slowly and surely, you will get two or three more people charged up, and they will each get two more people, and so on and so on, until the whole church is excited and those who do not want to dream big start to be infected by the excitement.

Give Your Participants Ample Opportunities to Become Involved

This may sound simple (or even stupid, since you obviously have opportunities open), but it's worth thinking about. Just because you have opportunities doesn't mean your members know you do. In fact, one of the most common problems churches have is that uninvolved people look around, see everything works fine, and assume there's no need for help. All the while, you have three volunteers working twenty hours a day in addition to their full-time jobs, just so everything at church runs smoothly.

Start a Connection Desk for People to Get Connected

One thing my home church does that works well is they have a connection desk. This is a central place where people can get information on small groups, learn about serving opportunities, fill out prayer request cards, and basically do anything else related to connecting into the body of the church. At the end of every service, they invite anyone new and interested in getting connected to stop by. Because they mention the connection desk in every service, people hear about it the first time they come. It's important to reach first time guests because there is a small window when people are willing to work at getting connected. Once people find friends in the church, they'll feel connected enough that they won't put forth the effort to try something new. But, if a first or second-time guest is interested in the church, they're desperate to get connected and meet more people and will work hard to do so. The connection desk meets that need and channels this desire toward integrating people into the heart of the church.

The First Serve or First Watch Test Drive

A first serve is where prospective volunteers are allowed to test drive a service opportunity with no strings attached. Too many times we in the church are so hungry for volunteers that we latch onto anyone who shows interest and never let them out, which makes people more hesitant to express interest. Because a first serve has no strings attached, it encourages people to try out different ministries and find one that fits them. Regardless of the strategies you develop and implement, focus on preventing persons from disconnecting in the first place. It is much easier to prevent people from disconnecting than to try to reconnect them.

Keeping Church or Class Members Connected

Prevention really is the best medicine when it comes to keeping people connected. How can you prevent persons from becoming so disconnected that you don't even have an accurate address or telephone number? Use the following suggestions to develop your own ideas for preventing the need to clean up rolls. Assign every church member to a Sunday School class (or other ongoing Bible study group). Avoid assuming classes or groups are staying connected. Use your records to flag people who have missed two consecutive weeks. Consider generating reports that ask classes or groups to fill in how they contacted those persons. Use care groups or teams in adult classes as the primary means of ministry. Coordinate with other age group leaders to share the ministry load. Adult classes should coordinate outreach and ministry with preschool, children, and youth leaders to avoid duplication of efforts and better use all available resources. Include in-service/associate members in adult care groups or teams. Recognize leaders in other age groups often slip between the cracks after they give up leadership roles in another age group. If they are not connected with adult classes as they serve, they most often do not connect again when they can attend an adult bible study group. Also they need ministry and fellowship with adults their own age or life stage as they serve. Plan quarterly, personal connections with every class and department. For example, on the second Sunday of each quarter, Sunday School classes and departments could hand deliver learner guides to those persons who missed the first Sunday.

Include Sunday School and church members in regular mail-outs including the request for forwarding and address corrections. This ensures you obtain correct addresses when people move if they leave a forwarding address. Use email as one way to keep people plugged in with prayer requests and praises. Make it a habit to obtain email addresses for the new church and small group members. Weekly emails of the prayer praises and requests will also notify you of email address changes. Consider using social networks to remind members and prospects of birthdays, anniversaries, and other life events. In addition, you may continue discussions throughout the week that arise during Bible study. Don't miss the family connection. Everyone wants to have a healthy, strong family. Coordinate your connecting strategies with other age group leaders. Focus on helping parents build strong families and marriages. Some people may reconnect because of something happening in their family (empty nest, death of parents/spouse, marriage or divorce, etc.). Build a reputation in your community of the church who cares. Enlist a mission's coordinator who coordinates monthly mission activities. Plan at least four servant evangelism activities in your community each year. Design "care cards" to leave when ministering throughout your community. Use the cards so people are constantly hearing or bumping into someone or something that shows them your church is serious about impacting the community around them. Your church will draw inactive as well as newcomers to your church family. Devise a ministry plan for meeting needs as you discover them. Recognize ministry windows are not open very long and when they close, they may close tighter than before. Evaluate your church-wide system for caring for members and prospects. Sometimes there are multiple groups with caring responsibilities, and this may cause someone to fall between the cracks because one person/group thinks another will pick up the ball. For example, a Sunday School class may think the deacons will provide ministry for the choir, or the Women on Mission group—when in fact no one is ministering because each thinks the other is doing so.

Wrapping it up!

The task of the Church is not to gather together a community of like minds, but to offer the world the good news of redemption, that it is the subject of God's unconditional love and grace. Declining churches must redevelop a strong and committed laity. In many churches, we still have no systematic development of the laity, no real educational process in the discipleship of people. The Church ought to be, and is, a lay-centered community in which all the vocations must move forward together. The primary mission of any church is not to serve itself but to serve the world. Someone has said, Church is 98% laity with only 0.5% clergy, and 1.5% religious spectators. You hear it all the time that twenty percent of the laity do all the work and eighty percent of the laity are drifting spectators allowing those more deeply committed to doing all of the work. I believe that this Pareto 80/20 Principle is not what the Lord had in mind for His church. In Acts we read: *"All the believers were one in heart and mind. No one claimed that any of their possessions was their own, but they shared everything they had."*55 Healthy churches should combat the Pareto principle, not perpetuate it. Every believer has a particular part to play in fulfilling God's plan for the world. The laity has an important role to play within the

---

55 Acts 4:32.

mission of the local Church. Many signs indicate that the
Holy Spirit is empowering them for an even greater role in
the future. A survey gathered from Protestant pastors
revealed that most pastors participate in at least sixteen major
activities on a regularly: casting vision, identifying and training
leaders, preaching and teaching, raising money, serving the
needy, providing strategy and planning, organizing church
activities and programs, overseeing all administration,
managing staff, and volunteers, resolving conflicts,
representing the congregation in the community, providing
congregation care and counseling, and evangelizing the
unsaved, administering the sacraments, and discipling
individuals.56 The underutilization of laypeople parallels
waning church member engagement and, as might be
expected, an overworked clergy. Often the declining or dying
church has become ossified – 'frozen' into a 'holy huddle'
such that it has neglected that it is there to serve the needs of
those outside of the church in the community. Releasing the
laity to be confident and faithful disciples is integral to an
effective mission and to building a healthy revitalized church.

---

56 The Barna Group, 2001, p. 1.

Chapter Twelve
What Leader's Should Know About Church Revitalization and Renewal

Granted when you first begin to be aware of church revitalization and renewal, there is a lot to learn. You will feel overwhelmed at times if you do not get a revitalization coach. The Renovate Group has coached coaches and pastors in church revitalization and renewal since 1997. When everyone was running around talking about church growth, we and a few others were talking about church health. What we want to do in this chapter is to provide you with some basic knowledge that will help you to initiate renewal in your church and allow you to speak authoritatively about the subject. It will be on you though to continue to learn. We offer you the assistance you need to grow as a leader in this area.

Let us first nail down for you what revitalization truly means. Revitalization means that the local church knew how, at one time previously, to renew, revitalize, and re-establish the health and vitality of the ministry. One of the challenges for the laity in the day in which we live is that they have lost the knowledge of church renewal and no longer want to cultivate the skill sets necessary to see their church experience revitalization. Sadder is when a congregation does not have the corporate memory that there was a day when the local church was reaching people for Christ Jesus and active as evangelistic witnesses into their community. Many churches consider revitalization and renewal only because they desire to avoid the death blow of the church. Yet, most laity find it hard to allow someone to assist them and reveal the very things that caused their decline. Here is a revitalization I want you as the leader of a potential renewal project to consider. Here it is: When a local church refuses to trade its fear of closing the door for a desire to see life come back within the congregation, the church revitalization experience will end promptly as soon as the danger of death has been eliminated. What happens next may mean another recycle of decline until it is bad again. Church Revitalization is focused upon the renewal of the membership as they begin to consider and understand their individual relationships with the Lord, their community, and the purpose of God for the local church to be located where it has been placed. Churches only experience renewal when their people experience renewal. Unless a church's leadership, both professional staff, and lay leadership, want renewal, it will not happen. There must be a commitment to lead the church towards revitalization. If not, nothing will be changed. The stages of church revitalization and renewal take some time. I have discovered that if you are not willing to invest a minimum of 1000 days you should not get into the effort of revitalization and renewal.

Answer These Four Fundamental Questions Relating to Your Church

Truthful evaluation is the best place to begin any effort towards renewal. We have found that there are four fundamental questions that need to be answered in a revitalization process. They are:

> What are the real problems and issues?
> What are God's biblical solutions?
> Who are God's Leaders?
> What are God's plans?

Incredible changes have taken place in the past hundred years. We are experiencing more change than ever in history. The rate of change is so great that we barely catch our breath before another blast of change slams into us. The starting point for unfreezing a stuck church is the development of a solid community of faith that includes spiritual leaders, the absence of major conflict, trust in one another, and a desire to connect with the unchurched world. Everything we are acquainted with is changing. If you are sensing you might be facing a little stuckness in your church, perhaps some of the, following ideas might help you:

Realize You are Trapped in a Habitual Routine

Become aware of what you have tried in the past that has not worked. Become willing to let go of what has not worked while honoring previous attempts. My testimony is often as a church planter and then a revitalization restart leader, I would take three steps forward and two steps back at times. But I was still gaining one forward step even in those times where we were breaking with routine.

Become More Accessible to Other Points of View

Focus on the solution, not the problem. Iron sharpens iron so allow others to assist you with big ideas that might help the revitalizing church to continue to advance. Remember that even your lay leaders have a vital stake in the renewal church's continual growth. Often, they are closer to a possible solution due to less of the responsibility for leadership being on their platter. While you are up to your ears leading, they often can step back and think about those things that might bring further growth to the church in need of revitalization.

Examine Your Daily Thinking and How It Has or Has Not Served You

Realize there is a choice of which path or action to take. Sometimes revitalization leaders just need to readjust their strategy a little as they move forward from the various phases of growth in the renewal effort. I sometimes reflect on why the Lord would not allow me to do the same thing in one church that I had just done in another. God is about the new and often the old has passed by and He desires to create something so new in you and your church that you need to let go of the old thinking that has not worked or is no longer working.

Assess Your Next Steps for Change

Ask the question: am I doing these things out of preference, practice, pattern, or panic? Many a church planter and pastor have said to me, "I do what I do!" and then wonder why it is getting harder to see growth and advancement. That is a preference! I see all over the country revitalization leaders who get locked into a predetermined pattern and just cannot see a way out to do something else. Assessing your next steps will greatly help you and your work of church renewal. As you are doing so, be sure to check your ideas out with others.

Understand That If You Make a Blunder, Recognize It As Part of the Journey

See what your part of any blunder is and apologize where and when necessary. Good church revitalization leaders are not free from mistakes so don't try to be perfect. When you do make a blunder as the solitary leader, acknowledge it, learn from it, and seek to discover the life lesson in it. What I have learned though is if you are transparent enough as a Revitalization Leader to admit your mistakes and your people sense it is a heartfelt confession, they will indeed forgive you and even respect you much more because many pastors just cannot admit it when they make a mistake.

Appraise Your Revitalization Plans by Whether They Fit Your Beliefs and Core Values

Then act accordingly. What are the core values? They often are unwritten statements that guide who we are and what we do.

They inspire our words and actions.

They are convictions about how a church operates not doctrinal statements about what it believes.
They are the foundation for developing relationships, church systems, ministries, and strategies.
They are the four to seven key statements that distinguish a church.

Remember what core values do? They clarify expectations. They clarify roles and relationships. Core values offer a compass for strategic planning. They help in sharpening your church's mission statement. Take a minute and consider whether or not your beliefs and core values reflect the beliefs and values of Jesus? Ask yourself how do these beliefs and values reflect God's Word? Revitalization transformation is difficult - if it weren't you would already be doing it. That is why we need support and guidance along the way as we prayerfully seek to revitalize the local church.

Pastor, What You Don't Know Might Hurt You

The hard reality in North America is that most churches and most, if not all, denominations are in a state of decline. The membership within these churches and denominations is plateauing and what used to pass for involvement and activity within churches is deteriorating. While all of this is happening, the rank and file of the church appear powerless to assemble the strength that is needed to get the American church growing again. Kevin Ezell, President of the North American Mission Board of the Southern Baptist Convention declares, "We must keep our denominations focused on the ministry of rebirth and redemption, not on the business of enforcing rules and rituals."57 In 1990 an editor for the *Wall Street Journal* Wade Clark Roof published an editorial article

---

57 David S. Dockery, Ray Van Neste, and Jerry Tidwell, *Southern Baptists, Evangelicals and the Future of Denominationalism* (Nashville: B&H Publishing Group, 2011), i.

entitled, "The Episcopalian Goes the Way of the Dodo," where he argued the decline of mainline denominationalism and its effect on Christianity.58 With the turn of the twenty-first century, sustained growth within our churches is an intermittent exception while decline seems to be more of the pronouncement. The mainline denominations, to which Roof referred, are still in the midst of severe decline and serious deterioration. Stuck in the status quo, new wine cannot be poured into the same old wineskins of outdated mindsets. A new sense of urgency is required for lasting change. Change is required and the church in need of revitalization and renewal cannot escape change. Will we allow the church of America to become mirrors of the churches all across Europe that find themselves empty urns holding the obvious; we must not.

The need for training today's minister with the tools and skillsets necessary to combat this rampant plateau and decline is crucial. Most ministers coming out of our seminaries today lack preparation for the challenge of church revitalization and renewal. If the estimates are accurate that, at a minimum, eighty percent or more of our churches need revitalization, then it stands to reason that the majority of graduates from our seminaries are going to begin their ministries in the majority of these churches. Less than five percent of these graduates will actually be going to healthy churches. Existing ministers will pastor the healthy pool of churches that make up the twenty percent so the seminarian needs to prepare for the eventual challenge of revitalizing a plateaued or declining church.

The Time is Right Now!

If there is going to be revitalization in American churches in the twenty-first century, the initial step must be taken

---

58 Wade Clark Roof, "The Episcopalian Goes the Way of the Dodo," *Wall Street Journal*, July 20, 1990.

immediately. Revitalization of our churches is not an insurmountable task. While we must start with re-encountering the divine and realizing any church which is revitalized or becoming revitalized is the work of our Lord God, we must do our part to provide tools and methodologies for today's ministers to assist them with new practices and approaches that can help today's declining churches. Our Southern Baptist churches must not remain in stained glass, red-bricked, spire castles giving out apologies for lack of renewal or mixed gestures towards revitalization efforts.

The time for revitalization and renewal is now; sick and declining churches are all across America. Will the people of God be led like days of old when the shepherds of God boldly served the church of God and led His people to remember why they exist and to whom they belong? With such an absence of missionary mandates from our missionary agencies, the challenge is for the theological institutions across the convention to pick up the slack and prepare the new army of church revitalizers.

Statistics are Our Friends in Church Revitalization and Renewal

That phrase is a familiar quote from my friend Ed Stetzer. It is a timeless quote and one we all should take to heart when examining the current realities of our churches. According to *Leadership Journal*, 340,000 churches need church revitalization today.59 Ninety-five percent (95 percent) of churches in North America average 100 or less. Over eighty percent (80 percent) of American Churches are in decline or on a plateau. Many people wonder where the original quote "85% of America's Protestant churches have plateaued or are declining

---

59 http://www.ctlibrary.com/le/2005/fall/8.24.html (accessed 3/20/11).

in membership!"60 Each year approximately 3,500 churches die in North America.61 Within my own Southern Baptist Convention the annual death rate averages between seven and nine hundred!62 Our Southern Baptist Convention reports that 26,000 of our churches have an average attendance of fewer than 125 people!63 Studies have shown that churches typically plateau in attendance by their fifteenth year, and by year thirty-five they begin having trouble replacing the members they lose."64 Only 7.3 % of small churches are growing in North America currently. Of the churches, which are fifty years old or older, only 9.2% are growing.

In North America, fifty to sixty churches close their doors every week. Among churches of all sizes, growing churches are rare! In fact, they only make up about "20 percent of our churches today. The other 80 percent have reached a plateau or are declining."65 In a study of more than two thousand churches, David Olson revealed that 69 percent of our churches in America have reached a plateau or

60 Anderson, Leith. *Dying for Change: An Arresting Look at the New Realities Confronting Churches and Para-Church Ministries.* Minneapolis: Bethany House Publishers, 1998.

61 Warren Bird, "More Churches Opened Than Closed in 2006," *Rev Magazine,* July-August 2007, 68.

62 *"Annual Change in the Number of Southern Baptist Churches 1973-2009"* Center for Missional Research, North American Mission Board, SBC. Alpharetta, Georgia.

63 McMullen, Shawn and Mary Elizabeth Hopkins. "Common Size, Uncommon Impact" *Outreach,* July/August, 2006.

64 *"Churches Die with Dignity" Christianity Today* Jan. 1991, Vol. 36.

65 Stetzer, Ed and Warren Bird, *Viral Churches: Helping Church Planters Become Movement Makers* (San Francisco: Jossey-Bass, 2010), 60.

even worse are declining.66 Jim Tomberlin and Warren Bird declare that "80 percent of the three hundred thousand Protestant churches in the United States have plateaued or are declining, and many of them are in desperate need of a vibrant ministry."67 The majority of these churches has fewer than two hundred people in attendance and a large portion have fewer than seventy-five weekly.68 Churches sometimes lose their sense of direction. Many churches never realize they are in trouble until it is almost too late. Ronald Keener says that eight out of ten of the approximately 400,000 churches in the United States are declining or have plateaued. Hurting churches must come to terms with their past and genuinely repent or there will be no future.69

Thom Rainer of the Rainer Group says that "between 6,000 and 10,000 churches in the United States are dying each year. That means one hundred to two hundred churches will close this week."70 The Southern Baptist research arm within the denomination; LifeWay Christian Resources, in cooperation with the Center for Missional Research from the North American Mission Board, conducted a study based on churches' five-year change in total membership. The study reports that 28.1 percent of our Southern Baptist Convention

---

66 David T. Olson, *The American Church in Crisis* (Grand Rapids: Zondervan Publishing, 2008), 132.

67 Tomberlin, Jim and Warren Bird, *Better Together: Making Church Mergers Work* (San Francisco: Jossey-Bass, 2010), xvi.

68 "Fast Facts." Hartford Institute for Religion Research. Retrieved from http://hirr.hartsem.edu/research/fastfacts/fast_facts.html#sizecong (accessed 3/20/2011).

69 Keener, Ronald E. "Pulling Back from the Brink" *Church Executive*, November 2008.

70 "Fact & Trends" Thriving in a Post-Christendom Culture, Winter 2018. *Hope for Dying Churches*, pg. 5.

churches are growing, 43.9 percent are in a state of plateau, and 28 percent are in decline.71 Bill Hendricks declares that 53,000 individuals leave the church each and every year! He further states that most of them never come back.72

A more recent series of studies were conducted by Bill Day, Associate Director of the Leavell Center for Evangelism and Church Health, who serves the New Orleans Baptist Theological Seminary as the Gurney Professor of Evangelism and Church Health, in his sequential studies on church health and growth from 2003, 2007, and 2010, where he reports that currently there are less than seven percent (6.8) of our SBC churches which are healthy growing churches. That means 3,087 of our 45,727 SBC churches are healthy.73 Leonard Sweet states that the declining mainline church has faced a "double whammy of postmodernity and post-Christendom."74 Harry L. Reeder, pastor of Briarwood Presbyterian Church in Birmingham, Alabama in a recent interview with *byFaith* magazine points to stagnancy in American churches as a serious problem that must be addressed. "Eighty-five to ninety percent of churches in the U.S. are stagnant. More churches are closing than are being planted. Planting more churches is not the solution. We need to focus on revitalization." Alan Hirsch discussing small churches stated recently that "it is a fact that we have had

---

71 Annual Church Profile data, LifeWay Christian Resources, Nashville, TN. Compiled by: Center for Missional Research, North American Mission Board, Alpharetta, GA.

72 Hendricks, William D. *Exit Interviews: Revealing Stories of Why People Are Leaving the Church.* Chicago: Moody Press, 1993.

73 Bill Day. *The State of the Church in the S.B.C.* (New Orleans: Leavell Center for Evangelism and Church Health, 1/3/2012), C.f. Appendix Two.

74 Leonard Sweet. *So Beautiful: Divine Design for Life and the Church* (Colorado Springs: David C. Cook, 2009), 20.

church growth and mega-churches for well over thirty years now, and the overwhelming majority of the 485,000 churches in the United States remain under eighty-five per congregation while laboring under the guilt of failure to perform like the bigger churches."75

Most Recent Discoveries Regarding the State of Church in North America

Less than 20 percent of Americans regularly attend church— half of what the pollsters report.

While Gallup polls and other statisticians have turned in the same percentage—about 40 percent of the population—of average weekend church attendees for the past seventy years, a different sort of research paints quite a disparate picture of how many Americans attend a local church on any given Sunday. Initially prompted to discover how church plants in America were really doing, Olson, Director of Church Planting for the Evangelical Covenant Church (covchurch.org), began collecting data in the late 1980s, gradually expanding his research to encompass overall attendance trends in the church. In his study, he tracked the annual attendance of more than 200,000 individual Orthodox Christian churches (the accepted U.S. church universe is 330,000). To determine attendance at the remaining 100,000-plus Orthodox Christian churches, he used statistical models, which included multiplying a church's membership number by the denomination's membership-to-attendance ratio.

The Numbers

His findings reveal that the actual rate of church attendance from headcounts is less than half of the 40 percent the pollster's report. Numbers from actual counts of people in

---

75 Hirsch, Alan. *Outreach*, July/August 2010, 68.

Orthodox Christian churches (Catholic, mainline and evangelical) show that in 2004, 17.7 percent of the population attended a Christian church on any given weekend. Another study published in 2005 in *The Journal for the Scientific Study of Religion* by sociologists C. Kirk Hadaway and Penny Long Marler—known for their scholarly research on the church—backs up his findings. Their report reveals that the actual number of people worshipping each week is closer to Olson's 17.7 percent figure which is 52 million people instead of the pollster-reported 132 million (40 percent). "We knew that over the past 30 to 40 years, denominations had increasingly reported a decline in their numbers," Marler says. "Even a still-growing denomination like the Southern Baptist Convention had reported slowed growth. Most of the mainline denominations were all reporting a net loss over the past 30 years."76

The Halo Effect

What Hadaway and Marler, along with Mark Chaves, author of the "National Congregations Study," discovered was at play is what researchers call "the halo effect"—the difference between what people tell pollsters and what people actually do. Americans tend to over-report socially desirable behavior like voting and attending church and under-report socially undesirable behavior like drinking. Gallup Poll Editor in Chief Frank Newport agrees that the halo effect factors into poll results. During a Gallup telephone survey of a random sampling of about 1,000 Americans nationwide, interviewers ask respondents questions such as, "In the last seven days, did you attend a church service, excluding weddings and funerals?" to determine their church-going habits. "When people try to reconstruct their own behavior, particularly more frequently occurring on-and-off behavior, it is more

---

76 https://www.proclaimanddefend.org/2019/03/21/7-startling-facts-an-up-close-look-at-church-attendance-in-america/

difficult, especially in a telephone interview scenario," Newport says. But he stands behind Gallup's 40 percent figure: "I've been reviewing [U.S. church attendance] carefully," he says. "No matter how we ask the question to people, we get roughly 40 percent of Americans who present themselves as regular church attendees." He adds, however, that if you were to freeze the United States on any Sunday morning, you may find fewer than 40 percent of the country's adults actually in churches. "Although about 40 percent of Americans are regular church attendees, it doesn't necessarily mean 40 percent are in church on any given Sunday," he explains. "The most regular church attendee gets sick or sleeps in. The other reason may be people who tell us they go to church but are worshipping in non-traditional ways, such as small groups, people meeting in gyms or school libraries."[77]

A Disconnect

In another study surveying the growth of U.S. Protestants, Marler and Hadaway discovered that while the majority of people they interviewed don't belong to a local church, they still identify with their church roots. "Never mind the fact that they attend church less than 12 times a year," Marler observes. "We estimate that 78 million Protestants are in that place. Ask most pastors what percentage of inactive members they have—they will say anything from 40–60 percent." Even with a broader definition of church attendance, classifying a regular attendee as someone who shows up at least three out of every eight Sundays, only 23–25 percent of Americans would fit this category. Olson notes that an additional million church attendees would increase the percentage from 17.7 percent to only 18 percent. "You would have to find 80 million more people that churches forgot to count to get to

77 https://churchleaders.com/pastors/pastor-articles/139575-7-startling-facts-an-up-close-look-at-church-attendance-in-america.html

40 percent." Clearly, a disconnect between what Americans say and what they actually do has created a sense of a resilient church culture when, in fact, it may not exist.

Fast Facts for Busy Pastors

I get asked often for a quick guide for pastors to help them understand the state of church decline. This series of fast facts for busy pastors provides a macro view of the challenges in renewal. Here is what we know:

The American Church Attendance is Progressively Fading

Well-known church growth consultant Thom Rainer notes, that the failure of churches to keep up with the population growth is one of the church's greatest issues heading into the future. In a 2002 survey of 1,159 U.S. churches, Rainer's research team found that only 6 percent of the churches were growing—he defines growth as not only increasing in attendance but also increasing at a pace faster than its community's population growth rate. "Stated inversely, 94 percent of our churches are losing ground in the communities they serve," he says.

There are Denominational Variances

A breakdown of overall attendance percentages by church type shows decreases across the board in evangelical, mainline, and Catholic churches. The most significant drop in attendance came at the expense of the Catholic Church, which experienced an 11 percent decrease in its attendance percentage from 2000 to 2004. Next, and not far behind were mainline churches, which saw a 10 percent percentage decline. Evangelicals experienced the smallest drop at 1 percent. Though scholars are hesitant to definitively acknowledge a decline, they do say that attendance is not increasing: "There's no good evidence to suggest that overall church attendance has gone up in the recent decade," Chaves adds that he believes there has been a decline. He cites the watershed book *Bowling Alone* (Simon and Schuster) by Harvard sociologist Robert D. Putnam as his primary reasoning. "I think church attendance is a close cousin to the other kinds of activities Putnam says Americans are doing alone—indicating that Americans have become increasingly disconnected from family and friends," Chaves says. "So if all those areas are going down and church attendance isn't, that would be odd." He identifies various implications declining attendance may have for church leaders: "If this is the reality, then I see a trend toward people being less involved, while maintaining a connection to the church. Maybe a pastor used to be able to count on seeing someone every week, but what's now happening is that people's lives are busier and they're attending more infrequently."78

Small Groups are On the Rise

Many individuals are finding greater connectivity with some form of a small group or home group for their spiritual nourishment these days. The large gathering has been replaced by the smaller intimate group of ten to twenty participants. Ed Stetzer, professor and dean at Wheaton College as well as the Executive Director of the Wheaton College Billy Graham Center, has found similar evidence of spiritual behavior occurring outside church walls. He recently finished a study on alternative faith communities and found that a growing number of people are finding Christian discipleship and community in places other than their local churches. The study found that 24.5 percent of Americans now say their primary form of spiritual nourishment is meeting with a small group of twenty or fewer people every

---

78 https://churchleaders.com/pastors/pastor-articles/139575-7-startling-facts-an-up-close-look-at-church-attendance-in-america.html/2

week. "About 6 million people meet weekly with a small group and never or rarely go to church," Stetzer says. "There is a significant movement happening."

The Number of Midsized Churches is Dwindling

One of the interesting phenomena is the discovery that midsized churches are shrinking while at the same time the smaller and larger churches are increasing. While America's churches as a whole did not keep up with population growth from 1994 to 2004, the country's smallest (attendance 1–49) and largest churches (2,000-plus) did. During that period, the smallest churches grew 16.4 percent; the largest grew 21.5 percent, exceeding the national population growth of 12.2 percent. But mid-sized churches (100–299, the average size of a Protestant church in America is 124, declined one percent. Today there exists a growing consumer culture in the western church. Stetzer adds that because today's large churches emphasize small groups and community, hoping to create a small church feel, they offer the best of both worlds. "There are multiple expectations on mid-sized churches that they can't meet, programs, dynamic music, quality youth ministries," he says. David Anderson of the Bridge Leader Network and pastor of Bridgeway Community Church in Columbia, Maryland has observed that mid-sized congregations tend to lose the evangelistic focus they once had, and instead adopt what he calls a "club mentality." He cautions the church when he states, "You have just enough people not to be missional anymore," he explains. "You don't have to grow anymore to sustain your budget." As for why the smallest churches have kept up, Shawn McMullen, author of *Unleashing the Potential of the Smaller Church*, notes that smaller churches cultivate an intimacy not easily found in larger churches. He says, "In an age when human interaction is being supplanted by modern technology, many younger families are looking for a church that offers community, closeness and intergenerational relationships."

Matriarchal and Patriarchal Churches are Declining

Long tenured established churches that are over fifty years of age are declining. These matriarchal and patriarchal churches which many were started before 1960 are showing either decline or rapid decline. Churches which were begun in the early 1800s are showing the greatest decline. Kirbyjon Caldwell, senior pastor of Windsor Village United Methodist Church in Houston shares that established churches in decline are suffering from a leadership crisis. While his church is fifty years old, Caldwell says he has been there twenty-five years and in effect has made a "DNA change." The church has grown from a struggling congregation under his charge to a revitalized church. Reversing the decline, he says, was about the leaders of the church—both clergy and laity—deciding to redefine the congregation and meet the needs of the community.

Church Revitalization and Church Planting Is Not Keeping Up with Population Growth

Our numbers are dismal in the field of church planting during the past ten years. We are not keeping up with the revitalization of plateaued churches and allowing them to cross over into rapidly declining churches which are hard to turn around. In my own denomination, we have seen our church planting numbers decline from planting between 1,300 and 1,800 new churches annually to now numbers in the 600 to 700 range. While there has been an increased emphasis on the mega metropolitan cities in North America which is good, we have all but left the rest of our communities and turned a blind eye to their needs for new churches. Additionally, the number of declining churches being worked with and saved from closure is at an all-time low as well. We have opted for church closure and the planting of a new church instead. The sacrifice that members made to these churches only to see them closed down and little or no effort made to save them is alarming. Our strategies have not kept pace with the population growth and we are a nation which is declining spiritually as the result. Morale in many declining churches is at an all-time low. Some say that we would need to increase our new church plants by seventy-five percent annually to keep pace with the population growth. In a day where that is not happening it is critical that we work to save declining churches. I love the planting of new churches and that is in my DNA, but if we keep throwing away the existing churches, eventually we will have no churches available to sponsor the new ones. Remember, churches usually fail because we place our individual wants, needs, and desires over the Lord's.

Some Practical Advice for the Church Revitalizer

For the church revitalizer here are a few practical things which could help you as you begin your initial one hundred and twenty days in church revitalization. They are tiny nuggets more designed to get you thinking. Fleshing them out would be a wonderful activity for you and your leadership team. The first has already been said in this work but should be a reminder again. Get praying for renewal and don't stop. I would also add that you should work towards placing an elevated emphasis on disciple-making in your renewal efforts. As Acts 2:42-47 reminds us most declining churches need to rediscover how they can connect with the communities they serve. When we as a church share our life within the community the community is blessed and the church is as well.[79] Another nugget is that you need to remember that the church is made up of people and they are the key to church renewal.[80] Begin equipping your membership for the work

---

79 C.f. 2 Corinthians 8:3-5.

80 C.f. 1 Thessalonians. 2:8.

that needs to be done outside of the four walls of your church. A wise church revitalizer will begin immediately discovering, developing, and training new leaders for the leadership of the church as it moves forward in renewal. I would also challenge you to move past the preoccupation with self-preservation and begin to focus on the self-sacrifice you and your members can make for the cause of Christ. The nugget of originality should not be overlooked as well. Far too many church revitalizers want to copy someone else's renewal plans. Far better is listening, discerning, and responding to the voice of the Lord concerning your church. Copycat revitalizers often find that cutting and pasting another's church revitalization strategy leaves the church distant from the Lord's promptings since the decision was made to do it your way over His. Listening to the Lord's leading is always the preferred way. Also begin to design ways for you, your staff, and your members to give themselves away to the community you serve. Think about a few new initiatives that could provide you with new avenues to reach new prospects. Ask yourself if there are any new entrance points (touch ministries) that could be begun. While you are doing that consider letting go of ministries that are no longer serving the church. Church Revitalization is a long-distance relay run by marathoners not sprinters. You must be willing to invest a minimum of 1000 days into church renewal. If you aren't willing to fully commit yourself to the 1000 days it would be best that you do not get involved in revitalization.

Wrapping it up!

What type of Church Revitalizer are you seeking to be? All of us are wired in different ways. Each one of us has various idiosyncrasies that while they may work for us individually might not work for someone else. Far too often we catch the peculiarities over the talents anyway. But as Church Revitalizers for church revitalization and renewal, we would do well to understand the sort of leader we are.

The Problem Resolver

The problem resolver is the type of church revitalizer who develops plans to unravel the difficulties change generates. A Church Revitalizer recognizes timing issues and is adept at communication. Those who are wired as a problem resolver are able to find alternatives, which can be offered to the whole group, which will be effective for church renewal.

The Catalytic Stimulator

The catalytic stimulator is a church revitalizer who often introduces change by expressing dissatisfaction with the status quo. When I think of the scriptures perhaps the best example are those who are blessed with the gift of being apostolic. It is more of a creative discontent than it is a guy who wants to whine about everything. The stimulator inspires others to creative discontentment as well. They are good at asking questions and willing to lead.

The Early Pacesetter

The early pacesetter is a church revitalizer who is more likely to embrace and implement a new idea before others embrace the concept. Typically, the early pacesetter is a very entrepreneurial idea person and is non-bureaucratic in their nature and generally, they are very supportive of the change process needed for church revitalization and renewal.

The Resource Connecter

The resource connector matches needs with available resources to keep the change process going in church renewal efforts. They are able to connect the process of revitalization to economic, or physical resources, as well as important individuals.

The Information Deliver

The information deliver are those individuals with strategic information for church renewal that provide it in a timely matter to those who lead change. The gift they bring to the pastor serving as a church revitalizer is timely, useful and helpful tools, which will advance the church renewal efforts.

The Transformation Associates

The transformation associates are those parties who silently or outspokenly share the concerns of those who lead change and provide supportive roles to the church renewal efforts.

The Systems Implementer

The systems implementer coordinates the church renewal systems for change with the other church revitalizers. They can see the big picture, identify needs, and develop the process to handle critical steps at specific points in the process. They often have the gifts of administration and pastoral care. The systems implementers are very likely to be at ease with handling various levels of conflict and adept at conflict resolution.

These seven types of church revitalizers are the most common. While each church revitalizer has a unique style and contribution to the process of change in a revitalization effort, understanding these styles and their contributions can help in understanding the role that God has for each person He has called to facilitate revitalization and renewal within a local church. Revitalization and transformation are difficult. If it were not so difficult you would already be doing it. That is why we need support and guidance along the way as we prayerfully seek to revitalize the local church. Church revitalization takes some time. Nearsighted consultants believe it can be wrapped into a six-month period. I have discovered that if you are not willing to invest a minimum of 1,000 days you should not get into the effort of revitalization and renewal. These are the things that every church leader ought to know before jumping into revitalization and renewal.

Chapter Thirteen
Generating Buy-In as A Church Revitalizer

Developing a vision and a series of action plans for the launching of revitalization in your church begins with the consideration of how you will get your members to buy-in to the vision and take part in the action plans required to bring complete renewal to your church. This is not an easy subject to consider as a church revitalizer, but it is one that you will need to consider early if you are going to invest your first 120 days of revitalization and even more so if you are committing to investing a minimum of one thousand days in the effort. The reason it is not easy is that most Church Revitalizers and Pastors have never been taught how to get buy-in in the first place. The reality is that in creating a strategic story for any revitalization strategy, there must be a positive preferred future in which to travel. Most Revitalizers do not know how to generate such buy-in by significant church audiences for continual advancement. I define the concept of generating buy-in as a church revitalizer as an agreement to join in the effort of renewal, even though those who are agreeing to the idea did not initially have anything to do with the process beforehand. Generating buy-in requires that the revitalization leader draws as many congregants together in a single vision of renewal even though most of them have not had any input in the strategy. Certainly, there have been church staff and church lay leaders contributing, but the average rank and file members have had little if any input or suggestions. Developing buy-in for the renewal process requires generating understanding while seeking commitment and requiring action from church members in support of the Church Revitalizer, the Revitalizer's ideas, the Church Renewal Teams Proposal, plan, outcome, and structure. For the revitalization effort, buy-in is the indispensable emotional ingredient needed for any cooperative revitalization effort to be fruitful. There is no simple cookie-cutter process for overcoming some church member's natural ambivalence toward, or even active resistance to, major church change.

There is something within many individuals that oppose change. It is as if we have a resistance towards the change button that turns on when we are challenged with a degree of discomfort. As human beings we naturally resist change, we like things to stay the same because that is where we are most comfortable. Yet in the business world, organizations evolve and new ways of doing things emerge. The same is true of healthy churches. Not so for unhealthy declining ones. Change is upon us before we realize it and the need to be more open to, and embrace change, has never been greater. The church revitalizer who desires to lead their church through revitalization and renewal must learn the art of generating buy-in from church members. Their ability to influence and persuade is often a large part of creating that initial thrust towards renewal. How a revitalizer navigates the negotiation revolution with church members often determines if the church can indeed get back to health and become a renewed church. If you are a top-down leader who calls out the commands from on high expecting those in the trenches to snap to it and get in line, you will have a difficult time being used as a church revitalizer. Your ability to raise the level of buy-in is paramount in revitalization. Facing the reality as a church revitalizer that we cannot turn around a church by ourselves but that it requires the buy-in from church members and church leaders is necessary. I need you as a brand-new church revitalizer to buy-in to the idea that you need to learn a series of things within your first one hundred and twenty days in order for you to become a successful revitalizer of your church. You need your congregants to buy-in to your vision for renewal. Let's face it, all of us need someone to buy-in to our ideas almost every day of the week. If we are going to succeed in church revitalization and renewal it will require that we seek the buy-in from others in the church and in the church's leadership structure. In fact, your ability to generate such buy-in will be a skill set, that once developed, you will use over and over in turning around dying churches.

Buy-in is viewed as your ability to gain others' understanding, achieve their willingness to make a commitment and to call from them an action that supports your vision for renewal. Sometimes it is as simple as a hand raised vote and at other times it requires a willingness to join in actual hard work in order to achieve the series of goals that will lead to the renewal of your declining or plateaued church. As you influence your member's thoughts, feelings, and actions you are generating their buy-in. If you can grow as a leader in the area of development of buy-in to your cause you will be well on your way to achieving church revitalization and renewal. This one single skill will be perhaps the greatest tool a church revitalizer can learn. No matter where the Lord calls him in the future once learned God will utilize this gift over and over in renewal of declining churches. Understand this if you will, in today's churches there are often those who do not desire to follow the one the Lord has called as their pastor to lead their church. Compelling others to buy-in and follow your lead will be a necessary factor towards the renewal of the church. Wise church revitalizers work hard at getting their church members to believe in the cause and to believe in you the one leading them towards renewal. Church members need to believe in church revitalization and the fact that the Lord wants to save their church. Also, they need to be growing in their belief in you as the leader who can lead them out of the wilderness and into the promised land. Buy-in is everything. Once you have it renewal seems to fall into place one piece of the puzzle after another. But if you have not invested enough time in achieving it, you will likely fail and chances for success are diminished. Take the time to create healthy buy-in to your vision for revitalization and renewal.

Positioning the Juncture for Buy-in from Church Members

No matter what your ideas are there will come a time where you must begin positioning the juncture or crossroads where ideas from the pastor leader are acknowledged and considered by the church members. Membership reaction to pastoral ideas for change is many times mere suspension of judgments against anything that moves the church off of the status quo. The moment there is tension in the fellowship about the new direction these individuals will jump in to massacre your revitalization effort and shatter it. Those in the lower ends of leadership within the church are the ones who usually grow uncomfortable with the new direction. In portion, this is due to the realities that this group will be required to make the most significant series of changes over the upper levels of church leadership. Thinking through the immediate, short-term, mid-term, and long-range benefits before proceeding towards renewal will equip you as the leader to embrace this group and help them see the best future for the life of the church. Here are a few of the benefits of generating buy-in for the vision of revitalizing the local church where you serve:

Juncture Positioning Allows You to Share Reality Without Any Judgment

Speaking the truth and reality as an opportunity for the Lord to do something great is important. Many members in declining churches have false-positive views of the health and vitality of the church. Facts in the process of revitalization are a church revitalizer's friend. When you launch the effort of renewal with a straightforward and thorough effort to determine the truth of the church's situation, the right decisions, choices, and conclusions often become self-evident. This single element in church renewal is the extent to which renewal leaders commit from the beginning to be forthright, above board, trustworthy, and willing to share with the congregation completely what, why, where, and how the revitalization effort is going to proceed. I have learned in working with churches in need of revitalization and renewal that fully disclosing everything allows the membership to not only have head knowledge but heart knowledge as you touch their emotions as well. It is a traction maker, not breaker. Appealing to feelings often proceeds an appeal to our thinking mechanisms. Showing a church membership is compelling. Pie charts of data only bore the member so paint a beautiful picture and tell an incredible story of what the church will be once renewal is accomplished. Declining churches are made up of members who would like to see the opportunity you present to them. They want to feel the feelings that will be the new norm of a healthy church. Change is then easier to embrace because of showing them how their challenges are going to be transformed into opportunities.

Juncture Positioning Allows You an Opportunity to Break the Renewal Process Down

It is always easier to take small bites over great big ones. When you as the church revitalizer break the renewal process down into smaller manageable portions, it is easier to see the journey. Because you are ultimately investing a minimum of one thousand days this initial segment of one hundred and twenty days is a more manageable piece to begin the effort. By painting the picture in manageable pieces often known as chunking, you are able to lower the threat level for many members who fear any and all portions of change. This allows for stages of buy-in and gives most church members the time to become accustomed to where the church is going in renewal. Chunking allows for bite-size steps to be taken and proven successful before you move on to the next piece of the renewal process.

Juncture Positioning Allows You as the Church Revitalizer to Hear from Others

Because relationships will either make you or break you it is vital that you begin to hear what fellow staff members, lay church leaders, and church members are saying and thinking. If you fail to do this one thing, your membership and staff will begin to become resistant. That resistance will then translate over into dislike of you and your ideas for renewal. As you hear from others you are given the opportunity to address, explain, and navigate the issues. Overcoming such resistance requires probing, analyzing, and listening. Relationships come first while ideas are secondary. Pastors, keep talking with your members. Keep the flock engaged in the process and do not shut them out.

Juncture Positioning Allows You as the Church Revitalizer to Change the Course

Just because you are called to your church to lead it through the process of revitalization does not mean you are to drive the effort by leading the effort like a Brigadier General. Rank doesn't mean much in a local church if you as the leader lose your followers. This is where high "D" on the disc scale leaders get in trouble in revitalization. Shouting out orders and expecting the privates to jump in line doesn't work in most churches. Churches renew better from the bottom up not the top-down form of leadership. Top-down leadership behavior often will harm the church's ability to be revitalized. Change comes best when the pastor leader works with the rank-and-file church members to devise plans for saving one's church. Keeping those who work hard within the church structure involved is critical to the effort. Listening to them and hearing them out will often lead to the proper change direction in setting the course for renewal.

Go Early and Often to Gain Stakeholder Support and Buy-in

You can be assured that everything around us is changing. Change is persistent and perpetual in renewal. As the revitalization leader, you will never change things by fighting your current reality. To change your church and move it towards renewal, begin building a new model that makes the existing model obsolete. Even the tiniest piece of change can have a rippling effect on a church in decline. Stakeholders are your committed church members which comprise the levels of the leadership structure within your church. It could be a series of various groups that are part of the church stakeholder organization. It could be a number of individuals that make up the matriarchs and patriarchs. It could be the parents of the younger children or the parents of the youth. A church choir is often a stakeholder group. Anytime you are beginning to launch out a renewal effort it will require that you as the church revitalizer work to gain the buy-in of key groups of people in your church. This buy-in is the cement that builds the foundations and the glue that connects the membership to the effort. Let's look at how you go about discovering who these stakeholders are:

Recognize Who are the Stakeholders Within Your Church

Early in my ministry, I was on staff as the Youth Minister of a church in South Florida. We had this very elaborate worship service one Sunday where we dedicated a set of church chimes which would ring out every day reminding the community of not only the time but it would ring out particular church hymns as well. I was surprised that a church service would be set aside to dedicate a piece of equipment that was no higher than four feet and no higher than three-foot square. It sat in a closet and piped out recorded chimes on the hour, quarter-hour, and half hour. Every evening at seven it would play a hymn through the chimes for all of the community to hear. I asked my Senior Pastor later that week why we took the whole service to do that and he replied that when your number one stakeholder at church wants to donate church chimes to the church you hold a dedication service. That was my early introduction in ministry to stakeholders within a church. I began to realize that every church has stakeholders. It was easy in that church to see who the stakeholders were but it might be harder for you even in a declining church. It would be wise for you to consider who they are and the influence they have over the future direction of the church as well as the rank-and-file membership. I remember a youth pastor getting fired in Augusta because he reached all kinds of youth who needed Christ Jesus. The stakeholders only desired to have youth who were family members of church members. Understanding who these members are is a good way to assess the impact they will have on the revitalization effort. Stakeholder evaluation also has the objective of developing collaboration between the stakeholder and the church revitalization team, assuring successful outcomes for the effort.

Distinguish Your Stakeholder Needs in Renewal

Often, I hear a stakeholder say in a well-meaning way that they want to see the church revitalized but that they hope the pastor does not mess with their 8:30 a. m. Senior Service. I understand that. They are letting you know that they will be open to an additional service focused on renewal of the church but wish that the early service of which they are part of remains about the same. When you analyze the needs of your stakeholders, it will give you a picture of whether or not the church can be revitalized. Keeping one service the same while adding or changing another is not too much to ask for their full support. Stakeholders have needs and are willing to share them with the pastor. As you meet with your stakeholders to discuss their needs it gives you the opportunity to let them know you value them as a church member and as one who loves their church. By understanding to what degree, you can expect buy-in from your stakeholders you are better able to navigate the issues which could sink the effort. It further allows you to consider any rising pockets of resistance towards the revitalization of the church. Tailoring your church communication towards each stakeholder cluster safeguards that you are communicating successfully how the proposed changes will affect each stakeholder and what the effort will bring to the declining church.

Stakeholders are Best Engaged Through the Three H's

What are the three H's in engaging your church's stakeholders? They are engaging their head, their heart, and their hands. As you engage these members through the utilization of these stages you are better able to keep most of them connected to the church. When you share with them why the need for revitalization through the facts, you are engaging the head and their knowledge. They can see the benefits of a church full again. As you engage the longtime member through their hearts, you enable them to come to see and believe in their heart that the change is the correct thing for the church and now is the right time. They will also in their heart see that there are health benefits for the church they love as well. When you engage their hands to become part of the effort you are allowing them to become part of the army which will bring renewal to fruition.

Engage Your Church's Leadership and Governance Groups

In churches, there are groups such as Elders, staff, and Deacons which also need to be engaged. These are busy individuals already doing the work of the local church so time is going to be a precious commodity for them. They need to be engaged but not required to add even more to their busy schedules. Find ways they can be engaged but not adding additional requirements above visual and vocal support.

What is not measured in churches gets pushed down further and further until it is trampled on. Keep everyone involved and ask for their opinion often. Stakeholders will appreciate you taking the time to ask them even if they have no suggestions at the moment for you to consider. Keeping them in the buy-in group is important to the success of the revitalization effort.

Activating Buy-in for Your Revitalization Plan

If you are going to activate buy-in for your church revitalization plan from your church members you will certainly need to become better prepared and equipped at the telling of the key story for renewal. Great preachers have developed their ability to tell great stories throughout their sermons and draw their participants even closer through a timely story. Granted some people are not awesome storytellers but every one of us could become better at the art of telling the story. Telling the story often triggers the buy-in needed to get the church connected to the plan for revitalization. I know, you might never have your membership hanging on your every word regarding the need for the revitalization of your church, but you can become better at telling the interesting portions that bring the congregation closer towards embracing the plan for renewal. I always say that I would rather be a writer than an author. That is because writers live in the story and the journey while authors live in the accolades of a work in print. Church revitalizers must learn how to paint the picture of renewal and then bring the congregation with them. That is often done through becoming a better teller of the church's story. Telling the story of renewal draws the congregant into what it would look like to see the church transformed and renewed into a vibrant church once more. Here are seven ways to use the telling of your church's story to activate buy-in for the revitalization plan:

Grab the Attention of Those Listening to You Instantly

In High School, I had a speech teacher who helped me prepare for the various speech contest I entered around the State of Florida. It was approaching the two hundredth birthday of our great nation and there were all types of contests designed to find the best youth speakers sharing a patriotic message about our nation. I entered everyone I could find and won a large majority of them. When I graduated and went on to college, I had a large number of savings bonds which I cashed in and helped with my first two years of college. My teacher said it all the time, "You need to grab the attention of those listening to you instantly." Grab their intention and tell them your intention was the way I liked to think about it. What my teacher was teaching me was that if you are going to get the audience to jump in with where you want them to go, you need to grab them through active engagement immediately. I have heard presented, so many boring Church Revitalization Plans that I can't even count them. What is missing in every one of them is that the one declaring is trying to do so via a litany of boring data points and lethargic details. If you are going to generate buy-in from your church members, you must grab them in such a way that they want more and more of what you are sharing. Far too many church revitalizers offer their listeners nothing more than a boring set of gallbladder x-rays. Do not be shocked if your church members hastily tune you out. Grab their attention right away. Snatch it really. If you will spend a little time preparing what you are going to say so that it will grab members' attention, you will draw them in and keep them there.

Envision for Your Members the Correct Image

All good storytellers know that if you want to grab someone's attention then you need to paint a picture or a series of pictures that convey the very mental picture of a church that is now healthy and vibrant. By asking those present to visualize along with you, you are helping them buy-in to the new vision for renewal. Verbiage such as: "I see a day in the near future when the sanctuary will be filled with happy voices of the young and old alike" helps the hearers to buy-in visually and begin to embrace the opportunities. I always repeat my own revitalization story over and over to myself as I prepare for the time when I will declare it before my people. That is really because repetition reduces resistance. I rehearse what I want to say and how I want to say it in preparation for the moment in time when I will share it for all the world to see (really my church members). I have learned that it helps me to be self-confident and allows me to fix anything that does not present well. A story is a great way to draw your members into the effort of revitalization. People remember stories while they forget figures. As the leader of the Renovate Conferences, I used to bring in the past a speaker or two that would dazzle us with their data. What I learned was that these presenters on the main stage were always the ones who received the lowest evaluations. Paint a picture, it will go further than your data.

Work Towards Developing Emotional Buy-in

Most of your church members want to see their church healthy and vibrant again. By seeking to connect them emotionally towards a day where that is achieved, you have a wonderful opportunity to draw the net. Church members are engaged emotionally when you paint a visual of the happy days ahead including wedding that will take place and young people who will be called to the work of the Lord. Our attention spans are expanded when we seek to provide emotional attachments. For the listening audience. I have learned also that your story explodes with excitement if you pickle it with some emotional tidbits. Gone are the Dragnet Days when Joe Friday would show you his badge and declare, "Just the facts, just the facts please." Felt needs are a part of gaining emotional buy-in as well.

Pace Not Race Your Story

As a teenage preacher boy, I would often fly through my message which left everyone in a tizzy. I then began to learn that while the pace needed to be somewhat accelerated, it didn't need to be like a rocket shot off of the launching pad. Rushing your one chance to gather buy-in is poor planning on your part. People want to hear what you have to say so stop thinking you need to run fast through the presentation. Give your people the time while you speak to think through what you are saying and how you are saying it. Often, I will utilize various paces in a vision presentation in order to connect with the likes of everyone in the audience. You must also enjoy what you have to say as well as being the one saying it.

Know When to Share and Declare

I am smiling right now as I think of the number of times I have had a pastor tell me that their presentation was the right words delivered at the wrong time. You need to know when to share your revitalization plan and when to declare we are moving towards the renewal of the church. In case you did not already know this, Labor Day weekend is not the time because that is often the least attended week of the church's calendar. If you know in your church that you will have more people in attendance on the second Sunday of the month then choose that as the time to launch your efforts. Make it a big day and a day everyone will remember for a long time. It is probably going to be the single date that your members will remember as the start of God's blessings upon the church once more.

Tell Enough but Do Not Tell Everything

In a previous church where I came in to be their revitalization pastor, I made the mistake of wanting to paint a blueprint rather than paint a picture. I had plans for the children, youth, young adults, middle adults, and senior adults and proceeded to share with them everything. I shared about sixty-nine various ministries we would develop that would take the church out of the sanctuary and into the community. That is the stuff they can learn about later. Keep your picture and your story simple and succinct. Important things win out over telling them everything. Henri Frederic Amiel said, "A man must be able to cut a knot, for everything cannot be untied; he must know how to disengage what is essential from the detail in which it is enwrapped, for everything cannot be equally considered; in a word, he must be able to simplify his duties, his business, and his life."81 Succinctness and simplicity are sometimes hard to achieve in church revitalization and renewal but is almost always close by. Sometimes you just need to know where to look for it, or how to look for it. Do not make the process of revitalization harder than it is really.

Get Good, Real Good

Granted that is poor grammar but a great reality when it comes to church revitalization. If you will take the time as a pastor to grow in your knowledge as a church revitalization leader, you will begin to be known in your church and others as one who is proficient and worthy to be heard. The church revitalization community needs more pastors like that, rather than those jumping into renewal because church planting is

---

81 https://sourcesofinsight.com/simplicity-quotes/

drying up. If you desire to get really good at church revitalization and renewal, then you will need to burst outside of your usual ministry bubble of influence by participating in revitalization events, renewal conferences, and church restoration discussions relevant to your desire for church revitalization. As you gain a series of expertise, you will become known outside of your current ministry realm and area network. If you want to learn from various denominational experts then begin receiving the *Church Revitalizer Magazine* which is the only multi-denominational magazine out there on church revitalization and renewal. Find ways you can submit your revitalization story to the magazine regularly. As to participate at a revitalization event on your dime until you are worthy of them asking you to be part of the larger group of national leaders. What you are seeking in this area is to begin to create followership of pastors and leaders in revitalization.

Grasping Buy-in for Church Revitalization

Seizing the opportunity to begin the revitalization of your church is the beginning while leading the membership to grasp the need for revitalization is the middle and developing the methodologies for renewal is the long-term final stretch. We want to focus on the grasping stage for you as the revitalization process. The best way to begin is by a straightforward approach that eliminates any degree of complication. Church members are looking for plans that are easy to follow and not complicated. Shocking to most pastors is the revelation that the majority of your church members really do not want to know what the Bible has to say in the Greek text. They are more of Eugene Peterson *The Message* type of people. Simplicity and simple language work best. Every church has language usage that floats around its people. That is why it is best to utilize the special language of your people. Lofty words only confuse the mass so simplicity is a key. Help them remember the plan by using everyday speech. Understanding their language for buy-in is helpful. One last recommendation: keep your story to no more than three points. People remember the law of three much better than a long list. While seven is a holy number, in revitalization the numerical trinity works much better. I learned this in college during a speech class as the trilogy of persuasion. Here are my three:

Design Your Buy-in Story for Renewal

Church members think in pictures of what could be in the future. The things they remember most about the Bible come from the great stories throughout the pages of scripture. Our dreams are filled each night with pictures fashioned into a series of images. We wake up and can tell another for a little while all about the story we had that night. When a say the words: "A healthy church looks like," if you begin thinking about the phrase a series of mental images begin to foster and present a story. If you are going to begin triggering buy-in the best way to do so is by designing your revitalization story filling it with mental pictures of a preferred future for the local church. Take a note pad and begin writing down a few keywords that demonstrate your story's highlights. Every morning when my wife and I wake up we roll over together and talk for a while. I usually ask her a regularly reoccurring question after a while, "Cheryl, what were your dreams last night?" I have told her all our married life that she should have written down her dreams as soon as she got up because her stories are awesome and if you get them first thing in the morning, they are full of vivid descriptions and brilliant details all amplified with color and grandeur. Stories are the documents of our minds. A revitalization story that is fashioned and worked on until it is perfect can activate and initiate buy-in from the membership of the church. It can be and often is the beginning spark for people to embrace the revitalization effort. Make the story bigger than you and bigger than just a few. Design it to be an all-in endeavor for renewal. First, you need to create and design your buy-in story for renewal, but it does not end there.

Learn Your Buy-in Story of Renewal

It would be an assignment half done if you only created and designed your buy-in story. Nothing would ever happen because you failed to do the next two portions of the work. Even as you are praying about your renewal plan you cannot help but think about it in story form. Mentally we have visions and images dancing across our minds every day. A challenge for most pastors when we arrive at this step is to try to write a few bullets down on paper and believe we can wing it and get the job done. We cannot. Just like my wife's dreams each night until they are told they are really nothing, but when they are asked to be summoned forth, they present a wonderful time of imagination which is a delight to me the hearer and seer of the story. Now because you are going to share this story over and over again for at least the next three years, it behooves you to not only design it but to memorize it as well. I entered many speech contests as a high schooler and I understood quickly that the judges rewarded those who learned their speech with the top prizes. Your church being brought out of the death spiral and brought into renewed life is worth your investment to learn this story of renewal.

Tell Your Buy-in Story of Renewal

I believe this is the most important part of the assignment and that is because it is through the telling of your revitalization story you paint a picture of a preferred future. Jesus and the writers of the gospels told stories. Paul the apostle was a masterful storyteller. Think of the great storytellers of our time. John F. Kennedy, Ronald Reagan, Winston Churchill, and Franklin Roosevelt were all great storytellers when everything was on the line and they needed to get full buy-in. Nothing less is required of us as well. In fact, you as the pastor will be telling your story of renewal for a minimum of the next three years. You will be telling it once a year to the entire church body. You will be telling it to your church's new member's class. You will be telling it out in the community to potential prospects so getting it designed and memorized is only the preparation for the most important part of telling the story. If you are going to lead the church through renewal as its leader you must become a great teller of your story for revitalization and renewal. If you want to impact your church's future then begin by telling the critical story of its bright future and bountiful blessings. Buy-in is necessary if you want to achieve renewal and win the war against Satan. Your revitalization story is key to grabbing the attention of your church members and calling them to action. Stories snatch the attention of our emotions and hold one for a long time. Seize the day for revitalization by telling your church's story of renewal. Call your membership to action and set about the renewing of the church. Believe in your story and tell it boldly with all of your heart.

Virtues of a Pastor Everybody Desires to Follow

If you are a student of your own denominations church history like I am, you are also amazed that once prosperous churches are facing plateau or decline. Usually, these churches were formerly led by a strong personality and dynamic preacher. Congregation size grew during this minister's tenure and followers were devoted to the godly shepherd. Then through the years decline began to seep in and eventually the once healthy church was in a state of decline. You must have the right leader for revitalization. In revitalization, churches get one single opportunity for church transformation and renewal. The church revitalizer must be one that others want to follow and are willing to embrace the mindset of the revitalization pastor. A church revitalizer needs to be wired in a way that draws people and enthusiastic followers. Here are some critical virtues of a pastor church members willingly follow:

Pastors with Great Conviction

The conviction that the church can and will be revitalized is a significant virtue for the pastor working in renewal. The only way for church members to see the end result of renewal is for the pastor to present it vividly. Members need to understand what the final win looks like. Pastors with a strong conviction focus on the Word of God in their portrayal of a renewed church. The direction you choose has to be clear so followers feel their participation is purposeful, and so they are willing to watch your back.

Pastors Who are Loyal

Revitalization pastors must be loyal to the church God has called them to lead. That means they need to stop looking over their shoulder for the next church down the road that is a little bit bigger and a lot easier to lead. When the Lord calls you to a church you need to go as a loyal and faithful servant willing to lay down one's life for the flock of that church. Loyalty is a virtue that defines a pastor's true intentions. They are a leader who looks beyond self-centered goals and seeks to serve others with pure intents. Being loyal to the Word of God is also part of this as well. They are loyal to staff and the church they lead.

Pastors Who are Responsible

A pastor seeking to renew a church understands that they carry the load of responsibility for their actions, exploits, conduct, and thoughts. Since the leader's thoughts and ideas transform into someone's deeds, they're responsible for its consequences. Church revitalizers stand their ground but also accept the blame when things go array. They are wise enough to be in charge. They use logic and they analyze, they change perspective if needed, and keep working. Their role does not involve accusation. Their calling is to help others, not to give up.

Pastors Who are Honest and Accountable

Without honesty and integrity, a pastor would likely lose credibility with his church members and might even face job termination. A pastor is expected to maintain moral standards so their character is unquestionable and followers can trust their decisions and guidance. Even if a pastor has a support staff, he is often accountable for the church's finances; the well-being of congregation members; business-related transactions; community involvement; and the integrity of the organization as a whole. Honesty is vital to the position. Being accountable to some group is wise for the revitalization leader.

Pastors Who are Boldly Positive or Optimistic

It takes boldness to be the leader of a revitalization effort. One of the essential skills of a church revitalizer is bold positivity. It does not mean, however, that they avoid problems, or they do not care. Actually, they care more than anyone else. Still, they find inspiration to keep moving. That is the boldness required to be a good church revitalizer. Complications do not alarm them. Leaders know their dreams are worth their efforts. Being optimistic is underrated. It is often synonymous with being positive. While optimism and positivity are similar, there are important differences. Positivity is not about wearing rose-colored glasses and rolling over when the going gets tough. It is about staying focused on the good in any situation. Church revitalizers are optimistic about the church's future regardless of the church's past history.

Pastors Who are Humble

A church revitalizer must be courageous and confident without letting their ego get in the way. Humbleness often makes a pastor more accessible, so staff and congregation members are not apprehensive about asking spiritual questions or seeking their counsel. Even though a pastor is a highly visible public figure, their ability to avoid pride and arrogance demonstrates their meek and humble nature. Humility helps a pastor lead with kindness and gentleness, so their teachings are respected and well-received.

Pastors Who are Active Listeners

Revitalization pastors do not seclude themselves from the very people they are called to lead. Hiding in the midst of a revitalization project only demonstrates that you were not the one that should have been called to the effort. Revitalizers are open to communication and collaboration. They listen and talk to their teammates. Being the revitalization pastor means you embrace the opportunity to meet your followers and listen to their suggestions. You must be attentive to their opinions. Even if you do not agree with their assessment and have another one, you show your respect and concern. You let them take part. You invite different people to your team. The diversity of opinions you embrace makes a huge difference. Appreciate it and be ready to reap the harvest.

Pastors Who are Life-long Learners

Pastors in the realm of revitalization are always learning. Being the leader is not the end of the journey where you can check out intellectually. It is the beginning of the journey where you are the one accountable for the local church. It is now essential for you to keep developing. You do not have the luxury to shift into neutral for a season. You must lead. So, you must keep learning. Leading and learning go hand in hand. Do you want your church followers to improve their skills? Then show them how you keep improving. One of the reasons many church revitalization leaders write books on revitalization is because they are learning and want to keep growing. A one-shot wonder as authors often demonstrate that they have ceased to be a writer and are only interested in being an author. Keep learning so others can learn from you. Consistently keep on learning for it is the only way to stay fresh in the task of renewal.

Pastors Who are Loving and Compassionate

Love your congregation and let them know it. Christ loved the church and we should also. A loving mindset finds ways to encourage, strengthen, and correct members who need guidance and spiritual counsel.

Wrapping it Up!

Generating the buy-in required to advance your church through the renewal process takes real effort and how you design, learn and tell your revitalization story is essential. Never underestimate the power of creating buy-in for the renewal plan. Our Renovate Research poll discovered that seventy percent of all church renewal efforts fail primarily because the pastors do not seek to achieve sufficient buy-in from their membership for their renewal plans. Persons who you often disagree with may support your new ideas for renewal and you as the leader because they were asked for buy-in early in the revitalization process. Buy-in fosters reverence and belief. One word of concern to be aware of is that your members can sense when their pastor is afraid to make reasonable sacrifices, and that is one reason that many strategic buy-in initiatives fail. Make sure to remain consistent in what you say and how often you communicate. Real buy-in involves at least some element of collaboration. It summons discussion, debate, and allows everyone to feel even more vested in the outcome. As the revitalization leader, your responsibility is to provide guidance and consistency throughout every stage of the effort. Your stakeholders need to know you are always there, always accessible, and reliable. This provides stakeholders with the much-needed stability necessary to remain vested in your vision for renewal. Understand that if you are going to raise the buy-in quotient, it will take time and in the hard revitalization efforts, it will take a lot of time. Patience in the development of congregational buy-in is essential. It will also require you to really get to know your congregation. Granted that is a low priority to many pastors today but vital to revitalization pastors. Your members need to hear your vision for renewal, but it needs to be delivered in a way they will embrace it. That requires that you really do know your members. Your lay leaders will ask you in meetings how you are proceeding in achieving buy-in and a non-committal answer only reveals you do not know your congregation. Buy-in takes time. The message takes time for all to hear and even longer for some to fully embrace. Your church members want buy-in for the revitalization plan and yet they do not always have the means to make it happen. You must lead them. You as the revitalizer move strategically to make it happen. Your staff and lay leaders help it happen. The rank-and-file members let it happen. The result is the buy-in for the renewal necessary to transform the church and save it.

Conclusion
One Hundred and Twenty Daily Nudges to Begin the Revitalization of Your Church

Everybody at one time or another needs a little nudge! Sometimes it is a simple prodding to begin something. At times it is a little elbowing to get back in the game. There are times when a gentle push is all that is required. Bumps in the road are most often the very thing that nudges a church to move forward because it realizes it can't stand still or it will die. I have personally seen times when a hearty jolt is required to get a leader off of neutral and ministering again. Each time I enter into another church revitalization project and begin working with a different church or set of churches, I think back to what I have affectionately called "The NUDGE List!" Remember when you were a kid and one of your parents gave you a gentle nudge to get you back to your homework assignment? It was a gentle nudge. Do you recollect when your Mom came into your room and saw the great big mess and nudged you to get at the process of cleaning it up? In both instances, it was gentle and got you going once more. Churches that are falling back into becoming legacy churches often need the nudge in a similar way! Here is my quick acrostic for the word Nudge in church renewal:

> **N**ew things not previously tried
> **U**niting activities that bring people together
> **D**iscipleship groups emphasized
> **G**entle plans that demonstrate a new day and direction
> **E**vangelistic projects and events designed to reach and reconnect into community

A nudge for most churches is all that it takes to begin working on the revitalization of your church. While it is a minimal investment of one thousand days, what you do during your first one hundred and twenty days will set the pace for your efforts and provide a foundation for renewal in the days ahead.

How Do You Create a Nudge List for Church Revitalization?

Think about ideas and ways that will send a message to the community that you are doing a new thing and doing something new. If you are the pastor think about ways you can share the dream using short-term, mid-term, and long-range ideas and goals for renewal and revitalization. What would your church's nudge list look like as it begins the revitalization process?

Your Initial Nudge List Activity

Please spend the next ten minutes thinking about some simple things you and your church can do to begin to lead it back to becoming a healthy church once more. **STOP HERE and READ NO FURTHER UNTIL YOU HAVE DONE THIS EXERCISE!**

I want to thank two dear friends and fellow church revitalizers, Doctors Jim Grant and Terry Rials fellow co-authors of mine for helping me think through this list. Their insight is deeply appreciated. They have been with me from the beginning of the Renovate Conferences and have contributed greatly to the effort of revitalization for so many churches and church leaders. Your initial days are extremely important, so do not allow a single one of them to be wasted. Here is a proven list that will help you as you begin your journey towards renewal. Well now that you have begun thinking about your nudges and at the request of those who have journeyed along with me during the writing of this book, here are a suggested 120 daily nudges for your initial one hundred and twenty days in church revitalization and renewal:

1. Begin praying and seeking the Lord about the revitalization of your church.
2. Admit that your church needs to be revitalized.
3. Consider if your church has a history worthy of revitalizing. Does it need to continue?
4. Determine if the church has a DNR (Do Not Resuscitate). Is there toxicity within the fellowship that is hurting the church?
5. Begin a ministry of care and concern for the members of your church. Enlist others to help.
6. Think about: How could I create a vision of something better for our future. Begin praying for two church implementers to come alongside of you to help make your vision a reality within the membership.
7. Determine if now is the time for renewal. Ask questions of your membership.
8. Decide if you have 30-50 engaged members willing to begin renewal (Critical Mass).
9. Select one book on Revitalization to read in the next two weeks (become a learner).
10. Begin prayerfully seeking a coach who will coach you weekly and monthly.
11. Ask the question: "Am I the guy to do this?"
12. Pray about your sense of calling to become the church revitalizer.
13. Begin letting go of "the way things have always been done" syndrome and determine if the church is wedded to the past and resistant to a new direction.
14. Is there lay leadership willing to assist in leading change? Begin praying about reaching new generations over preserving the past ones.
15. Begin praying about who you should ask to serve on the Church Renewal Team.
16. Write out on paper the names of those who you believe to be committed to the effort of renewal.

17. Ask yourself: what needs to be done in church renewal?
18. Ask yourself: what can be done in church renewal?
19. Ask yourself: what your members are willing to do in church renewal?
20. Determine if you have your own personal house in order before beginning renewal.
21. Take a day to do a community windshield survey of your ministry field and write down what you observed.
22. Find your revitalization legitimizer in your church.
23. Begin to communicate Church Renewal to everyone all the time and anytime.
24. Remind your membership that renewal is a spiritual process that begins with prayer.
25. Lead your people spiritually.
26. Be bold when talking renewal. Declaration always comes before Revitalization.
27. Begin practicing patience with your entire congregation.
28. Begin to exegesis your community discovering potential groups to become part of your renewal effort.
29. Take the Renovate Church Passivity Assessment as leaders, lay leaders, and congregation. Notice similarities in the three groups and differences.
30. Conclude if the people structure in the church is helping or hurting your chances of renewal.
31. Form the Church Revitalization Assistance Team within your church. Select them, don't ask for volunteers. Get the team you want and need.
32. Take the Church Revitalizer Assessment from the Renovate Group as the potential church revitalizer.
33. Select a second book on Revitalization to read in the next two weeks (become a learner).
34. Begin preaching one sermon a month on church renewal (for the next 1000 days).

35. Determine if there are any support networks for Revitalization near you such as cohorts.
36. Prayerfully consider if you really have the tenacity to endure resistance that will come as the result of revitalizing your church.
37. Begin creating a sense of urgency for renewal over desperation for renewal.
38. Discover what was your church's defining moments in the past.
39. Seek new defining moments for the renewal journey.
40. Learn who the community civic leaders are and begin meeting with them asking appropriate questions relating to culture.
41. Ask yourself if you are willing to embrace the longevity required to bring about Renewal?
42. Determine if your church has a network of caregivers.
43. As the Pastor do you have a strong sense of God's calling upon your life?
44. Find renewal support from living in the Bible and boldly preaching the Bible.
45. Study during your personal study time the books of Ezra and Nehemiah with a journal in hand.
46. Make prayer a big thing upfront and not as an afterthought. A prayer covering is critical and it must be first and foremost. Revitalization efforts move forward on its knees. God works through the fervent prayer of His people.
47. Preach on confession, repentance, and renewal of the individual first and church second.
48. Renew, reinvent, and refresh your church's mission statement so that everyone can catch it! Keep it short so it can be embraced with ease. Work together with members on this statement and make it theirs as well as yours.
49. Keep personal evangelism on the front burner and lead lost people to Christ!

50. Light a salvation candle when some gets saved! Remember the responsibility for keeping evangelism a top priority is the senior pastor and no one else!
51. Keep your commitment to evangelism public.
52. Share the plan of salvation in your new member's class.
53. Give your church fellowship, handles for doing evangelism.
54. Work hard to include all age groups in evangelism.
55. Allow evangelism to become the driving force in revitalizing your church! Make reaching people the new priority.
56. Keep the fires of evangelism burning.
57. Establish a Church Revitalization line item as part of the Churches Budget.
58. Ask the chamber of commerce who lives in your target area.
59. Hang out around the mall and see who lives in your area. Become an observer of the masses.
60. Openly and outwardly display to your community your love in specific practical ways that demonstrate this love.
61. Conduct Special Evangelistic Events that will create awareness of your church's love for the community.
62. Become known as a church of compassion for its community.
63. Develop a working strategy for the present, near future, and long-term growth.
64. Work on ways to accommodate growth. Get your people ready for new prospects.
65. Connect your laity to the work of ministry.
66. Select a third book on Revitalization to read in the next two weeks (become a learner).
67. Find ways to reconnect with former members.
68. You must see the vision as a possibility and then lead your people to see it as a possibility as well. Paint a clear picture.

69. Cast a gripping vision of what the church could become.
70. Begin doing the groundwork to achieve the vision.
71. Within your organization structure, begin new classes and programs to meet new needs. New groups grow faster than existing ones.
72. Allow God to provide for the financial resources needed for the church.
73. Add services early and often.
74. Build relationships as early and often as possible.
75. Train staff and laity in renewal.
76. Utilize the media to help you share your story.
77. Be the provider of hope to your congregation and community.
78. Ask the question: Is my leadership the issue?
79. Ask the next question: Is the laity's leadership the issue?
80. Discover the deadwood and remove it.
81. Preach on spiritual renewal.
82. Preach on individual repentance.
83. Lead church to corporate repentance.
84. Hold a Solemn Assembly.
85. Ask the question: Do we have enough time or have we waited too long?
86. Begin enlisting and develop prayer coalitions within your church. Get the church praying throughout the day.
87. Ask the congregation who we are?
88. Ask the leadership what diseases do we have?
89. Consider the state of decline within the church.
90. Consider what are the things that are working?
91. Select a fourth book on Revitalization to read in the next two weeks (become a learner).
92. Engage your community and provide for them.
93. Examine the things that are not working.
94. Consider what needs to be done.
95. Consider what can be done.

96. Consider what you as the leader are willing to do?
97. Consider what you as a layperson is willing to do?
98. What are you willing to give away?
99. Start by exegeting the church.
100. Follow up by exegeting the community.
101. Consider the things that keep your church from growing.
102. Determine who are the organizations and partners we could connect with?
103. Consider who is on the bus (staff wise) and needs to be let go.
104. Consider who is on the bus but sitting in the wrong seat.
105. Thinking about the necessary changes required to revitalize the church.
106. Begin to develop your revitalization plan and strategy.
107. Discuss with leadership the sustainability of a renewal effort.
108. Determine if the church membership is in favor of renewal.
109. Determine if the church leadership is in favor of renewal.
110. Begin talking about church health not church growth first and foremost.
111. Analyze your music program and revise if outdated.
112. Renovate your church nursery and get it ready for bed babies. Recruit workers for the ministry of childcare.
113. Begin to implement your revitalization plan and strategy.
114. Consider facility improvements. A little paint goes a long way.
115. New member's class redesigned in light of renewal initiative and initiated.
116. Begin emphasizing the importance of discipleship.

117. Who in the next generation could be included in the leadership pipeline?
118. Share your pastoral dreams for the church's future.
119. Begin holding quarterly Church Fellowships to connect prospects.
120. Develop a Pastor, Staff, And Deacon Plan for visiting weekly.
121. Have your church signage renovated with a new and exciting slogan.

Wrapping it up!

At the beginning of this book, I suggested that you would become a better church revitalizer if you would do something each and every day, almost anything. While the point was made that it takes a daily nudge of a church towards revitalization, I did not direct you to things worth considering as the revitalization leader. Now as we wrap up this book, you have a list of things that could go into your own personal 120-day list. Many have found this list useful as a means to begin thinking about the things required of you as the leader and your members as followers of the one leading the effort. Do not squander your first four months as the church revitalizer. Diligent work during the initial portion of the revitalization will set the stage for greater things to come along the way. You can do this and it will be the most rewarding thing you have ever done in your ministry. Imagine being used of the Lord to save a declining and dying church to bring it back to glorious health and vitality. That is heady stuff. Know that the Renovate Group is here to help you. Press onward and lead them upward. Be a blessing.

APPENDIX

RENOVATE Church Revitalization Action Plans

As a response to the action priority:

_____

We will proceed by: _____

_____

_____

Who	When	Where

How		Resources

Your First 120 Days in Church Revitalization

	ACTION	PERSON (S) RESPONSIBLE	DATE ASSIGNED	DATE COMPLETED

RENOVATECONFERENCE.ORG/COACHING

RENOVATE SWOT Analysis Form

Strengths	Weaknesses	Opportunities	Threats

ABOUT THE AUTHOR
Dr. Tom Cheyney
Founder & Directional Leader
Renovate National Church Revitalization Conference
The Renovate Group
RenovateConference.org
ChurchRevitalizer.guru
tom@renovateconference.org

Tom is the founder and directional leader of the RENOVATE National Church Revitalization Conference, The Renovate Group, Executive Editor of *the Church Revitalizer Magazine,* and founder of the RENOVATE Church Revitalization Virtual Coaching Network where he mentors pastors, churches, and denominational leaders in Church Revitalization and Renewal all across North America. He serves as the National Co-Host of the weekly *Revitalization Today Podcast.*

Dr. Cheyney has written over 5,000 print, audio resources, guides, or books for church revitalizers, pastors, church planters, and lay leaders. His most recent books include: *Life After Death: A Strategy to Bring New Life to a Dead Church, Slaying the Dragons of Church Revitalization: Dealing with the Critical Issues that are Hurting Your Church, Church Revitalization in Rural America: Restoring Churches in America's Heartland, The Seven Pillars of Church Revitalization and Renewal, Practical Tools for Reinventing the Dying Church, The Church Revitalizer as Change Agent, Thirty-Eight Church Revitalization Models for the Twenty First-Century, The Nuts & Bolts of Church Revitalization and Renewal,* and *Preaching Towards Church Revitalization and Renewal.*

Cheyney has also written along with his friend Rodney Harrison *Spin-Off Churches* (B&H Publishers). Tom is a nationally recognized conference speaker and a frequent writer on church revitalization, church planting, new church health, and leadership development. Others have labeled

Tom as the *Father of the Church Revitalization Movement* as his influence has stretched across multiple denominations and countries. He leads a monthly training lab for all those desiring to see their churches brought back to life.